NAFTA
STORIES

NAFTA STORIES

Fears and Hopes in Mexico and the United States

Ann E. Kingsolver

LYNNE
RIENNER
PUBLISHERS

BOULDER
LONDON

Published in the United States of America in 2001 by
Lynne Rienner Publishers, Inc.
1800 30th Street, Boulder, Colorado 80301
www.rienner.com

and in the United Kingdom by
Lynne Rienner Publishers, Inc.
3 Henrietta Street, Covent Garden, London WC2E 8LU

Library of Congress Cataloging-in-Publication Data
Kingsolver, Ann E., 1960–
    NAFTA stories :   fears and hopes in Mexico and the United States   /   Ann E.
Kingsolver.
        p.   cm.
    Includes bibliographical references.
    ISBN 1-55587-974-8 (alk. paper)
    1. Canada. Treaties, etc. 1992 Oct. 7—Public opinion.   2. Free trade—North
America—Public opinion.   3. Public opinion—Mexico.   4. Public opinion—United
States.   I. Title: Fears and hopes in Mexico and the United States.   II. Title.
HF1746.K56   2001
382'.917—dc21

                                                                    2001019617

British Cataloguing in Publication Data
A Cataloguing in Publication record for this book
is available from the British Library.

Printed and bound in the United States of America

The paper used in this publication meets the requirements
of the American National Standard for Permanence of
Paper for Printed Library Materials Z39.48-1984.

5   4   3   2   1

for all the storytellers

Contents

Illustrations

Acknowledgments

This project was collaborative in many ways, as I have tried to explain within the text. For their insights and time, I thank all who participated in the interview conversations that informed this book—whether as those being interviewed or as fellow interviewers. I also give many thanks to Jorge Carrásco Araizaga and L. Miguel Morayta M., colleagues who have borne with the comings and goings of this project over the long term.

I appreciate the comments and assistance of my colleagues, including students, at Lawrence University, the University of California–Santa Cruz, and the University of South Carolina during the decade of this research. In particular, I thank Adriana Sandoval, Erika Rand, Aaron Howe, Steve Spellman, Bill Aurand, Ulrika Dahl, Elizabeth Sanín, Marcela Moya, Tantuashia Hutchinson, Olga Nájera-Ramirez, Norma Klahn, Guillermo Delgado, Patricia Zavella, Ivelisse Rivera Bonilla, René Ortega, Annapurna Devi Pandey, Nancy Chen, Alison Leach, Elaine Lacy, Michael Scardaville, Faye Harrison, Marilyn Thomas-Houston, Sara Gillies, Lessie Jo Frazier, Tom Leatherman, and Laura Liger—indexing maven. I thank also Jonathan Spencer, University of Edinburgh.

Claudio Lomnitz-Adler and Fran Rothstein provided useful comments in 1993 as panel discussants, and I thank the many writers and conference presenters over the years from whom I have learned in this work. The comments of two anonymous manuscript reviewers from fields other than my own (anthropology) were enormously helpful. With their permission, I can now thank those reviewers by name: KarenMary Davalos and Jonathan Fox.

The researchers and staff members of the Centro de Investigaciones Sobre América del Norte (CISAN) at UNAM (Universidad Nacional Autónoma de México) in Mexico City offered a warm welcome, a wonderful library, and thoughtful criticism in 1995. I thank Ma. del Carmen Trejo, V. Hugo Machorro, Dagoberto González, and Alejandrina Ortega for their archival skills, and Rosa Cusminsky Mogilner, Julián Castro Rea, Lucy Luccisano, and so many others who discussed shared research interests. I especially want to thank Graciela Martínez-Zalce and Teresita Cortés Díaz for their abiding friendship and helpful intellectual exchanges.

I appreciate the scholarly hospitality of Ma. Eugenia de la O., José Manuel Valenzuela Arce, and colleagues at El Colegio de la Frontera Norte when our working group from the Chicano/Latino Research Center at the University of California–Santa Cruz visited Tijuana in 1996.

Bridget Julian has been a most patient, perceptive, and encouraging editor. I appreciate the work of Karen Williams, Sarah Whalen, and others at Lynne Rienner Publishers who saw this book through production. My extended family—the Kingsolvers and the Whitakers—has been supportive of this project as well. Finally, in addition to my heartfelt thanks to all of those listed above, I am grateful to Dana Frank, Laura Ahearn and Rick Black, A. L. Anderson, Barbara and Randy Johnston, the Riley family, Sivaram Dharmeratnam, Vaishnavi and Vaitheki, and especially Mark and David Whitaker for various kinds of critical support and good humor as I completed this manuscript.

—A. E. K.

1

Introduction:
NAFTA Stories in
the Space of Absence

In 1993, a man named Ángel ran into the sundries shop of Don Modesto in an industrial zone of Mexico City, blurting out that he had seen some television commercials that said NAFTA would bring Mexico into the first world. So, he went on, he got really excited and went to a fortuneteller (who had a Ph.D. in economics from Harvard but found fortunetelling to be a less speculative profession) to ask what riches he would have after NAFTA went into effect. The fortuneteller, Ángel told Don Modesto in panic, related some scary things about the future for people like them. Don Modesto tried to calm his friend by saying that the television had assured them NAFTA would be the most ambitious economic project in the history of Mexico and that it represented the only viable future for Mexico. Ángel pointed out the distinction between NAFTA as the only solution, according to television and newspapers, and as the only solution imaginable. He began to raise questions about the North American Free Trade Agreement (el Tratado de Libre Comercio—el TLC) that were not being answered clearly in the news accounts: "What is a free trade treaty? What treaty has been negotiated? How was it negotiated? Who will benefit? Who could it affect? How could it affect them? How has it already affected the industrialists, workers, and farmers of Mexico, Canada, and the U.S.A.? How has the free trade treaty that Canada signed with the U.S.A. several years back affected Canadians?"[1]

Ángel and Don Modesto were political cartoon characters drawn by El Fisgón in a book called *¡Me lleva el TLC!* *(NAFTA Is Killing Me!)*, which was published as the legislative bodies of the three nations of North America were making decisions about the North American Free

1

Trade Agreement. It was sometimes hard, at that moment, to determine the real and the surreal in the public space where stories to make sense of NAFTA were being told. Political cartoonists could articulate questions like Ángel's that, as I found from interviews, were on people's minds but were seldom raised in formal public venues. U.S. Senator Paul Wellstone (D-Minnesota), in an exception, put to his colleagues some very similar questions (with as much formal response) as the Senate prepared to vote on the NAFTA-enabling legislation on November 20, 1993. Senator Wellstone suggested that "this NAFTA agreement goes to the heart of the issue of representation." He said:

> Regular citizens, which I mean in a positive sense, ask the question: Who decides to sign this trade agreement and who might lose their job? . . .
>
> They ask the question: Who decided that we cannot have an adequate appropriation of funding to make sure that there are programs for job retraining to address worker displacement, and whose families are going to be without jobs?
>
> They ask the question: Who decides that we cannot invest in our economy and invest in high-paying jobs and invest in education and invest in opportunity, and whose families pay the price?[2]

This book is about the questions asked and the stories told in the public space opened for discussion, ironically, by the largely inaccessible North American Free Trade Agreement. In the absence of the document itself, NAFTA/el TLC[3] became a symbolic entity invested with hopes, fears, and agency—the power to change lives and nations.[4] It became a vehicle for discussing the particular ways individuals understand, experience, and explain global capitalism. There is no proliferation of virtual "town meetings" in North America (except perhaps in Canada) on the shifting social contract between citizens and national governments regarding the right to regulate capital; the decisionmaking powers of transnational corporations in relation to individual and community livelihoods; or the relationship between stereotypes of migrants and North American nations as they are linked to fears of job loss. NAFTA became a catalyst for the necessary discussion of these issues as they affected citizens' lives in Mexico, the United States, and Canada.

I do not want to separate the "real" or lived effects of NAFTA from the symbolic space I focus on in this book. They are intertwined. The very legitimacy of national governments to negotiate a treaty (as the document is called in Spanish) or an agreement that is meant to benefit capital more than a general public has been called into question through events symbolically linked to NAFTA, as in the challenge to the Mexican government by the EZLN on January 1, 1994—the day NAFTA began to go into effect.[5] The stories we tell as citizens grant the collective agency that we give as a "public" to the entities, which then seem inevitably constituted (e.g., nation-states and transnational corporations, nongovernmental organizations, and entities like the World Trade Organization invoked through the General Agreement on Tariffs and Trade). Rather than constructing this book from the narrative perspective of the larger entity (i.e., the Agreement itself and the regulatory bodies it creates), I follow the various story lines of "situated individuals" in Mexico and the United States as they imagined and interpreted NAFTA. By situated individuals, I mean that the storytellers in this book have perspectives shaped by their particular experiences of identity, place, and occupation; I thought it important to include stories from multiple perspectives, but by doing so I do not intend to imply that their voices universally represent their regions, vocations, or identity groups. Each of us, as individuals negotiating multiple social contexts in daily life, is strategic in the way we tell stories. I include here stories of farmers, scholars, factory workers, teenagers, treaty drafters, hunger strikers, and others. There are contradictory perspectives, sometimes in the stories told by the same individuals about NAFTA and North America. My aim here is not to provide a coherent story of what NAFTA really is and does but to demonstrate through a few of the many NAFTA stories told between 1991 and 1996 some of the private and public interpretations of global capitalism being debated. Storytelling, like silence, is not innocuous. As NAFTA stories representing nationalist, neoliberal, capitalist visions of prosperity for all were being told, other stories representing racialized stereotypes and threats on the lives of migrant workers also circulated. As Liliana Goldin (1995, 8) put it, "A xenophobic environment has developed parallel to one that presents multicultural affirmations at the national level [in the United States]."

Because my job is an academic one, I punctuate this text with academic references; those interested can read that story line through the endnotes. I do not see scholarly narrators as more legitimate or more theoretical than any other storytellers I invoke here, nor do I see the stories elaborated in the endnotes as less important than the other lines followed. I appreciate notes as an option for constructing multidimensional texts. I have seen attempts to write anthropology using hypercard computer programs,[6] and if the technology were more widely available, that would have interesting possibilities. It would be especially helpful if readers could identify themselves at the beginning of the text; for example, those who read Spanish would not need translations. As it is, I must apologize to those whose familiarity with Mexican culture(s) and politics may make some of my explanations tedious at best. Because I must choose a particular audience for this text, I have chosen to address those in the United States whose experiences of Mexico may be more imagined than direct. I was motivated to write this book, in part, because of stereotypes of Mexican people and perspectives that I heard in public discourse in my own country. In these stereotypes, Mexican perspectives seemed to be represented as more accepting of NAFTA and less sophisticated than those of U.S. commentators. Such misconceptions have dangerous implications, and thus I have chosen to address them as an activist form of academic storytelling. Another readership I envision for this book includes those who also employ activist storytelling to counteract stereotypes, wherever they may be situated.

I see theory as the stories we tell ourselves to make sense of life and to determine where we are as we navigate social space. My young son tells stories about trains to make sense of his experiences; that's what he reads about. I see the world in terms of multidimensional stories about capitalism because I chose to be trained as a political economic and interpretive cultural anthropologist—that's what I read about. We each have our vantage point as a storyteller. I tried to pay attention, in listening to these stories about NAFTA, to how the storyteller's position mattered in relation to what was being said, without assuming that a worker spoke for all workers or one woman spoke for all women. These are the stories I asked for and was told, organized in relation to particular events I was following: the formal and informal discussions of NAFTA/el TLC before its passage in 1993 (see Chapter 2); a week in the fall of 1994, when President Carlos Salinas de Gortari of Mexico delivered his sixth annual, and final, summary address and California voters passed Proposition 187 (see Chapter 3); and the fall of 1995, when President Ernesto Zedillo gave his first annual summary address and the Alianza Cívica (Civic Alliance) administered a national poll related to the political alternatives represented by the EZLN in Mexico (see Chapter 4). Chapter 5 concludes the discussion, even as the Agreement continues to go into effect by degree. I was interested in following these stories, so I wrote grant proposals and found ways to be in particular places at particular moments. There are myriad other stories to be told. As the narrator, my choices reflect my own position as an anthropologist from Kentucky, a teacher, and an activist.

In the interest of transparency—the word often used in calls to reveal the strategies of global policymakers—I explain how I came to collect the stories discussed here. Listening to people's stories is what we do in cultural anthropology. The texture of individual experiences and interpretations complements quantitative analysis in social research. As a cultural anthropologist, or ethnographer, with an interpretive perspective, I believe that meaning and social relations are constructed through language and action and that, within limits related to assertions of power and memory, we negotiate in public discourse concepts like *globalization* and *national identity*. Guillermo Bonfil Batalla's (1966) reminder to anthropologists that we must look historically, internationally, and politically at interpretations that are specific and general, local and nonlocal, informed this research project on NAFTA. This research, in turn, is part of a longer-term project in which I am listening to how differently-situated individuals interpret transnational capitalist processes. But listening implies a powerful silence on the part of the researcher, and stories emerge in conversation. I agree with Kirin Narayan (1995) that ethnographic fieldwork is "shared stories" rather than dispassionate data collection.[7] What we have to say as cultural anthropologists is always rooted in relationships, often between people in different class positions (Behar 1993, 338) or with different national identities. Faye Harrison (1997a, 1) notes that such anthropological relationships and projects have most often served the interests of those "belonging to or with allegiances to the world's White minority." She asks the question, "Can a genuine study of humankind arise from dialogues, debates, and reconciliations amongst various non-Western and Western intellectuals—both those with formal credentials and those with other socially meaningful and appreciated qualifications?" (Harrison 1997a, 1). I agree with Harrison and others that anthropological research needs to be decolonized. For this reason, I think of all narrators in this book as storytellers rather than some as experts and others as folk; each one is a theorist, explaining NAFTA and neoliberal capitalism from his or her particular vantage point.

Inspired by activist anthropologists—especially those writing in the late 1960s whose work was published in *Reinventing Anthropology* (Hymes 1969)—and participatory researchers Paulo Freire and Myles Horton,[8] as well as women who told me during my undergraduate thesis work on both sides of the Mexican–U.S. border that I should study capitalism "in the belly of the beast," I did my dissertation research in the 1980s on interpretations and experiences of capitalist development in my rural Kentucky hometown.[9] At that time, both tobacco and Toyotas were being produced there in multinational industries, and Mexican workers were beginning to be seen by tobacco farmers as a labor source in "stretch" times (Kingsolver 1991). It seemed to me that if communities in Mexico, the United States, and elsewhere could have direct opportunities to exchange stories about their experiences of working in multinational industries, for example, there would be less stereotyping and more understanding of how economic benefits and uncertainties are distributed in transnational capitalist development. As I have followed NAFTA stories, I have seen exciting efforts to establish such communication between workers in multiple nations, and some of those stories are included here. We need much more transnational collaboration to interpret the effects of neoliberal capitalism, as many others have pointed out and demonstrated. Those whose work cycles take them between countries, like the tobacco workers coming to rural Kentucky from Mexico, are positioned to critically interpret national identities and work identities in the context of capitalist globalization.[10]

The focus on countering stereotypes in this book also stems from my work in Kentucky. Stereotyping, or attributing negative qualities to an "other" group, is a complex process, usually having to do with power relations. Residents of my home county might be stereotyped as insular hillbillies by some, and yet a broad range of life experiences and work roles (including sitting on multinational corporate boards) are represented there. In turn, a legacy of slavery in the county (with the forceful stereotyping that sustained it) was written out of our schooling there, and as Mexican citizens began to move into the county in larger numbers, I wondered how the images of Mexico might be critically reexamined. For example, one section of the county called Mexico was rumored to have been deeded to that nation over a century before because it was so "wild" that no surrounding county wanted to incorporate it.

I thought that working in my hometown, where most people already knew me, would help check the ethical problems of power imbalances between researcher and researched and make collaborative research more possible. I learned that the problems of one researcher representing multiple voices are equally present, if perhaps different, whether one is doing research as an insider or an outsider; with all the hats we wear as individuals, we are usually a bit of both in any social context. Thus when I began to think about a project on interpretations of possible regional integration in North America through NAFTA, I was concerned with issues of ethics and power in research relationships. I agree with Douglas Foley, Clarice Mota, Donald Post, and Ignacio Lozano (1988, xviii) about their collaborative research in South Texas: "Indeed, it is clear to us that the idea of a single, all-purpose ethnographer in the multi-ethnic communities of a complex society is not altogether reasonable and methodologically defensible. There is much to be gained by having a racially and sexually diverse research group."

I was also concerned about both the political implications of another itinerant gringa asking questions in Mexico and in the United States, then disappearing with the answers, and the use of resources—storytellers' time particularly—invested in just one person's research project. I wanted to engage in collaborative research but did not assume others would necessarily want to produce the same kind of documentation that I did, simply because I found the funding and organized the collaboration. As an academic working in the United States, I had access to resources that could serve such transnational collaboration, but I wanted to do multisited work with persons who had as much depth of experience in a particular place as I had in rural Kentucky. I see research as a convergent process, with multiple possibilities for representation, so I looked for others who also wanted to talk about NAFTA, with their own projects in storytelling. As I envisioned this project, in grant proposals and conversations, I thought interpretations of transnational capitalism as focused through the lens of NAFTA could best be studied through three forms of collaboration: first, between researchers from different nations; second, between different disciplinary perspectives; and third, between those working inside and outside academic contexts. Ethnographic research is always, of course, an act of collaboration between the interviewer and the person granting the interview.[11] I wanted to find ways to make learning, teaching, and research more of an integrated cycle so, whenever possible, I collaborated with interested students, learning from them as I learned from the narrators in these NAFTA stories. An ideal situation would have been to work with Mexican, Canadian, and U.S.-based colleagues and students in a project on interpretations of NAFTA that involved transnational collaboration in all three nations. But since my immediate focus in 1991 was on countering representations of Mexico in public discussions in the United States, as well as on shifting notions of transnational identity, I concentrated on initiating collaboration both with Mexican intellectuals also interested in those topics and with students from the United States and Mexico. Just as I had multiple roles in relation to the storytelling here (e.g., California voter, white, upper-middle class woman, ethnographer, teacher, activist, Spanish speaker, English speaker), each of my collaborators had multiple roles and interests that motivated them to join me at times in conversations where our concerns met.

Here, then, is the account of how I came to select the particular moments emphasized in this book and how I came to collaborate with those whose questions and stories also shape this account. In 1992, with support from Lawrence University, I spent the summer in the national archives in Scotland, studying the history of the European Union for parallels with possible North American economic, if not political, regional integration. Before I left for Scotland in June I attended a conference at the University of California–Riverside, called "Myths in U.S.-Mexican Relations."[12] Among those I met there was Jorge Carrásco Araizaga, a financial journalist covering the presidential beat in Mexico City—which at that moment meant President Salinas de Gortari and his neoliberal internal and external economic policies. He was in the United States with a colleague, David Torres, to collaborate on an article about stereotypes of Mexicans in the United States. Because our research and writing projects were convergent, Carrásco Araizaga agreed to collaborate with me in research involving conversations in the United States and Mexico. With support from Lawrence University through a Mellon grant for language learning, he came to Appleton, Wisconsin, during the winter quarter of 1993 to teach students I was preparing for a summer fieldschool in Mexico that year, which was focused on NAFTA, how to listen to and interpret Mexican news in Spanish. The students were Bill Aurand, Aaron Howe, Erika Rand, and Steve Spellman from the United States and Adriana Sandoval from Mexico. Each student chose a topic of interest in relation to the North American Free Trade Agreement (e.g., labor or the environment) and did background reading on that topic. We discussed ethics and research design. Because of both ethical and legal requirements that I collaborate with a Mexican anthropologist in conducting ethnographic research in Mexico and because we shared an interest in rural identity and development policy, I contacted Miguel Morayta M., who works for the Instituto Nacional de Antropología e História (INAH, or the National Institute of Anthropology and History) in Morelos. We had taught there together in a summer ethnographic fieldschool for the

University of South Carolina in 1991, and had discussed at that time the possibility of long-term transnational collaborative research involving students. The North American Free Trade Agreement and its interpreted effects on identity seemed a good place to begin. The interviews done through the 1993 fieldschool are all archived, with the story-tellers' knowledge, in the INAH offices in Morelos as well as in the Department of Anthropology at the University of South Carolina. Jorge Carrásco Araizaga has copies of the tapes of interviews done jointly with him.

During the 1993 fieldschool, the students and I stayed in Mexico City part of the time and in Cuernavaca and Cuautla in Morelos. In Mexico City, we did many interviews together with Jorge Carrásco Araizaga, particularly those with journalists and government represen-tatives. In rural Morelos (communities near the borders of the states of México and Puebla), we did many interviews either with or arranged by Miguel Morayta; he had been working in rural Morelos for nearly twen-ty-five years and could vouch for the accountability of our collaborative project to the region. Adriana Sandoval did some interviews with stu-dent friends in Cuernavaca; these are the only ones used here that I did not participate in directly. The six of us met each morning, with either Carrásco or Morayta joining us, depending on where we were. We would go over the questions we wanted to ask in interviews, serving each person's writing project. Carrásco was writing a series of newspa-per articles for *El Economista* on the financial aspects of the proposed NAFTA. Morayta was writing a book on articulations of rural identity in relation to public policy. I was writing papers related to this book project, and the students were working on their course papers. In an interview, I would explain the project to the person who agreed to speak with us, and how the resulting information would be made accessible to that person, who would then define the terms of his or her consent to be interviewed (e.g., taped or not taped). To give the students interviewing experience, sometimes we all took turns asking questions. The inter-view transcripts are available through the INAH offices, and whenever possible we gave them to the person interviewed and followed up with later conversations.

In succeeding years, I did interviews alone, except for some revisits with Miguel Morayta in Morelos and interviews done with Tantuashia Hutchinson, a UC–Santa Cruz undergraduate who accompanied me to events in Mexico and California in 1995. I have not used the analyses of collaborators in this book, but our questions are certainly interwoven in the conversations, and I am indebted to them for what I have learned from working with them. Miguel Morayta and I have collaborated in writing for anthropologists (Kingsolver and Morayta 1995), and his attention to how people shift between identifying as *indígena* or *campesino* has contributed to my thinking about strategic alterity,[13] or "othering" by political convenience. Jorge Carrásco and I have had many conversations about the different priorities of journalistic and ethnographic research and writing; the pseudonyms used throughout this book are an ethnographic convention, for example, and not usually a journalistic practice. The students, especially Adriana Sandoval and Erika Rand, shaped this book in their focus on the views of young Mexican citizens regarding NAFTA/el TLC. As they pointed out, the majority of Mexico's population is under eighteen and that constituency was not represented as a significant public for most discussions of NAFTA.

I moved from Wisconsin to work in the Department of Anthropology at UC–Santa Cruz (1993–1996) and became associated with the Chicano/Latino Research Center there, which presented many opportunities for learning in relation to this project.[14] Through working in a research cluster with Guillermo Delgado, Norma Klahn, and Olga Nájera-Ramirez, participating in a research exchange with colleagues at the Colegio de la Frontera Norte in Tijuana, and helping to organize the binational conference, "Bridging Borders, Crossing Centuries: U.S.-Mexico Relations After NAFTA," I learned from activist scholars whose long-term projects include theorizing binational identity and studying and participating in plurinational social movements.

As an academic, I used my attendance at conferences as an opportunity to fund travel to do further interviewing and observation for this project. In November 1993, for example, at the annual meeting of the American Anthropological Association in Washington, D.C., I co-organized a session called "Interpreting the North American Free Trade Agreement: Anthropological Perspectives on Transnational Policy" and presented a paper in it (Kingsolver 1993). The timing of that meeting coincided with the congressional votes on the NAFTA, so I witnessed the voting myself. In October 1994, I returned to Mexico City for the "9th Conference of Mexican and North American Historians: The History of Three Nations: Mexico–United States–Canada" and gave a paper on interpretations of NAFTA, which was heard by two researchers from CISAN at UNAM, the national public university. Mónica Verea Campos, CISAN's director, invited me to be a visiting researcher there, and I received leave and funding from UC–Santa Cruz to be at UNAM for the fall of 1995. The experiences provided opportunities for more interviewing and also meeting with researchers from Mexico, Canada, and the United States about issues related to this project. These and the library at CISAN allowed me to understand more about Canadian perspectives on NAFTA; I did not visit Canada and talk with researchers/activists there until January 2000, when I presented a paper on the NAFTA research at a conference on race, gender, and class in Vancouver. In between, I interviewed fellow protestors at Proposition 187 rallies and continued visiting Kentucky and talking with people there.

In 1997, I returned to Mexico City for follow-up interviews after attending the Latin American Studies Association meetings in Guadalajara. Although serendipity plays a part in all research, I did not simply pop up at strategic political events in one nation or another. My goals for this documentation project included using resources in multiple ways, such as getting equipment to my collaborators and having interviews serve the interests of the storytellers and various writing projects. Similarly, where statements had been made in the public record, as in public speeches or press interviews, I incorporated them into the NAFTA stories to make the point that ethnographic listening need not always involve one researcher and one researched, in a room with a microphone. As citizens, we are involved constantly in larger patterns of storytelling to which we contribute and from which we learn.[15] Especially on topics like white supremacy, which have both private and public silences, it is important to balance individual interviews with analysis of public discourse. (White supremacy is discussed in relation to NAFTA in Chapter 3.)

The conversations in which these NAFTA stories were told, then, were sometimes group conversations; sometimes drawn from government documents or political cartoons; and were in Spanish or English and occasionally nonverbal. I have translated the Spanish into English, which I find problematic for reasons explained below. A Spanish co-edition is planned for publication in Mexico.

Some U.S. readers may be those whose attention to free-trade agreements and accountability of global capital has been focused by public contestation—in Seattle in 1999 and Washington, D.C., in 2000—of the role of the World Trade Organization and other transnational regulatory bodies in shaping life conditions around the planet. In many ways, the U.S. national public is the last in the world to inform itself on the lived effects of neoliberal capitalist trade policies,[16] and I see this book as contributing to that activist project. I do not see the U.S. public as a single, stable identity; there are many stories of identity encompassed in "a national public." I include accounts of Mexican cultural and political practice that may be less familiar to some readers than to those who navigate the borders of the North American nations more easily than I do.

NAFTA, the Document

An article in the *Economist* (1993) sports a photograph of President Clinton in a baseball cap that says "NAFTA, WE HAFTA." Why did the U.S. administration see the North American Free Trade Agreement as so crucial when, as the same article points out, the nation already had a free-trade agreement with Canada and Mexico's economy in 1993 represented only 5 percent of the combined U.S. and Canadian economies?[17] The Agreement was part of a larger trade liberalization agenda[18] that included the impending Uruguay Round of GATT negotiations and plans to eventually link the various free-trade areas in the Americas to increase jobs and markets. The question many critics were asking about such plans was: *whose* jobs and markets? A pamphlet published by the Office of the U.S. Trade Representative (1992a)—meant to encourage support for NAFTA during the administration of President George H. W. Bush, who had asked Congress for permission to negotiate the Agreement—advertised that "NAFTA will expand U.S. imports" and generate "over 1 million [U.S.] jobs by 1995." NAFTA would do this because it

> eliminates all tariffs . . . ; opens Mexico's $146 billion service market . . . and improves our access to Canada's $285 billion services market . . . ; phases out restrictions in the North American auto market to create important new U.S. export opportunities . . . ; opens access to Mexico for U.S. agricultural exports . . . ; offers a higher level of protection for U.S. copyrights, trademarks, patents, and other intellectual property rights . . . ; establishes an effective dispute settlement mechanism . . . ; provides fair rules for investment in North America by ensuring non-discrimination, ending local content requirements, and dropping export performance quotas; and provides substantially increased access for U.S. firms to

Mexico's state-owned energy companies. (Office of the U.S. Trade
Representative 1992a, 1–2)

The pamphlet did not mention that PEMEX, the Mexican national
petroleum corporation, would retain control over the Mexican oil industry or that truckers would be able to cross the border with increasing
freedom, which was interpreted in Mexican promotional literature as
making it more likely that U.S.-based industries would locate at least
part of their operations in Mexico. In "Myths & Realities: The North
American Free Trade Agreement," another pamphlet published that
summer by the same office (1992b, 1–2), Carla Hills directly addressed
some of the public questions circulating (Hills's answer follows each
question):

> Will Mexico's lower wages and workplace safety standards encour-
> age U.S. companies to move to Mexico? No. . . .
>   Will NAFTA lead U.S. companies to move their operations—
> and jobs—to Mexico to avoid U.S. environmental standards?
> No. . . .
>   Will NAFTA turn Mexico into an export platform for products
> from outside of North America? No. . . .
>   Will NAFTA mean that cheap imports from Mexico will flood
> the U.S. market? No. . . .
>   Will NAFTA increase immigration from Mexico? No. . . .
>   Will anything be done to help displaced workers? While
> NAFTA will create good, high-paying jobs for Americans, workers
> dislocated as a result of the NAFTA will be eligible for adjustment
> assistance.

While all tariffs on goods marketed in the North American free-
trade area would eventually be removed under the Agreement,[19] the sectors seen by labor activists and others to be most strongly affected by
this change included agriculture; textiles; automobiles; investment,
insurance, and telecommunication services; pharmaceuticals; entertain-
ment and electronics; and transportation services. The North American
Free Trade Agreement was proposed by President Salinas of Mexico in
1990, and negotiations began during the administrations of President
Salinas, President Bush, and Canadian Prime Minister Brian Mulroney.
Before it was approved by the legislative bodies in each country to go
into effect January 1, 1994, national administrations had changed from

presidents Bush to Clinton and prime ministers Mulroney to Kim Campbell and then to Jean Chrêtien. The change in administrations meant that trade representatives in charge of negotiating the Agreement changed also; U.S. Trade Representative Carla Hills was replaced by Mickey Kantor, and Prime Minister Campbell appointed Thomas Hockin to replace Michael Wilson as Canadian trade minister.

The North American Free Trade Agreement was signed by Salinas, Bush, and Mulroney (each in his own country) on December 17, 1992, and then went to the legislative bodies for approval; the struggle for ratification was greatest in the United States, but there was strong and organized opposition to the Agreement in each nation. President Bush had negotiated fast-track status for the Agreement, which meant that after it was signed and implementing legislation had been submitted to Congress, members of Congress were obligated to vote on it (without amendments) within ninety days of legislative session activity. The U.S. Congress extended the fast-track option during the Clinton administration with the provision that side agreements be negotiated to strengthen protection of the environment and workers' rights. These side agreements established regulatory bodies to oversee labor and environmental conditions, with particular attention to the U.S.-Mexican border region, but support for these was divided: many felt the protections were weak and would not be enforced. The Canadian House of Commons voted to ratify the Agreement on May 27, 1993. President Salinas's party, the PRI, controlled the Mexican legislature, so its support for the Agreement (and for Salinas's broader neoliberal economic agenda) had been assumed all along. The side agreements on environment and labor were signed by representatives of all three nations on September 14, 1993, and the U.S. Congress voted to approve the Agreement on November 17 and 20, 1993. It began to go into effect January 1, 1994.[20]

The story of NAFTA's implementation is a much longer-term one than its stint as front-page news throughout North America. It began to go into effect on January 1, 1994, but it was written to go into effect over a fifteen-year period, to protect various sectors seen by the authors as economically vital or to protect political constituencies from a sudden lifting of tariffs. Senator Charles Robb (D-Virginia) called NAFTA a "living agreement" because of its gradual implementation and the ways potential change were built into it: "And I should point out to those concerned about particular facets of NAFTA, that this is a living agreement. Like the United States/Canada Free-Trade Agreement, standing committees will adjust the implementation of the deal as it goes forward to make . . . up for abuses, injustices, or situations that may not have been foreseen."[21]

The notion of the NAFTA as a living agreement parallels the agency that was granted to NAFTA by many storytellers. As I report in Chapter 2, NAFTA was described as being something alive to wield power, to make decisions, to bring either salvation or doom to families and communities. Such imagination of this tremendous entity was facilitated by the document itself being largely unavailable to readers in the United States and Mexico.

There have been many books written to explain the Agreement.[22] It is easy to see why, looking at even a paragraph of the document without an eye trained to read legal language.[23] The North American Free Trade Agreement between the governments of the United States, Canada, and the United Mexican States,[24] written in 1992, was inaccessible to the publics that those governments represented, both in its language and in the availability of the document itself.[25] Some people who work regularly with legal and political documents have told me that my focus on the document's inaccessibility is unfair. I realize that government documents are not usually written in straightforward prose or mailed out—except for U.S. ballot initiatives that may be accessible to voters through the mail, which are seldom written in accessible language. What was different about this one? Millions of dollars were spent by governments (the most by the Mexican government) to promote the policy, yet it was singularly unavailable for the publics, being lobbied by their governments, to peruse. At the time of this writing, I can find government documents on the Internet or walk to the library and read the text of NAFTA for free, but this was not the case in 1992 and 1993 when it was being discussed before its passage by the three legislative bodies.

In the rest of this section, I first tell stories of degrees of access to the document and then stories of what NAFTA was said to be, in summaries prepared through various lenses. These summary stories became especially important in the absence of the document itself. I leave it mostly to other texts to describe the legal, political, and economic details of the Agreement. In this book, I focus on the use of NAFTA as a metaphor because in 1993, without access to the document, so many people in North America invested it with meanings that came to be associated with it but were not actually part of the Agreement. Xenophobia, the fear of strangers or foreigners—immigrants, for example, or anthropology's "others"—is an issue that I argue was closely associated with NAFTA in the U.S. public imagination, even though the NAFTA negotiators took care to avoid detailed discussion of worker migration and immigration policy in the central document.

The time that NAFTA was a prominent topic in North American news and conversations was a moment, I think, when "public" was being contested. Did the social contract between publics and the representative governments in the three nations authorize signing a treaty that could reduce the accountability of those controlling transnational capital to national publics? Throughout this book, I recount stories of who the public for NAFTA was imagined to be. Different publics were strategically invoked for different audiences, especially by political leaders. Important questions to ask about this process related to the presentation and representation of policy include the following: How is the invocation of "public" used as a gloss for inclusiveness that effectively excludes? An example here would be the representations (discussed in Chapter 2) of each national public of North America as a single-raced and -classed individual (e.g., the Mexican as a migrant worker). This thought style[26] obscured President Salinas de Gortari's motivation to promote el TLC to Mexican millionaires to attract capital investments in the national economy. Other questions are: Who feels entitled to represent a public? Who feels left out of any representations of national publics? These questions are raised in this section describing the contents of the Agreement because they have everything to do with its writing and negotiation. How much agency did each national public have in authorizing it? What would an "informed public" mean in relation to it?

In 1992, while at the National Library of Scotland, I found a DOCEX document published in the United States that listed the members of the Mexican negotiating team and their credentials. I spoke with Jorge Carrásco Araizaga, who was assigned as a reporter at that time to Los Pinos (the presidential home/office in Mexico, parallel to the U.S. White House). He said that even that basic information was unavailable to the Mexican public, including himself. This prompted me to learn more about differential access to information about the NAFTA negotiations and the document itself. In 1993, I heard a news report that Bill Clinton, then a presidential candidate opposing incumbent George Bush, could not get access to a copy of the Agreement until just before he had to announce his position on the hefty document. (It is hard to say how many pages it runs because the pagination starts over in every chapter of the five-volume set; the figure of two thousand pages was most commonly estimated in discussions of its inaccessibility.)

There was differential access to the document by nation and by class. The document was most available to the national public in Canada, perhaps because of experience: another contentious trade treaty (the Canada–U.S. free-trade treaty of 1988) had already been debated and followed in the public sphere.[27] In the United States and Mexico, the document was most accessible to the business and investment community, which it seems the authors of NAFTA envisioned as its main audience.[28] In 1992, the Mexican SECOFI (Secretaria de Comercio y Fomento Industrial, or Secretary of Commerce and Industrial Development) office made a fifteen-year time line of the implementation of el TLC available, without charge, to businesspeople through its library (SECOFI 1992). But as I saw personally, access to that library is strictly regulated. The more than $30 million spent by the PRI government to publicize el TLC (Heredia 1993, 27) did not include money for broad public distribution of either the document or the SECOFI summary. In the United States, the more one could pay, the more access one had to information about NAFTA and to the document itself. A private printing company in Virginia, for example, was selling copies for $102.84 each—the most reasonable price among those investigated in an article in *Nation's Business* (Holzinger and Manzella 1992, 25). Access to technology was a factor in access to the Agreement as well. The "Bits & Bytes" section of *Business Week* in October 1993 advertised a CD-Rom copy of the entire NAFTA document for $99. This was just before public libraries made CD-Rom technology widely available, and even if they had computers equipped to read compact disks, whether libraries had funds to purchase copies of the document in any form was another issue. Although the U.S. Government Printing Office made the document available for $41 to individuals or over $200 to public libraries in 1993, I was told by my library in Wisconsin that it could not be purchased with the budget available for government documents. Some U.S. public libraries offered the document for consultation and others did not.

So what is in this document of questionable pagination? From a well-thumbed library copy of the 1992 document, I list here the general contents. After a preamble, reproduced below, there are eight parts (with internal chapter divisions) in the first volume: "general part"; "trade in goods"; "technical barriers to trade"; "government procurement";

"investment, services, and related matters"; "intellectual property";
"administrative and institutional provisions"; and "other provisions."
The second volume includes Annex 401, "specific rules of origin," and
Annexes 1–7, "reservations and exceptions to investment, cross-border
trade in services and financial services chapters" [capitalization
removed]. Volume 3 contains the tariff schedule of Canada, Volume 4
the tariff schedule of Mexico, and Volume 5 the tariff schedule of the
United States. Here follows the complete preamble to the North
American Free Trade Agreement between the government of the United
States of America, the government of Canada, and the government of the
United Mexican States (Executive Office of the President 1993):

> The Government of the United States of America, the Government
> of Canada, and the Government of the United Mexican States,
> resolved to:
>
> STRENGTHEN the special bonds of friendship and cooperation
> among their nations;
> CONTRIBUTE to the harmonious development and expansion of
> world trade and provide a catalyst to broader international coopera-
> tion;
> CREATE an expanded and secure market for the goods and services
> produced in their territories;
> REDUCE distortions to trade;
> ESTABLISH clear and mutually advantageous rules governing
> their trade;
> ENSURE a predictable commercial framework for business plan-
> ning and investment;
> BUILD on their respective rights and obligations under the *General
> Agreement on Tariffs and Trade* and other multilateral and bilateral
> instruments of cooperation;
> ENHANCE the competitiveness of their firms in global markets;
> FOSTER creativity and innovation, and promote trade in goods and
> services that are the subject of intellectual property rights;
> CREATE new employment opportunities and improve working
> conditions and living standards in their respective territories;
> UNDERTAKE each of the preceding in a manner consistent with
> environmental protection and conservation;
> PRESERVE their flexibility to safeguard the public welfare;
> PROMOTE sustainable development;

STRENGTHEN the development and enforcement of environmental laws and regulations; and PROTECT, enhance and enforce basic workers' rights;
HAVE AGREED as follows:

There ends the preamble, without a period. I found in talking with citizens of Mexico and the United States about NAFTA that many did not feel their interests were protected or strengthened by it. As Karl Marx pointed out in reference to the rhetoric of the French Revolution,[29] the unitary, liberatory language of such documents masks the very divergent interests held by members of those groups of people glossed as national publics.

Since the document itself was largely unavailable, the stories told about its contents and possible consequences mattered all the more, and one's view of NAFTA was likely to indicate other forms of allegiance as informed through particular sources. The sources, of course, were often in direct conflict about the contents and implications of the Agreement, and because readers or listeners (and perhaps those making the arguments themselves) were not directly consulting the document, the charisma of stories and speakers was in full play. For example, in the proceedings of a Heritage Foundation conference, "The North American Free Trade Agreement: Spurring Prosperity and Stability in the Americas" (Wilson and Smith 1992), Don Newquist of the International Trade Commission stated:

> There were a lot of red herrings raised during the debate over fast track authority, and one of the biggest ones was *maquiladoras.* Now, the maquiladora issue is a red herring because, first of all, maquiladoras already exist. Secondly, they will not be more advantaged under free trade but less so, because under the NAFTA the special advantage of being a free trade zone within a free trade country isn't such a hot deal. The expansion of the maquiladora cities would tend to be diminished, not increased. (Bostick, Newquist, and Reynolds 1992:36)

On the other hand, Ralph Nader (1993, 7) said:

> Want a small-scale preview of the post-GATT and NAFTA free trade world? Check out the U.S.-Mexico border region, where hundreds of U.S. companies have opened up shop during the last two

decades in a special free trade zone made up of factories known as *maquiladoras*. When U.S. factories have closed down and moved to Mexico, this is where they have gone. The attraction is simple: a workforce that earns as little as four to five dollars a day and does not have the means to defend itself against employer aggression because it is effectively denied the right to organize, and environmental and workplace standards are either lax or largely unenforced.

Don't make the mistake of thinking the maquiladora system is benefitting the Mexican people; they have to live in the polluted areas and accept the low wages and dangerous work.

Although this was not a direct debate, it is an example of the kind of information that was available to the U.S. public about NAFTA. Maquiladoras were either extraneous or central to the NAFTA debate. There seems to be an underlying agreement in these two texts that the difference between maquiladora zones and the rest of North America would diminish with the Agreement's implementation, but there is disagreement about whether that would be positive or negative—a key question then becomes, "For whom?" Revisiting the same two collections with that question in mind, here are some answers supplied by Senator John McCain and Vandana Shiva.

Senator John McCain summed up for his Heritage Foundation audience just who would benefit from the Agreement and the Uruguay Round of GATT:[30]

The conclusion of the NAFTA would place the U.S. in the center of a market of 360 million consumers, with a collective output of $6 trillion, a market much larger and much richer than the European Community. The recent explosive growth of our exports to Mexico, more than doubling in the last four years, portends much greater growth in a fully free trading relationship with our southern neighbor. The Commerce Department estimates that 538,000 American jobs are related to our exports to Mexico. Half of those jobs are a direct consequence of the trade liberalization policies that Mexico has undertaken since 1986.

As I stated, the best tonic for popular apprehension about free trade is a simple, direct connection of the benefits of free trade to the economic welfare of individual Americans. To most Americans the Uruguay Round of the GATT negotiations is little more than

some obscurely threatening process with an exotic name. But if the
one-third cuts in global tariff and non-tariff barriers which the U.S.
envisioned for the Round were effected over the next ten years,
they would generate a $1.1 trillion increase in our GNP. On aver-
age, that amounts to a $16,700 real income gain for every American
family of four. (O'Beirne and McCain 1992, 74–75)

Are any U.S. households waiting for the NAFTA check to come in the
mail? In her discussion of intellectual property rights—a significant
topic in the NAFTA text—Vandana Shiva points out that free trade is
freeing for corporations but not necessarily for communities. She refers
to intellectual property rights as rendering into corporate commodities
what was part of the commons—seeds and knowledge about resources,
for example. Privatization of knowledge and rights does not mean private in terms of household ownership but private in terms of corporate
rather than public ownership (Shiva 1993, 110–115).

The confusion about who would actually be served by the North
American Free Trade Agreement is rooted in the document itself, with
reference to what a person is actually considered to be. On page 2-2 of
the Agreement (1992), in the section called "General Definitions," there
is this statement: "*person* means a natural person or an enterprise."
Although this may be considered an obtuse reading from a legal perspective, as a social science researcher I find it necessary to read it from
various vantage points. The Agreement was signed by representatives of
national governments that exist because of social contracts as expressed
by their most recent constitutional documents; therefore does this mean
that a business has the same constitutional rights as a person? What
does this imply for the agency of a public as it intersects with the
process of approving and implementing a treaty/accord like the North
American Free Trade Agreement? In my reading of it, the document is
crafted in favor of those "persons" who are actually enterprises. This
builds on conventions of business law in each country, but one of the
stories I follow in this book is how the specific language and practice of
neoliberal trade policy might be read by a growing number of citizens
who feel that corporations have more rights than communities under
transnational trade law and the World Trade Organization and that
nations have decreasing regulatory powers over corporations. There are
many kinds of transnational businesses, of course, and the purpose here
is not to follow the specific effects of the Agreement by industry.
Instead, I listened for the ways people were articulating a shift in the

meaning and relative legitimacy of entities, including corporations, nongovernmental organizations, and nation-states, as varied as those are.

I suggest you consult the Agreement itself, if you have not already, to learn what is in it, especially since it is now much more available than it was in 1992 and 1993. Here is a brief summary from my perspective. The North American Free Trade Agreement, with its side agreements stipulating protections for workers and the environment (especially focused in the U.S.-Mexican border region),[31] lays out changes to occur in trade policies (and national protection of specific industries) among Canada, the United States, and Mexico over a fifteen-year period that began January 1, 1994. Much of the Agreement deals very specifically with intellectual property and trademark rights. One could ask a question about the Agreement and the pharmaceutical industry, for example. If a worker with Mexican citizenship in a Canadian-owned pharmaceutical plant in Buffalo, New York, created a new drug that could cure uterine cancer, who would own the patent? The Agreement provides a framework for the adjudicating bodies it establishes to address this kind of question (among a myriad of others), giving rights to corporations—if I may say this so sweepingly—over nations or individuals. Another dimension of trade negotiated in the Agreement had to do with rules of origin. If a product or a specified percentage of its components has been manufactured in the United States, Mexico, or Canada, the Agreement specifies a relaxing of import tariffs over time within the North American trade area for marketing these commodities. The schedules for eliminating tariffs over the fifteen-year period of implementation comprise the last three of the original five NAFTA volumes.

The schedules for the United States of America and Canada are written in English, and each has a single column listing the schedule for eliminating tariffs on goods imported from both of the other North American nations. The schedule for the United Mexican States is in Spanish and has two columns to distinguish the schedules for the elimination of tariffs on items from the United States and Canada. In a majority of cases, the schedules are the same, but the differences reveal the significance of the proximity of the United States for the Mexican government in protecting some of its nation's industries, given that tariffs are lifted first for Canadian goods and later for those from the United States, where there is a difference in the NAFTA schedule of easing duties on specific imports. The schedule in all three cases is connoted basically through a system of letters: "A" indicates that the item was already duty-free at the time of implementation on January 1, 1994. "B" is used to describe tariffs to be removed in five equal stages between January 1, 1994, and January 1, 1998. Items with "C" rankings would have tariffs removed in ten equal stages between January 1, 1994, and January 1, 2003. The lettering system continued to indicate items already duty-free at the time the Agreement would go into effect and with more complex schedules for tariff reduction.

Some examples of tariff schedules for specific items from each nation's schedule follow; these items caught my eye in a random reading of the Agreement. I do not want to trivialize these lists, because the reduction of tariffs in specific industries could be related directly to employment in those sectors in each country; these schedules were, therefore, key to labor union responses to the document in each North American nation. The fact that I select a few items as examples should be seen as exemplifying how different NAFTA stories can be and how much that has mattered in what were represented as straightforward summaries of the document.

The schedules were published as three volumes of Annex 302.2. The Canadian and U.S. schedules are paginated; the pages of the Mexican schedule are not numbered sequentially throughout the document. Therefore, I provide page numbers for the Canadian and U.S. schedules but not for Mexico's, from the 1992 version of the Agreement.

In the Canadian schedule, examples of goods listed as "A" (duty-free in January 1994) included lavatory (toilet) seats and covers (p. 188), oysters in the shell (p. 11), sunflower seed oil (p. 48), and "magnetos for use in the manufacture of internal combustion engines" (p. 445). "B" goods, to be duty-free on entry to Canada by January 1998, included saws (p. 444), iron oxides and hydroxides (p. 99), potatoes and mushrooms (p. 64), and "baby carrots (of a length not exceeding 11 cm) in airtight containers" (p. 65). Some examples of "C" items, to be free of tariffs by January 2003, were school supplies, belts, doormats (p. 166), and vacuum cleaners (p. 444).

In the U.S. schedule, "A" goods included "margarine, excluding liquid margarine" (p. 91), "sweetcorn (*Zea mays* var. *saccharata*)" (p. 143), brass-wind instruments (bagpipes were already duty-free in 1994) (p. 689), and "new pneumatic tires, of rubber: of a kind used on motor cars (including station wagons and racing cars)" (p. 350). Examples of "B" items scheduled to be duty-free by January 1998 included cottonseed oil (p. 90), "cherries preserved by sugar (drained, glacé or crystal-lized)" (p. 143), and truck axles (p. 640). "C" items included Roquefort cheese (p. 42), avocadoes (p. 146), kerosene (p. 179), and slip joint pliers (p. 553).

The schedule of Mexico (which is in Spanish) lists the following as having matching tariff-removal schedules for the United States and Canada. "A" items include rosins, ginseng roots, and Clementines; "B" goods include shovels and trapezoidal vulcanized rubber transmission sections that weigh less than or equal to 5 kilograms, excepting dentated ones. "C" items, to be duty-free by January 2003, include metallicized paper, spades, potassium carbonate, sugar cane, and dressed dolls representing human beings. An example of an item for import into Mexico with tariff schedules differing for the United States and Canada is the *seta,* a kind of mushroom; the Mexican government set a tariff rating of "A" for Canada and "B" for the United States.

The differences in tariff schedules might reveal anything from labor lobbies to the access to information about the NAFTA negotiations by leaders of companies in specific industries. It is difficult to read backward through the now-available document to the processes behind the negotiations. For that, I turn to particular NAFTA stories at the time of the negotiations (see Chapter 2).

NAFTA Stories Told Here

In this book, I follow some NAFTA stories and not others. Of the NAFTA stories told in the world, some had a lot of money behind them (like the stories national governments told in publicity campaigns), while others did not. I tend to emphasize stories told to me by particular people in particular places rather than those a reader had access to through magazines, newspapers, and video footage of political speeches from the moments represented herein. The ethnographic tradition has been to follow stories deemed less powerful in relation to processes like government decisionmaking.[32] This ethnography is about the intersections of differently empowered stories and how NAFTA was used as a signifier in working out new interpretations and alliances.[33]

What is the range of NAFTA stories followed in this text? Some are new, some old, some were widely heard, and others either silently told or silenced after the telling. There were fearful, hopeful, racist, and community-building NAFTA stories. I follow some of those. There were state stories, scholars', workers', and capitalists' stories. If I were composing this in a control room in a sound studio instead of at a desk in a library, and you were listening to these NAFTA stories instead of reading the way I've edited them together, then I would be boosting the volume on some stories and lowering it on others to find a sound that I imagine to be corrected for the distortion that capital can bring to the telling of stories. Just as many people in the late 1990s talked about how political races are won based on the amount of money spent on air time, I heard and read many critiques of the amount spent to *promote* rather than *publicize* NAFTA while the three North American national publics were involved in imaginary decisionmaking about it.

A subtle reading is unnecessary to discern that my perspective both as an ethnographic listener and storyteller is critical of the privileging of capital over communities. I think of Karl Marx as the first ethnographer of the impulses for global capitalism. He was not a good ethnographic analyst of colonialism (e.g., the unreflective but contemporary use of *barbarian* in the following quote), but he was an excellent documentarian of the form of liberalism echoed in today's neoliberalism, which is reflected in policies like NAFTA. In 1848, Marx and Engels wrote about the goals of investment and merchant capitalists (the bourgeoisie) in terms quite relevant to those today trying to make sense of the emphasis on tariff reduction and intellectual property rights in relation to NAFTA and GATT:

> The need of a constantly expanding market for its products chases the bourgeoisie over the whole surface of the globe. It must nestle everywhere, settle everywhere, establish connexions everywhere.
>
> The bourgeoisie has through its exploitation of the world market given a cosmopolitan character to production and consumption in every country. To the great chagrin of Reactionists, it has drawn from under the feet of industry the national ground on which it stood. All old-established national industries have been destroyed or are daily being destroyed. They are dislodged by new industries, whose introduction becomes a life and death question for all civilized nations, by industries that no longer work up indigenous raw material, but raw material drawn from the remotest zones; industries whose products are consumed, not only at home, but in every quarter of the globe. In place of the old wants, satisfied by the productions of the country, we find new wants, requiring for their satisfaction the products of distant lands and climes. In place of the

old local and national seclusion and self-sufficiency, we have inter-
course in every direction, universal inter-dependence of nations.
And as in material, so also in intellectual production. The intellectual creations of individual nations become common property.
National one-sidedness and narrow-mindedness becomes more and
more impossible, and from the numerous national and local litera-
tures there arises a world literature.

The bourgeoisie, by the rapid improvement of all instruments
of production, by the immensely facilitated means of communication, draws all, even the most barbarian, nations into civilization.
The cheap prices of its commodities are the heavy artillery with
which it batters down all Chinese walls, with which it forces the
barbarians' intensely obstinate hatred of foreigners to capitulate. It
compels all nations, on pain of extinction, to adopt the bourgeoisie
mode of production; it compels them to introduce what it calls
civilisation into their midst, *i.e.,* to become bourgeois themselves.
In one word, it creates a world after its own image.[34]

The NAFTA stories that attempt to make sense of global capitalism
are not entirely new stories, then. As I write in Chapter 2, one elderly
farmer in rural Mexico, "Don Hugo," answered my questions about
NAFTA in 1993 with stories about history—the century-old history of
Porfirio Diaz, the liberal free-trade Mexican president who emphasized
European investment in Mexico over the welfare of the Mexican people. The Porfiriato, as the period of his presidency was called, brought
the reaction of campesinos led by Emiliano Zapata, and the Mexican
Revolution led to the Mexican Constitution of 1917, which established
guaranteed access to agricultural land for generations through the *ejido*
system.[35] It took years to understand what Don Hugo was explaining to
me and how he was using history.[36] In the 1990s, the fall of the Berlin
Wall and the Zapatista rejection of NAFTA in Mexico figured in a story
that was anticipated in the above passage from Marx and Engels. Is
there a unified, inevitable momentum to global capitalism that tran-
scends democratic decisionmaking, national sovereignty, and the long-
term well-being of families and communities? These questions, in the
stories I heard of NAFTA's power as an agent to transform lives for better or ill, are difficult to ask because they violate a strongly enforced
thought style. Is the United States a neocolonial power through free-
trade policy and the guise of the World Trade Organization and other
international bodies?[37] Some U.S. leaders seem to make this claim to

U.S. dominance of and responsibility for the world economy. Here is a portion of a speech by Senator Phil Gramm (R-Texas), for example, in the November 20, 1993 Senate debate about NAFTA:

> We created at the end of World War II a world trading system that rebuilt Europe, that rebuilt Japan, that created economic miracles in Korea, and in Taiwan, and Hong Kong, places that had never had economic growth on a sustained basis before. This wealth creating machine was so powerful that it changed first the economic balance of power in the world, and then the military balance in the world. It tore down the Berlin Wall, liberated Eastern Europe, transformed the Soviet Union, and changed the very world that we live in. That was all accomplished because of American leadership, under President Truman and President Eisenhower and President Kennedy and President Reagan, to expand world trade.
>
> I have behind me a map which I find to be interesting. The map has the continents as they look in the atlas, but I have superimposed on the map some circles which represent the ability of the various nations to produce goods and services.
>
> This whole debate is about trying to merge the Mexican market, which is a relatively small economic market, with the huge American market and with a large Canadian market. But I ask my colleagues, in looking at this chart, to realize that it was American policy and leadership that created the European Economic Community, one of the world's greatest free-trade areas. It was our policy and our leadership under Democratic and Republican Presidents that created this economic miracle. It was our policy and our leadership that rebuilt the Japanese economy. And in doing so, we not only made them rich, but we made ourselves rich through that trade, and we won the cold war. It was a little twig off the American tree that we stuck in the ground in Korea, and it grew into a world economic power—and the same in Taiwan and the same in Hong Kong. This is a process that we built, and today we take a gigantic step forward in seeing it grow, in nurturing it and seeing that the world benefits from it.

Later in Senator Gramm's speech, he read from a speech made by U.S. Democratic Congressman Bourke Cockran in London in 1903, to establish that he and Winston Churchill were right in being strong supporters of free trade:

Your Free Trade system makes the whole industrial life of the
World one vast scheme of cooperation for your benefit. At this
moment, in every quarter of the globe, forces are at work to supply
your necessities and improve your condition. As I speak, men are
tending flocks on Australian fields, and shearing wool which will
clothe you during the coming winter. On Western fields men are
reaping grain to supply your daily bread. In mines, deep underground, men are swinging pick-axes and shovels to wrest from the
bosom of the earth the ores essential to the efficiency of your industry. Under tropical skies hands are gathering from bending boughs
luscious fruit which, in a few days, will be offered for your consumption on the streets of London. Over shining rails locomotives
are drawing trains; on heaving surges sailors are piloting barks;
through the arid desert Arabs are guiding caravans all charged with
the fruits of industry to be placed here freely at your feet.

You alone, among all the inhabitants of the earth, encourage
this gracious tribute and enjoy its full benefit, for here alone it is
received freely, without imposition, restriction, or tax, while every-
where else barriers are raised against it by stupidity and folly.

Senator Gramm followed this quote with the statement: "Great Britain
rejected this system, and they lost their position of world leadership.
Today, we embrace it and we commit to the principle that America will
not lose its position of world leadership."[38]

Clearly, arguments about NAFTA were intertwined with references
to historical colonial and current neocolonial power in the world and the
complex relationship between nation and capital (in both senses). Is
there a difference between the United States as a democratic nation and
as a tenuous home base for various forms of capital? Is it "anti-
American," with all the threatened force brought to that phrase by the
McCarthy era, to ask whether policies made in the interest of capital are
made in the interest of the public in a democracy? What if the trickles
do not come down but pool together and move away? A vague anxiety
about what a public has been trained not to articulate floated to the surface in the U.S. public discussions of NAFTA, which were compressed
in time, compared to those in Mexico and Canada.

There has always been, in U.S. culture, a tension between egalitari-
anism (the equal creation of all *men*) and individual economic competition.[39] Many have written about this (see, for example, de Tocqueville
1838). How that story of contradictory interests figures in NAFTA sto-

ries, though, is in the way NAFTA was represented to present opportunities for economic betterment for all citizens of North American nations (implied in Senator McCain's comment about dollar amounts per U.S. family), even as the document was distributed only to those controlling capital through corporate entities. Whose story was NAFTA, anyway?

In the political rhetoric associated with NAFTA, it seemed to be important for speakers to lay claim to NAFTA through an origin story. There are many such stories, and they do not converge as one. In many accounts, President Salinas de Gortari is represented as the author of the idea of NAFTA. In others, President George H. W. Bush receives credit for proposing the Agreement, and in a few, Prime Minister Mulroney figures in the origin myth.[40] In speeches with a deeper history, I have seen President Theodore Roosevelt credited with authorship of the idea. Like most of the NAFTA stories I invoke, what I see as most important is not a resolution of the differences between accounts but of the ways in which the stories are told and how NAFTA is being symbolically invoked to service other claims and concerns, difficult to express for various reasons.

One NAFTA origin story I heard in Mexico was that President Salinas de Gortari and his neoliberal advisors had proposed the Agreement in order to improve Salinas's chances for becoming the first leader of the World Trade Organization, which was to be implemented through the Uruguay Round of GATT.[41] Another related story was that he was trying to attract the capital of wealthy Mexican investors back to Mexico from European markets. Both of these stories run counter to the dominant stories in the United States, prior to the Agreement's passage, about Mexico representing (in the North American free-market-to-be) a source of labor rather than of capital or world leadership. As I see it, the complex field of assertions of power and agency associated with NAFTA give credence on one hand to Foucault's model of power as "something which circulates" (Foucault 1980, 98) and on the other— especially given the secrecy with which this public document was crafted and handled—to Gramsci's (1971) notion of hegemonic power. The elected national leadership of Mexico,[42] the United States, and Canada (Mulroney and Campbell much more than Chrêtien), along with the advising corporate leadership, were asserting the right to decide for national publics what would benefit them in terms of trade policy, and—as Gramsci might have noted—the right to promote an interpretation of NAFTA as beneficial to everyone even though it was phenomenally more so to those with capital than those without it. Simultaneously, the right of elected and corporate leaders to negotiate in secret and to make decisions (about both actions and their interpretation) on behalf of national publics or consumers of policy and goods in the free market in question, was being contested in myriad ways daily throughout the Agreement's negotiation and implementation. Some of that contestation was organized—as in the armed movement in Chiapas that directly confronted the power of national and state governments to impose neoliberal economic policies and the protests calling for transparency and delegitimization of World Trade Organization decision-making—and some was more "capillary," to use the Foucaultian term, as individuals in all three nations refused to see themselves as powerless in the face of global capitalism and chose personally not to recognize the Agreement, for example.[43] Thus many of the interpreters included here, whether legislators or busdrivers, were positing theories about power through their stories about NAFTA.

Related to those theories of power were theories of identity. For example, in characterizations of each North American nation by NAFTA storytellers, who were Canadians, Mexicans, and (U.S.) "Americans" imagined to be? Assertions of national identity reinforced through the telling of some NAFTA stories were countered by others, for example, the plurinational organizing by First Nations/Native American/indígena (depending on where the telling took place in North America), activists who came to world attention at moments such as in Chiapas at the beginning of 1994. I use the term *plurinational* here to indicate that more nations or polities were interpreting and affected by NAFTA than the three nations of North America recognized in the document. Canada, Mexico, and the United States are themselves pluralities of nations, if we take into account cultural and political entities like the Mohawk Nation and the Nation of Islam. One story I follow in this book is that of plurinational, not simply transnational, organizing. For example, representatives of indigenous nations or *pueblos* (peoples) from throughout the North American continent traveled to Chiapas in 1994 to monitor human rights there.

NAFTA Stories Not Told Here

NAFTA stories one might expect to find in this book that are *not* included are those told by Canadians and members of the EZLN in Chiapas.

These stories are not the central ones here for several reasons, one, of course, being where I chose to be—Morelos, Mexico City, Kentucky, or California—during the moments documented. Another is that many books have already been written about Canadian perspectives on NAFTA and events in Chiapas as they related to neoliberal policies like el TLC. A few other reasons, though, bear some explaining.

Vigorous public debates in Canada linked free trade, the future of jobs, national sovereignty (whether for Canada, Québec, or the Mohawk Nation), and cultural identity before the 1988 free-trade agreement between Canada and the United States. That agreement was not very popular with Canadian citizens;[44] it was clear in 1993 that the government of Canada, rather than the public, was supporting NAFTA. This point seemed to make Prime Minister-elect Chrêtien uneasy about the Agreement as he faced its implementation without having negotiated it himself or sent it through a popular referendum; he made a television announcement late in 1993 to the effect that the Canadian legislature or prime minister might not have the power to make such a decision. But the Agreement was signed, and it stands. With even the new prime minister expressing doubts, perhaps it was more widely apparent in Canada than in the other two North American nations that the Agreement was an act in the interest of representatives of capital—carrying the sense of inevitability that global capitalism as a concept conveys.[45] After all, Canadians were still sorting out what had happened in 1988. I do not mean to say that the Agreement was not actively contested in Canada, but since there had been sustained action against neoliberal free-trade policies in Canada since the mid-1980s, I have focused on the newcomers to the debate about North American free trade in Mexico and the United States.[46] What is curious to me, as a U.S. citizen, is that strong public debate about NAFTA occurred in the United States, much more than with the free-trade agreement between it and Canada, perhaps, in part, because the fear of integration with the "other" is more focused on a Mexican "other" than a Canadian one.

The text of the Canadian-U.S. free-trade agreement had been published widely in Canada, along with its implementing bill. Both were posted in libraries and published in newsmagazines. A Senate-Commons committee held thirteen thousand public hearings across Canada on trade with the United States in general and on the free-trade agreement in particular (Citizen's Forum on Canada's Future 1991, 131; Bain 1988, 55). Despite opposition, the treaty went into effect on

January 1, 1989.[47] There was an economic recession between 1990 and 1992 in Canada, which many Canadians attributed to the free-trade agreement (Cameron 1993, x).

Public distrust in Canada of free-trade negotiations with the United States has a long history. In 1854, for example, the Canada-U.S. Reciprocity Treaty took effect. It took eight years to negotiate that treaty, which waived tariffs on forty-three commodities, and the United States broke the treaty in the next decade (Kerr 1986). Michael Bliss (1987, 23) pointed out that following the failed free-trade agreement of 1854, there were other attempts to establish free trade between Canada and the United States:

> In 1874 we [Canada] negotiated another one that Congress never passed. In 1878 we had an election on tariff policy and made tariff protection our National Policy. In 1891 we had another election on the free trade issue. In 1911 we had another. In 1891 the opposition slogan was "Ottawa, not Washington our Capital" and in 1911 they declared that Canada should have "No Truck nor Trade with the Yankees."

NAFTA stories, then, perhaps especially for Canadians, were not new stories. The 1988 Canadian-U.S. free-trade agreement staged tariff reduction over ten years, so by now that free-trade area exists.

Within the United States, "the border" has been used more often to signify the border between it and Mexico than the longer U.S.-Canadian border, but silence about the latter in the accounts from the U.S. press and public conversations should not be taken to mean the Canadian-U.S. free-trade agreement has slipped into place without hitches. The first challenge through the adjudicating mechanism had to do with the quality of plywood coming into Canada and with the definition of wool (Tedesco and Clark 1989, 15). There were concerns about many industries, among them Canada's cultural industries. Magazines, newspapers, recordings, cable television stations, and other enterprises could no longer be protected, either as Canadian products with national tax breaks or from competition from U.S. cultural products without tariffs (*Maclean's* 1988, 21). One kind of NAFTA story is told about the resistance of national culture in the face of consumption of transnational (or often, in the case of Mexican and Canadian storytellers, U.S.) goods and services. Collins (1990, 328), for example, remarked that "consumption of U.S. broadcast programming, whether delivered by radio or television, has been the norm in Canada for more than sixty years. In spite of the absence of boundaries in the 'aether,' Canada, and Canadian nationalism survive in robust health." This is very similar to a statement about the persistence of Mexican national culture despite the consumption of U.S. goods, which a Mexican news producer made to me, as relayed in Chapter 2. In sum, examples from Canada are used in this book primarily as background and comparison for the NAFTA stories told in Mexican and U.S. contexts at the specific moments highlighted here, because Canadians had a long history of considering free trade with the United States and its implications for national culture and sovereignty.

The other major story not followed is the EZLN's armed resistance to neoliberal policies. Its leadership, often represented in press accounts to be Subcomandante Marcos (but much more a collective one in EZLN accounts), strategically invoked the symbolic power of NAFTA in its show of arms on January 1, 1994, the day NAFTA became whatever it is imagined to be: an entity, a policy, an oppressor, a liberator. In addition to the many written accounts of the EZLN, I want to bring attention (parallel to the point about multiple global capitalisms) to the many social movements—throughout Mexico and North America—that were resisting neoliberal policies before the commodification of ski-masked neoliberation. For example, in 1993, I was in rural Morelos when the townspeople of Jonacátepec jailed the police force, claiming they felt safer with the policemen behind bars. This exemplified the frustration and fear felt by many people I spoke with about the untried killings of young adults, practically every weekend, by soldiers and policemen around the state of Morelos (see Chapter 2). The political terrain in Mexico was already complex when President Salinas de Gortari and legislators made constitutional changes in anticipation of the North American Free Trade Agreement, and those changes themselves had a tremendous impact throughout the nation. The EZLN was one of a number of popular responses to the neoliberal changes in Mexico's social contract (exemplified by the Constitution of 1917) that included privatization of national industries, the potential sale of ejido lands, and acknowledgment of Mexico's pluriculturality, which did not go so far as to recognize the sovereignty of *pueblos indígenas*. The EZLN does figure in some of the NAFTA stories related in this book, especially in connection with the Alianza Cívica, but it is not the main strand of the text.

Notes on Words

Apart from the obvious logistical problems of multisited ethnography, the major challenge of this interpretive project had to do with words—their translation, in particular. In Spanish, for example, the North American Free Trade Agreement is the Tratado de Libre Comercio, or TLC, which means the Free Trade *Treaty,* not Agreement. The differences between those two words and the strength of commitment behind them formed an area for discussion in the interviews. Related to symbolic consideration of how Mexico is included in and excluded from North American identity, as when distinctions between first world and third world are invoked, is the term *norteamericanos.* In Spanish, this term refers to citizens of the United States and Canada, not Mexicans. Another example of the significance of words through translation is the Spanish phrase *la política.* This can refer to either politics in general or a specific policy, so care had to be taken in interviews to facilitate later translations of these stories into English. In the planned Spanish edition, as well, there will be translation problems in going from English to Spanish. For example, is the term *alien* from California's Proposition 187 (discussed in Chapter 3) to be translated as *extranjero*? Where does intentionality come in, in the use and translation of particular words? In the case of alien, for example, I need to explain that while the term *illegal alien* technically refers to all noncitizens in the United States without recognized immigration status, it is often selectively used to stigmatize those from particular countries, including Mexico. I agree with poststructuralists[48] that the use of words can constitute an expression of power.[49] Words are empowered by force, as when the stigmatizing phrase *illegal alien* is combined, sadly all too often, with beatings and other deprivations of human rights.

Some challenges presented by particular terms have to do with translation and others are related to contextual meanings. The word *sovereignty* provides an example. When I gave a talk on this project in Spanish at UNAM (National Autonomous University of Mexico), sociologist Julián Castro Rea warned me that when I spoke in English to U.S. audiences about this work, I might want to substitute the term *national security* for *soberanía,* or sovereignty, in order to convey the emotional significance of the term in Mexican contexts. Evidence of the importance of the word *soberanía* to Mexican national ideology is the very first statement of the National Development Plan (Plan Nacional de Desarrollo), 1995–2000, published by the Zedillo administration:

La soberanía es el valor más importante de nuestra nacionalidad; su defensa y su fortalecimiento son el primer objetivo del Estado mexicano. La soberanía consiste en asegurar la capacidad de los mexicanos para tomar libremente decisiones políticas en el interior, con independencia del exterior.

Sovereignty is the most important value of our nationality; the primary objective of the Mexican State is the defense and strengthening of our sovereignty. Sovereignty consists in insuring Mexicans' right to make [political or policy] decisions freely among ourselves, with independence from any exterior influence. (Poder Ejecutivo Federal 1995, 3) [author's translation]

Social theorists Gilberto Giménez (1993, 27) and Akhil Gupta (1992, 63, 67) have pointed out that assertions of nationalism are, paradoxically, given their strength through being posed against a transnational background or, in this case, the invoked threat of another nation usurping the agency of a nation's citizens. Since there are many reasons and ways to use words, a project in interpretation must pay careful attention to context. One cannot be sure what is meant when someone speaks of national identity, the nation, or sovereignty, unless elaborating questions are asked. As Federico Reyes Heroles (1995, 159) has said, "Soberanía como ética de Estado, soberanía como instrumento político, soberanía real y soberanía como emoción popular se mezclan y cruzan creando confusión." ("Sovereignty as a state ethic, as a political instrument, actual sovereignty and sovereignty as a popular emotion cross over one another and mix together, creating confusion.")[50] In a project like this one, then, it has been necessary to ask a speaker to what sovereignty or what nation he or she referred. In the answers sometimes lay NAFTA stories about plurinational movements crossing national boundaries, for example, and the sovereignty of indigenous (which does not carry quite the same meaning in English as the word *indígena* in Spanish) nations in conflict with that of the North American nations as they appear on dominant geopolitical maps.

Words like *democracy* can also be problematic as labels for nations in NAFTA stories. In this book, perhaps the reader can find specific points of comparison between Mexican and U.S. contexts, for example, that elaborate the meanings of *public* and *democracy*. Voting is often the litmus test for democracy, as noted by representatives of the Carter Center observing elections in Mexico, which have long been dominated by PRI party tactics; bags of ballots sighted downriver after elections exemplified such tactics. Voting was also called into question as a measure of democracy in the United States when, for example, the registered voters of California passed Proposition 187, which affected a resident population unable to vote. In a reversal of voting stories in 2000, Mexican citizens elected the first president in seventy-one years *not* representing the PRI, Vicente Fox Quesada, and the U.S. presidential election was shadowed by stories of missing and uncounted ballots.

What about access to information as a measure of democracy? In Mexico City, street vendors sell copies of national laws at the cost of printing. It would be interesting to see the U.S. Government Printing Office take to the streets with vending vans. How accessible are laws— the documents, the language, and the process by which they are made? In this sense, I think democracy was another theme running through the NAFTA stories followed in this book.

Listening Moments

There is a genealogy to the ethnography of public events, often traced in anthropology and sociology by the study of religious and political rituals throughout history—how these both structure and reflect collective sense-making, how they address symbolically the tensions in cultural thought worlds, how they are planned and performed, and how they reveal for a moment what is left unarticulated most of the time (cf. Gluckman 1962; Turner 1957; Ortner 1978; Handelman 1990; Nájera-Ramírez 1997). Attention to performance, storytelling, and the ways ethnographers can misinterpret such events as "pulling one's leg" was the central work of Américo Paredes (cf. 1993); the field of folklore has not received the credit it is due for shaping interpretive ethnography.[51] What has most informed this book is the work of those who are also trying to combine interpretive attention to storytelling with documentation of the lived experience of structural inequalities and the responses to those inequalities. June Nash, for example, demonstrated how political economic and interpretive approaches can be united productively. She told a story (1992) of an event, situating it within the structural frame of policies imposed on Bolivia through the International Monetary Fund and the interpretive frame of how individuals made sense of and responded to the national debt crisis. Women, marching in support of miners in 1986, laid a Bolivian flag in the road in front of Bolivian government troops armed to fire on them as (what Nash interpreted to be) a symbolic invocation of the national identity that strikers and soldiers both shared. Judith Adler Hellman (1994) listened to the effects of structural adjustment policies on the lives of Mexican narrators and related the stories of fifteen of those storytellers in her book *Mexican Lives.* She closely followed the experiences of individuals working and living in various economic sectors and regions of Mexico. Another inspiring author is Pablo Vila (2000), who used photographs to elicit stories about the "other" from many perspectives in the U.S.-Mexico border region and then discussed the ways narratives and metaphors were used to construct identities, stereotypes, regional "coherence," and plans for social action and reaction.

As ethnographers, whose stories do we follow? Nancy Lutkehaus (1995, x) likened what we do as crafters of accounts with multiple story lines to photographers making images through multiple exposures. As critics of ethnography have pointed out, the author is not only a listener but is definitely controlling how stories (or images) are retold and combined, including multivocal accounts. Too much emphasis on that point, however, sets the ethnographic storyteller artificially apart from everyone as storyteller (theory maker). All persons whose stories we hear and then try to retell are also weaving stories together.[52] I like Laurel Richardson's point (1990, 119–120) that the separation of scientific writing from literary attention to narrative took social scientists on a long detour away from paying attention to the significance of narrative "as both a mode of reasoning *and* a mode of representation" in social life (1990, 118). Richardson reemphasizes how "narrative creates the possibility of history beyond the personal" (1990, 127) and that unofficial collective stories have transformative possibilities, which social scientists have a responsibility to consider.

These are some of my colleagues in intention, then, as I attend to storytelling at particular moments in relation to the symbolic space and the transnational document, NAFTA. The reader, too, is an active storyteller. As Van Maanen notes (1990), there are three moments of ethnography: the first is when someone tells a story heard by the ethnographer; the second is the retelling in writing by the ethnographer; and the third is the act of reading it, with all the stories brought by the reader to the interpretation of, in this case, these NAFTA stories.

The moments I chose in which to attend to NAFTA stories were listed earlier in this chapter and will be discussed in detail in Chapters 2, 3, and 4. Chapter 5 does not document a specific moment but follows NAFTA stories told in 1996 and since. In the moments selected, there were both official storytelling performances—as on the U.S. Senate floor or on the presidential podium in Mexico—and either official counterperformances—as when Cuauhtémoc Cárdenas delivered a simultaneous state of the union address from his political party's perspective (the PRD) in the streets of Mexico City—or individual NAFTA storytelling for families, coworkers, friends, journalists, anthropologists, and so on. Through these multiple layers of storytelling at particular moments, it seemed to me as a listener that however amorphous a public conversation may have been, there were themes that marked the anxieties and hopes of the moment. Just as we structure our stories individually from the cacaphony of thought and possibility, I have retold these NAFTA stories by focusing on particular issues at particular moments: xenophobia in 1994, for example, and sovereignty in 1995. As a positioned listener, I was in Mexico City and small communities in western and eastern Morelos the summer of 1993; in Washington, D.C., during the Senate vote on the Agreement in November 1993; in Mexico City and north-central California, the fall of 1994; in Mexico City, the fall of 1995; and making visits to rural Kentucky throughout this period. I was told some stories specifically because I or a co-interviewer asked. Others were formal public addresses I heard because I was in the crowd.

Notes

1. These questions and all of the preceding description and dialogue appear in a panel on page 18 of *¡Me lleva el TLC! El tratado retratado,* by Rafael Barajas (El Fisgón), 1993. The NAFTA commentary in cartoon form, in Spanish, is followed in the text by documents on the NAFTA negotiations prepared by the Red Mexicana de Acción frente al Libre Comercio (RMALC, or the Mexican Action Network Against Free Trade), and selections from Cuauhtémoc Cárdenas's alternative proposal to the Agreement.

2. This text is taken from page 4 of the *Congressional Record*–Senate (20 November 1993), 103rd Cong., 1st sess., 139: 16602; the reference as it appears on the Congressional Universe website is 139(163), <http://web.lexis-nexis.com/congcomp/documen . . .>.

3. In this text, I use "the North American Free Trade Agreement" or "the Agreement" to refer to the document itself, as distinct from "NAFTA" the entity invested with meaning in public space. "El TLC" is the equivalent of NAFTA in Spanish, in terms of the public entity. Agency is interesting to think about in relation to NAFTA, both in the way the document was invested with it by speakers making claims about what NAFTA would do, for good or ill, and in

the way the document defines a person as either "a natural person or an enterprise" (North American Free Trade Agreement 1992, 2-2).

4. Following Sherry Ortner (1973), a cultural anthropologist, NAFTA could be called a "key symbol" because it was used as a central point of invocation of so many other domains: national identity, globalization, migration, and so on.

5. Ejército Zapatista para Liberación Nacional (Zapatista Army for National Liberation), the name of which was inspired by Emiliano Zapata, the campesino leader of the earlier Mexican Revolution that resulted in the Mexican Constitution of 1917, which was changed in the 1990s to accommodate the passage of NAFTA.

6. Steve Kurzman demonstrated the possibilities of hypertext ethnography while a student in a graduate anthropology seminar I taught at the University of California–Santa Cruz in 1994; Michael M. J. Fischer (1999, 295–296) also discusses the possibilities of hypertext ethnography.

7. All the authors in the collection (Grindal and Salamone 1995) in which Kirin Narayan's essay "Shared Stories" appears address how research intentions are intertwined with the lived experience of friendships and other social relationships that make sharing stories possible. This project, in turn, is embedded within a larger conversation in anthropology about research praxis, or the combining of theory and practice with attention to the power relations between researcher and researched. Much work and experimental writing in cultural anthropology in the last fifteen years have reflected this dilemma of representation. It is widely acknowledged that fieldwork is always a collaboration and that that should be reflected in our writing.

8. I met both Paulo Freire and Myles Horton through a seminar and conference at the University of Massachusetts at Amherst organized by Peter Park. Their approach to research as community problem solving, truly collaborative throughout the entire research process, seemed much more suited for social change than did the apparatus of the academy. Sources on their approaches to participatory research include Adams with Horton (1975) and Freire (1973, 1984).

9. I did ethnographic fieldwork in Kentucky from 1986 to 1989, for my dissertation, "Tobacco, Toyota, and subaltern development discourses: Constructing livelihoods and community in rural Kentucky" (Kingsolver 1991). In the dissertation, I used a local theoretical concept of "placing" individuals and ideas in social, historical, and physical space to frame an analysis of how people "placed" ideas and practices of capitalist development (Kingsolver 1992).

10. The authors collected in Smith and Guarnizo (1998) discuss the possibilities for agency afforded by multilocal or transnational experience, countering state control of the construction of individual and community identity and economic life. I would add that the structural inequalities conditioning migrant work are not discounted, but it is an important point (and one made also by a storyteller in this book) that transnational workers are observers and agents of social change and not simply economic victims.

11. The person being interviewed is often called the interviewee or the subject in social science analysis. Because I believe the person interviewed has power or agency in shaping analytical discussions, in this book I sometimes refer to him or her as the narrator. He or she is always a collaborator in a story-telling project of this kind.

12. That conference and another led to the volume *Common Border, Uncommon Paths: Race, Culture, and National Identity in U.S.-Mexican Relations* (Rodríguez O. and Vincent 1997).

13. *Strategic alterity,* a concept I have elaborated in several papers and articles (cf. Kingsolver 2000), refers to the way in which alterity, or the imagining of a different—and often stigmatized—"other," can be strategic or encouraged at specific moments to partition a workforce through capitalist rhetoric and practice, keeping one group in debt peonage, for example, which is justified through the "othering" rhetoric. Many other ethnographers of capitalism have written about this, including Eric Wolf's (1982, 380) discussion of an ethnically segmented labor force.

14. The Chicano/Latino Research Center provides immensely valuable opportunities for presenting and discussing research. I appreciate the comments of those who attended my talks that resulted in working papers nos. 5 and 11 in the CLRC series, "'Publics' speaking: Multiple perspectives on NAFTA, GATT, and California Proposition 187 in Mexico and the U.S." and "Plurinationality and Multilocality: Some explanations of identity and community before and after NAFTA in Mexico and the U.S.," which I drew from in writing this book.

15. George Marcus, Judith Stacey, Sherry Ortner, James Faubion, Don Brenneis, Peter Dobkin Hall, Kim Fortun, Michael Fischer, Paul Rabinow, and David Brent came up with the term *citizen anthropologist* in their conversation about the changing context of ethnographic practice (Marcus 1999, 15), which is useful for seeing anthropologists as connected and accountable to a wider set of relationships than those usually discussed as ethnographic encounters; postcolonial and feminist ethnographers have often pointed this out.

16. Latin American researchers and writers have long discussed the persistent inequalities associated with capitalist development in the hemisphere and the complexities of transnational identity that have been recently taken up in globalization literature in the United States. One of the realities of globalization is plural identity. As Edna Acosta-Belén (1995) points out, over a century of Latin American scholarship exists on the notion of transnational, pan-ethnic, and multicultural identities. She says (1995, 85–86) that José Martí's 1891 concept of *nuestra América* acknowledged both the divisions wrought by racism in colonial encounters and the possibilities of pan-ethnic and pan-national collective action against U.S. imperialism.

17. An economy is a nebulous entity to tabulate; for this reason, various relative percentages were published during this period to demonstrate the relationship between the economies of the three nations of North America. Sidney Weintraub (1988, 32), for example, stated the relationship this way: "One-fifth of U.S. exports go to Canada, by far the largest U.S. foreign market. Together Canada and Mexico are the recipients of more than 25 percent of U.S. exports. Thus there is an informal de facto trading bloc in North America."

18. In an article in the *New York Times,* Thomas L. Friedman wrote:

> As President Clinton has thrown himself into the campaign to win approval for the free-trade agreement with Mexico and Canada, he has shifted away from emphasizing its impact on jobs and begun to stress a different argument—that failure to pass the accord will undermine American foreign policy.
>
> About once in a generation, former Secretary of State Henry Kissinger said in speaking in favor of Nafta at [sic] White House ceremony last week, "this country has an opportunity in foreign policy to do something defining, something that establishes the structure for decades to come. . . . Now we live in a world in which the ideological challenge has disintegrated and a new architecture needs to be created, and Nafta is the first and crucial step in that direction." (1993, A1, 12)

Of course, the leadership of each nation had a larger trade agenda of which NAFTA comprised only a piece. For example, "the Council of the European Community and the Mexican Government drew up a Global Agreement on Economic Cooperation in 1975 whereby the contracting parties conferred most favored nation status on each other and promised to promote greater economic cooperation between themselves" (De Mateo 1987, 17). That mutual interest continued through the end of the twentieth century, with Mexico's oil industry being significant to the EEC, then the EU, since that body was not self-sufficient in terms of oil production (Coffey 1987, 30). It was important to Mexican negotiators in drafting the Agreement that the United States not gain control of Mexico's oil industry, because it gave the nation economic leverage with other nations of strategic trade importance.

19. All or nearly all tariffs will be removed in the North American free-trade area within fifteen years of implementation; different sources state this differently. Frederick W. Mayer observes that "the agreement is also interesting for what it did not include. A few politically privileged industries in all three countries were largely exempted: for example, Mexican oil, Canadian cultural industries, and U.S. shipping (1998, 110)." Some areas related to North American commerce, then, were simply left out of the negotiations of this treaty which so specifically removed trade barriers over time.

20. I have assembled this chronology from multiple sources. A useful chronology can be found at the beginning of Cameron and Tomlin's book, *The Making of NAFTA: How the Deal Was Done* (2000); that text also includes a list of the negotiating team members for all three countries, which was not widely available at the time of the secret negotiations. There is also a chronology of NAFTA-related events at the end of Pastor's book, *Integration with Mexico: Options for U.S. Policy* (1993).

21. This text is taken from page 21 of the *Congressional Record*–Senate (20 November 1993), 103rd Cong., 1st sess., 139: 16602; the reference is 139(163), as it appears on the Congressional Universe website.

22. A few of these, which represent a range of political and national perspectives, include: Ackerman and Golove (1995); Bognanno and Ready (1993); Calva (1991); Cameron and Tomlin (2000); Cameron and Watkins (1993);

García Canclini (1996); Castañeda (1993); El Colegio de la Frontera Norte y la Universidad Autónoma de Cuidad Juárez (1992); Dávila-Villers (1998); Erfani (1995); Calzada Falcón and Gutiérrez Lara, with Herrera Núñez (1992); Fernández de Castro, Verea Campos, and Weintraub (1993); Alarcón González (1994); Huchim (1992); Mayer (1998); Nader et al. (1993); Orme (1996); Pastor (1993); Perot, with Choate (1993); Whiting (1996); and Witker (1992).

23. Here, for example, is a partial paragraph from Volume II, p. ANNEX 401-1:

> (e) paragraph 1 of Article 405 (De Minimus) does not apply to:
> (i) certain non-originating materials used in the production of goods provided for in the following tariff provisions: Chapter 4 of the Harmonized System, heading 15.01 through 15.08, 15.12, 15.14, 15.15 or 17.01 through 17.03, subheading 1806.10, tariff item 1901.10.aa (infant preparations containing over 10 percent by weight of milk solids), 1901.20.aa (mixes and doughs, containing over 25 percent by weight of butterfat), not put up for retail sale or 1901.90.aa (dairy preparations containing over 10 percent by weight of milk solids), subheading 2009.11 through 2009.30 or 2009.90, heading 21.05, tariff item 2101.10aa (instant coffee, not flavored), 2106.90.bb (concentrated fruit or vegetable juice of any single fruit or vegetable, fortified with minerals or vitamins), 2106.90.cc (concentrated mixtures of fruit or vegetable juice, fortified with minerals or vitamins), 2106.90.dd (preparations containing over 10 percent by weight of milk solids), 2202.90.aa (fruit or vegetable juice of any single fruit or vegetable, fortified with minerals or vitamins), 2202.90.bb (mixtures of fruit or vegetable juices, fortified with minerals or vitamins) or 2202.90.cc (beverages containing milk), heading 22.07 through 22.08, tariff item 2309.90.aa (animal feeds containing over 10 percent by weight of milk solids and less than 6 percent by weight of grain or grain products) or 7321.11.aa (gas stove or range), subheading 8415.10, 8415.81 through 8415.83, 8418.10 through 8418.21, 8418.29 through 8418.40, 8421.12, 8422.11, 8450.11 through 8450.20 or 8451.21 through 8451.29, Mexican tariff item 8479.89.aa (trash compactors), Canadian or U.S. tariff item 8479.89.aa (trash compactors), or tariff item 8516.60.aa (electric stove or range, . . . (Executive Office of the President 1993)

The paragraph is actually two pages long, but this ends item e (i).

24. To clarify the difference between the formal national titles of the United Mexican States and the United States of America, I use "Mexico" and "the United Sates," respectively. As "America" encompasses a hemisphere, it is not used to refer to the United States of America.

25. Ralph Nader (1993, 5) has also written about both the physical and verbal inaccessibility of the Agreement. He asserted that "this difficulty in obtaining and understanding the actual agreements is not an accident; it reflects a purposeful effort by government negotiators to conceal the terms and effect of the agreements from the public, the news media, and even Congress. They would rather have citizens read a sanitized summary suitably interpreted by the

agreements' boosters." Lori Wallach (1993, 50–51), writing in that same volume, described how negotiations of both NAFTA and the Uruguay Round of GATT were so secret that they were closed at times even to some negotiators, and how difficult it was for public interest groups or members of the press to obtain copies of the documents to review and distribute.

26. See Fleck's discussion of thought style as employed by Mary Douglas in *How Institutions Think* (1986, 12–15). A thought style is a way we are socialized to think, one in which concepts are naturalized—linked to the natural, observable world—so strongly that it is very difficult to question one's thought style or the fact that it might not be the only way to think.

27. See Thomas-Houston (1997, 348–351) for a review of theories of the public sphere, especially Jürgen Habermas's work, with her important notes on differential power and access in relation to the public sphere by segments of national publics.

28. Chief executive officers of several major corporations, including Kodak and American Express, helped facilitate the NAFTA negotiation. They were members of the U.S. Advisory Committee on Trade Policy and Negotiations (ACTPN), which had access to the secret talks in which it was negotiated. (Mayer 1998, 42, 114)

29. Marx wrote in "The German Ideology" (1978, 161) about representing a specific group's interests as those of the whole society; he was discussing the rise of merchant capitalists to power as the new bourgeoisie. As this point relates to the French Revolution, we can now see plainly that the phrase "liberty, equality, fraternity"—represented as goals in the general interest of a new French society—did not include women, children, servants, or slaves, and how unexamined that fact was in what others would later call the public sphere.

30. The General Agreement on Tariffs and Trade was proposed as a post–World War II policy by representatives of the United States. It was signed in January 1948, by representatives of Australia, Belgium, Brazil, Canada, Chile, China, Cuba, Czechoslovakia, France, India, Lebanon, Luxemburg, the Netherlands, New Zealand, Norway, South Africa, the United Kingdom, and the United States. Mexico did not join until 1986.

The International Trade Organization (ITO)—precursor to the World Trade Organization (WTO) that came into being in 1994—was proposed at that time (Contracting Parties to GATT 1949). The negotiating countries disagreed about the power to be held by the ITO, the U.N.-related governing body linked to GATT, and in 1950, the U.S. administration declared there would be no congressional debate or approval of the International Trade Organization. As many have pointed out (cf. Pastor 1992; Semo 1993), the United States has consistently dominated transnational trade negotiations.

31. See these useful sources for more detailed discussions of the side agreements and which unions and environmental organizations supported and opposed them: Moisés Beltrán (1995); Dreiling (1997); and Dreiling and Robinson (1998).

32. Ethnographies are what cultural anthropologists write based on what they do—listen to people. Listening to people is not so innocent or neutral an occupation as it sometimes is presented. Thus I attempt here to provide at least

some markers to indicate the vantage point from which I elicited and heard NAFTA stories. That active listening, though, was contextualized within a very full environment of storytelling from all directions, and that is why I try to interweave official with unofficial (and otherwise contrasting) stories. It is, as Whitaker (1996) says in drawing on Wittgenstein to inform ethnography, a "try." I do not believe this is the only or best way to tell these stories but I am writing down, as an aural witness, what I thought important at these moments in a longer-term process of making sense of what is happening in the world.

33. Frederick W. Mayer (1998) also looks at NAFTA as a symbol and at the importance of stories told about it as part of his interpretation of NAFTA from the perspective of political analysis. Readers in the field of political science might particularly appreciate his approach to incorporating interpretive and quantitative elements of analysis.

Matthew Gutmann (1998), an anthropologist, provides a useful account and analysis of perspectives on NAFTA of the "urban poor" in Mexico. He also reminds readers that persons who feel too disenfranchised for political action should be considered in discussions of popular responses to NAFTA.

34. This passage is from Marx and Engels's *Manifesto of the Communist Party* (1848; 1973, 37–38).

35. The ejido system set aside communal lands, which were parceled into lots that individuals could pass down within families but not sell. They were meant to provide the Mexican people with access to subsistence so that they would not become a dependent or indentured labor force.

36. A. L. Anderson has written thoughtfully (1999) about the process of learning history through an ethnographic apprenticeship with a Garífuna community historian in Livingston, Guatemala. She, too, describes the importance of telling history through telling stories that at first may seem far from the issue at hand to the ethnographic listener.

37. Faye V. Harrison (1997b) argues that neocolonialism is indeed being experienced by Jamaicans through structural adjustment and free-trade policies imposed through the International Monetary Fund, the World Bank, and the U.S. government in such policies as the Caribbean Basin Initiative. Further, she argues that the effect of such policies is structural violence, which is not only "raced" and "classed" but also gendered in the way it is enforced and experienced.

An example of neocolonialism by free-trade policy is the use of the World Trade Organization to force one country to accept and market goods from another country. A colonial strategy, of course, was to control the markets of the colonies through tariff regulation and forcing products into one colony's markets that were produced in another (Lappé and Collins 1977, 99–111). Will there be a neocolonial round of tea parties, like the Boston Tea Party recently recontextualized in terms of nationalism and global capitalism by Dana Frank (1999)?

38. These excerpts from Senator Gramm's speech are taken from pages 14–17 of the transcript of the *Congressional Record* 139(163) referring to the North American Free Trade Agreement Implementation Act, which appears on the lexis-nexis website.

39. The tension between community and individual interests is embodied

in the very phrasing of the Declaration of Independence (Congress of the Thirteen United States of America 1776). The unalienable rights asserted in that declaration included "Life, Liberty, and the pursuit of Happiness." This last word was a telling turn from Locke's wording (read by the authors of the Declaration of Independence) regarding the "lives, liberties, or fortunes of the people" (Locke 1689; 1982, 135) and the existence of the state to protect private property. A month after the Agreement began to take effect, the Republican U.S. House representatives met in Salisbury, Maryland, and agreed on "five principles to describe their basic philosophy of American civilization: individual liberty; economic opportunity; limited government; personal responsibility; and security at home and abroad" (Gillespie and Schellhas 1994, 4). The Contract with America to implement those principles was, I believe, intended to rearticulate the kind of social contract documented with the Declaration of Independence. Tensions between individual and community, however, have been evident in every attempt to articulate such a social contract for the United States, and the Contract with America did not seem to address the general interest of the national public, at least as noted from Newt Gingrich's step down from leadership of the House.

40. If President G. H. W. Bush were credited with proposing the Agreement, then he would have been following up on a proposal that Ronald Reagan made in 1980 for a North American accord (Mayer 1998, 37) or "North American common market" (Orme 1996, 34). Reagan's proposal met with little response at the time.

41. The General Agreement on Tariffs and Trade is called in Spanish, el Acuerdo General Sobre Aranceles Aduaneros y Comercio.

42. See Claudio Lomnitz's (2000) account of how the presidency came to be the focal point of capitalist development in Mexico.

43. Civil society as an alternative to state society has been discussed by many people, with many meanings, but one useful way to talk about it is to look across the grain of U.S.-dominant accounts of public policy and consider alliances and struggles in alternative political blocs (compare those of Latinos living in the U.S. and Latin Americans, discussed in Bonilla et al. 1998).

44. In one account of the Canada-U.S. free-trade agreement's lack of popularity in Canada, after it had been in effect for less than two years, John Daly (1990, 48) wrote in *Maclean's,* a mainstream Canadian newsmagazine:

> Politically, the prospect of continental free trade carries a number of risks for Prime Minister Brian Mulroney. For one thing, public opposition to the FTA has grown steadily since it took effect 21 months ago. In a *Maclean's* Decima poll in May, 57 percent of the respondents said that they believed that the FTA had hurt the Canadian economy, while only seven percent said it had helped. And labor leaders blame the FTA for most of the roughly 105,000 jobs lost in Canadian manufacturing since the beginning of 1989. They add that jobs are likely to become scarcer if companies take advantage of a three-way trade agreement by moving to Mexico. Wage rates for skilled labor in that country average $1.60 an hour, compared with more than $12 an hour in Canada.

45. I find J. K. Gibson-Graham's critique of imagining global capitalism as a unified, totalizing system useful, as well as the reminder that if we can keep particular representations of capitalism distinct, there are more possibilities for agency in understanding and responding to decisions that are glossed as part of a seamless global capitalism (1996, 3).

46. For a discussion of networking between activists in Canada and Mexico opposing NAFTA, as well as a very clear framework for thinking about such transnational networks, see Howard (1997).

47. Of the major political parties in Canada, members of the New Democratic Party wanted to break the free-trade agreement of 1988, the Liberals wanted to renegotiate it, and the Conservative Party wanted to expand the policy of free trade through the passage of NAFTA (Cameron 1993, ix).

48. My favorite explication of this point is by Umberto Eco in his essay, "Language, Power, Force," in *Travels in Hyperreality* (1986, 239–255), in which he discusses the relation between language and power as articulated by Roland Barthes and Michel Foucault.

49. Poststructural critique has been caricatured (and deliberately misunderstood) by some as saying that power rests solely in language. I believe the point of poststructuralism is to pay attention to exactly how meaning is constructed in each interaction and each context, rather than taking it for granted that sovereignty, for example, always has the same meaning.

50. Federico Reyes Heroles (1996) published a chapter (in English), "Sovereignty: Concepts, Facts, and Feelings," in a collection called *NAFTA and Sovereignty: Trade-offs for Canada, Mexico, and the United States.* I highly recommend his review of the many ways sovereignty may be understood and used in public discourse.

51. José Limón makes this point also, in his discussion of Américo Paredes and other ethnographic folklorists in a larger argument about the need to explore the intersections between Chicano studies and cultural studies, getting beyond the stereotypes of *mexicanos* to see that "in varying historical moments, these expressive discourses give evidence yes, of 'resistance' and 'domination' but also of seduction, anxiety, internal conflict and contradiction in race, class, and especially gender dimensions conditioned always, as always, by a changing 'Anglo' capitalist political economy" (1994, 15).

52. Some examples of recent texts on ethnographic fieldwork that acknowledge ethnographers are just one set of storytellers about culture, embedded in a vast network of individuals explaining their social worlds, include: Amit (2000); Behar and Gordon (1995); deMarrais (1998); Lamphere, Ragoné, and Zavella (1997); and LeCompte et al. (1999).

2

1993: Stories of Anticipation

On November 20, 1993, I stood in line with friends at the U.S. Capitol to enter the Senate gallery. I wanted to see the senators debate the North American Free Trade Agreement in the final moments before their vote on the NAFTA Implementation Act. It was a long wait for a short shift in the gallery, but it seemed worth it to be an eyewitness to policy being enacted on behalf of millions of U.S. citizens. I was a disappointed citizen and eyewitness. It seemed emblematic of the entire NAFTA debate up to that time that we in the gallery were told not to read or write and not to make any noise. I looked down, expecting to see the exchange that we had been asked to observe with dignity, but there was hardly any dignity to observe. The senators, it became apparent as the presiding individual allowed his annoyance to be more and more transparent, were nowhere to be seen by the public. They were not engaged in a public debate of NAFTA. Those speeches were already written or waiting to be written for submission to the *Congressional Record*. The Agreement had been approved by the House on November 17, and perhaps this vote seemed a "done deal." Most of the senators, having abandoned the lone speaker discussing grain production with a great deal of animation aimed at the C-SPAN camera, were in a back room watching a college football game on television and listening to others on the radio. Notre Dame lost to Boston College 39–41, West Virginia defeated Miami, and the senators voted 61–38 to approve the North American Free Trade Agreement.

An excerpt from the *Congressional Record* reflects the absurdity of that moment:

47

MR. ROCKEFELLER. Mr. President, I ask unanimous consent that the order for the quorum call be rescinded.

MRS. BOXER. I object.

THE PRESIDING OFFICER. Without objection, it is so ordered. The Chair did not hear an objection raised.

MRS. BOXER. I object.

THE PRESIDING OFFICER. Objection is heard. The clerk will continue the call of the roll.

The legislative clerk continued the call of the roll.

MR. ROCKEFELLER. Mr. President, I ask unanimous consent that the order for the quorum call be rescinded.

THE PRESIDING OFFICER. Without objection, it is so ordered.

WEST VIRGINIA DEFEATS MIAMI

MR. ROCKEFELLER. Mr President, I have been living in West Virginia for 29 very happy years, and this is not a statement that meets the moment of trade relations in the world, but I wish to share my joy with my colleagues that the West Virginia University football team just defeated the University of Miami, which is probably the biggest athletic triumph in the history of our State. I am trying to contain myself and be as dignified as I can, and I am not doing it very well, but I wanted to share that with my colleagues.

I thank the Chair.

MR. FORD. I suggest the absence of a quorum.[1]

Events in the public arena surrounding NAFTA's passage seemed just as surreal[2] outside the Capitol as inside. As my friends and I walked down the steps into the cold November dusk, we saw those waiting to play their part in the chain reaction to a fait accompli. A millenarian man, dressed in a superhero suit with a long cape, loudly proclaimed the evils of NAFTA and the impending end of the world as he paced back and forth across the steps, defending a position between any departing senators and the members of the press. The press, in turn, stood under a sprouting of lit silver umbrellas, each reporter telling a tale of NAFTA and waiting for a Senate spokesperson to stride toward the silver toadstools and pronounce the deed done.

What did the passage of NAFTA/el TLC mean, and to whom? In this chapter, I follow multiple strands of anticipation related to the document. What was being voted on in the legislative bodies of each North American nation? From what I heard and read in the pre-NAFTA moments of 1993, the NAFTA vote—more than being a decision about the information contained in the policy—constituted a symbolic assertion of national identity, a version of history and sovereignty based on a particular understanding of who constituted each nation's public. The NAFTA strands I chose to follow in 1993 are gathered loosely into five sections: nation stories, stories in metaphor, neoliberal stories and counterstories, student stories, and farm stories.

As noted in the previous chapter, information on the North American Free Trade Agreement was conspicuously absent from public discourse, and this lack became a feature of how the Agreement was summarized. For example, in 1992, the law firm of Paul, Hastings, Janofsky, and Walker (with seven offices in the United States and one in Japan) prepared a summary of the freshly negotiated Agreement for its clients. Here is an excerpt:

> The North American Free Trade Agreement is one of the most dramatic developments to appear on the legal and business landscape in recent memory. It presents opportunities and challenges to nearly every business, and in nearly every industry, operating within the U.S., Mexico and Canada. Understanding these opportunities and challenges will quickly become an essential element of business strategy not only for American and Mexican companies, but also for Asian and European firms competing for position in the North American Market. . . .
>
> The careful secrecy that surrounds most of the negotiation process kept even close observers guessing as to what the various NAFTA chapters would contain. . . .
>
> One purpose of this report is to aid clients and friends in spotlighting areas in which the implementing legislation may affect their interests. (Loeb and Owen 1992:1-2)

Corporate lawyers and their clients, then, were not necessarily party to the contents of the legislation (until closer to the vote), unless those clients belonged to the U.S. Advisory Committee on Trade Policy and Negotiations. Political figures were being asked to comment on the Agreement without having seen it, including U.S. presidential candidate Bill Clinton. In Mexico, these included Mateo Emiliano Zapata Pérez, the son of Emiliano Zapata (a leader of the Mexican Revolution), who continues the family tradition of being a strong advocate for agrarian rights.[3] What about those who were considered to constitute the public (rather than the spokespeople) for the Agreement? In southern Mexico in the summer of 1993, my colleagues and I asked questions about how information about the Agreement was being distributed and received. Some of the answers given follow (I have translated them from Spanish).

"Elena," a radio journalist in Mexico City, stated in answer to how she learned about el TLC:

> The first information that [the government] began to give out, in Mexico, was that the establishment of free-trade treaties was some-thing that everybody in the world was doing. They began to inun-date us with radio and television announcements that said, for example, that the European Community was establishing a free-trade treaty. So it seemed like a bright idea. Once a free-trade treaty would be in effect, there would be free circulation of commodities, and this would generate jobs—generating jobs was always a very important point they were belaboring. Information was given out to the media from two sources: the government and private enterprise. Private enterprise has been, practically, the source filtering out more particular information, about more precise areas. Because governments always talk about global progress, don't they?
>
> There is a list of points about this list of points and they have covered 75 percent, leaving only 25 percent. The most difficult areas are one, two, three. And this is what is being negotiated. But in the end it had been a bombardment of information. That is to say, one knows that the critical points at a given moment have to do with the auto industry, because that is what they are talking about constantly. Then the discussion moved on to textiles. And following that, the counterinformation was about the critical situation facing the textile industry in Mexico. If the free-trade treaty goes into effect and does not protect that industry, then let's say in a period of ten years and without going into details, that industry will fold. It will collapse because there is insufficient technology, insufficient quality, and the industry will not be able to compete with the prod-ucts that come from outside the country. But at the same time, as the free-trade treaty negotiations have advanced, the counterinfor-mation is the uncovering of things, the grave crises that exist in this country. So the discussion moves in little steps. The thing is that people don't have a concrete idea of what is going to happen in spe-

cific cases. . . . People could use specific details in organizing to stop them from doing certain things [she gave the example of shifting the printing of national textbooks to foreign printers], but these things simply never come to a public debate.

So what we have is bombardment of very general information and very few discussions of concrete specifics. I don't want to say that information is closed, because if a journalist goes in search of this information, it can be found. . . . But one would have to be a specialized journalist to understand the language of the treaty and to be able to translate what it means in simpler words, to make it clear to everybody. When they finally tell us that they have signed the free-trade treaty and that there are a few remaining points to be worked out, we will have to keep pursuing that discussion.

This is the image that we have in the media: that there is no information. But really what we mean is that there is no specific information. Even I don't know what they mean by specific terms, even though I have a professional interest and I have tried to investigate a little more. . . . All the information [about the free-trade treaty and the negotiations] comes to us in fragments.

Elena was asked: "But do you think that most people in Mexico know where to go to become informed about el TLC?"

No, information is restricted to the members of the media. It is restricted. In this case, it would have to be a journalist who manages the information. And even then, it would require full-time research. In the case of this radio station, we have five reporters to cover all the national stories. It would take two of those reporters full-time to cover el TLC, but that would take reporters away from other stories. And we have a nation of eighty million inhabitants to cover. So what we end up with is superficial coverage [of the free-trade treaty]. Always superficial.

An eighteen-year-old student at UNAM said this about information circulating about el TLC:

Somewhere I read that the more informed we are, the more misinformed we are going to be. In other words, the more we are hit with information, the less we are going to grasp things. So if we have a huge scope of information about it and daily we are told that, I think we'll end up sick of the topic and basically not giving it any importance. It is for that reason I say we are so misinformed even though the same information is reaching us from all sides.

A farming cooperative leader in a small community in the state of Morelos near the border with the state of Puebla would have liked more than superficial information about the constitutional changes and other preparations for el TLC made by the Mexican government. He told us:

> It seems that this treaty already is not going very well for us. It seems that things are not well defined. It is likely that the treaty will affect us if it is passed; there could be advantages, like they say, but I think it's going to be a little difficult. . . . We are lacking in information. We don't know what's going to happen. We're not very familiar with it yet.

On the other side of Morelos, near the border with the state of México to the west, another *ejidatario*[4] talked with us about the information his community was receiving in anticipation of the treaty's passage: "Information is what's missing. They only give us half so that one will remain up in the air."

If, as he said, the public of Mexico was up in the air about the meaning of el TLC, the same could be said of the publics of the other two North American nations, and even of those governments ("they" in the above quotes) busily constructing publics for the consumption of NAFTA stories. Telling NAFTA stories in 1993 was for government representatives, I think, a way of *asserting* a relationship with national publics as well as *constituting* publics.

Nation Stories

Telling NAFTA stories in 1993 became a sort of nation-telling: spinning a history for a particularly imagined public and implying a social contract empowering North American governments to negotiate with and on behalf of capital in ways that facilitated the Agreement. NAFTA stories themselves became "symbolic capital"[5] in discussions of national identities in North America. Who constituted each national public for the storytellers? What would an "informed public" mean? How much agency would that public have in making the decision about NAFTA?

Does decisionmaking power mean sovereignty? These were some of the questions on my mind as we listened to NAFTA stories that summer.

A plurality of nations was invoked in the stories, and the discursive space opened for NAFTA stories allowed for some serious play with national identity. For example, Québec (imagined as either a province or a nation in political discussions there) had negotiated a separate free-trade plan with Mexico in 1992. In English, it is called the Québec-Mexico Action Plan, and its aims (from the Québecois government perspective) were to find Mexican markets and to publicize within Mexico Québec's technical expertise and possibilities for mutual business development in Mexico City and Québec City. The Québec government's report on the action plan considered NAFTA favorable for Québec:

> If Québec is to meet the challenges that lie ahead, its domestic policies must incorporate an international dimension, and reflection on changes in North America and the world must serve as a starting point when government policy is elaborated. This is the approach adopted in the Québec international affairs policy unveiled in the fall of 1991.
>
> To enable Québec products to gain access to growing numbers of markets, the government will continue to prompt the gradual, orderly elimination of barriers to international trade, while ensuring that appropriate transitional periods and adaptation measures apply to the most vulnerable sectors of the Québec economy. (Gouvernement du Québec 1993, 78)

In Canadian political structure, as I understand it, provinces have extensive trade agreements with one another and are more sovereign under trade law than, say, states in the United States (although in 1996 I heard a California government official speak of that state as though it, too, were a sovereign trading nation). What I mean to invoke here is the complexity of nationalist arguments and trade stances in the telling fields in which NAFTA was made. The Mohawk Nation's assertions of sovereignty had been countered with armed force even as Québec's were entertained at the Meech Lake negotiating table by the Canadian government in 1990 (Whitaker 1992, xi). Elsewhere in North America, the leadership of the Nation of Islam called for economic sovereignty, and in Mexico, a number of pueblos indígenas rejected the changes made in the Mexican constitution in preparation for NAFTA, for example, the change in Article 27 that could be seen as encouraging individual profiteering and dismantling communal property rights. NAFTA stories, then, were told and heard in a plurinational atmosphere.

National publics of Mexico and the United States cannot be easily separated or characterized, as Mexican journalists Jorge Carrásco Araizaga and David Torres noted in 1992. They looked at changes in the representation of national identity in NAFTA discussions in both countries before the document's passage. Significant to this consideration of NAFTA stories, they pointed out that the listeners' memories affect interpretations of the arguments:

> In the U.S. press, there has been a significant departure from the depiction of Mexico that was standard until a few years ago. Mexicans still remember from the early '80s *New York Times* articles by Jack Anderson on former president Miguel de la Madrid Hurtado, which portrayed Mexico as a land brimming with corruption and electoral fraud. They remember the broadcasts of congressional hearings on the drug trade. Until just before NAFTA, the U.S. media presented a steady stream of editorials, articles, and television programs about the problems with drug trafficking, as if it were the only activity in Mexico. This theme was a determining factor in the negative relations between Mexico and the United States.
>
> A prime example of this sort of portrayal was the case of Enrique Camanera Salazar, the U.S. Drug Enforcement Administration agent assassinated in Mexico. Soon afterward, newspapers across the United States printed a cartoon showing the Mexican national shield, with its Aztec eagle and serpent smoking marijuana. This image became the subject of a diplomatic conflict between Mexico and the United States in 1984 and '85. (Carrásco Araizaga and Torres 1992)

The power of images in conveying national identity (or insults to it) and stereotypes will be taken up in the next section and Chapter 3, but the point is that representations of national identity were very interconnected with stories told in anticipation of NAFTA.

We decided in the summer of 1993 to interview someone whose job involved manipulating images and telling nation stories: a television news director in Mexico City. National symbols were all around us as we talked: the flag standing in the corner and the president's portrait on his office wall. As in interviews with government officials, I was not allowed to record the interview but could take notes.

The news director predicted that, in fifty years, all of North America would be a single country. He said that in ten years, Mexico would be an entire *maquila* nation, selling its labor power like the "Little Tiger" nations of the Pacific Rim. In the current economic world war, as he saw it, he said that el TLC would have to be passed in order to create a North American economic bloc to combat the European Community and the Japanese. He saw such a union as merely a legal arrangement, however, not as an opportunity for the United States to invade Mexico culturally. He was not worried about Mexico losing its sovereignty in the face of the other two North American nations, even with such an economic partnership. When I asked him if he saw NAFTA bringing a decrease in national identity or sovereignty for Mexico in relation to the United States, he said this:

> Mexico has three thousand years of history—the U.S. has little more than two hundred. It is going to be difficult to lose national identity. We've had U.S. [radio and television] programs for forty years. Half the population is under twenty-five, and it's a generation formed by television. We are products of television, yet we continue recognizing the tricolor flag. English is part of the language, for example "hot dog," like "taco" is now part of English, but it does not affect national culture or identity. [author's translation]

The news director told us, acknowledging that several of us were from the United States, that "a racist current against Mexico" exists there and "a belief that we are not at the same level." He explained to us that the main purpose President Salinas de Gortari proposed el TLC was to attract the capital of wealthy Mexicans back to Mexico. He predicted that a Mexican capitalist would buy the Empire State Building within the next ten years.

Further considerations of nation stories and the class position of storytellers appear in the "Student Stories" section below, and the relationship of racialization and racism to NAFTA stories is taken up in Chapter 3. Here, I discuss how metaphors are used in NAFTA stories, as in the news director's equation of the Empire State Building with modernity and with the United States's traditional position (which he implied was weakening), at least since World War II, as the first nation of global capitalism.

Stories in Metaphor

In NAFTA stories, the trade agreement itself has been attributed agency—the power to help or harm as though it were a person. In this section are examples of how metaphorical representations (with their verbal or visual allusions to already known domains of meaning and power) gave NAFTA agency over human futures in North America in these stories.

El Fisgón, the cartoonist whose characters discussed el TLC throughout the summer of 1993, titled his book of cartoons, *¡Me lleva el TLC!,* or (*NAFTA Is Killing Me*). That amount of agency—the power to take a life—even invoked in jest implied that NAFTA was a force to be taken seriously and understood in its effects on individuals' futures, if the information could be found.

At the other end of the spectrum of NAFTA expectations portrayed by Mexican political cartoonists that summer was the neoliberal argument that it was a panacea: free trade would be the answer to all the nation's problems. This was conveyed with iconic power by the cartoonist Ahumada in the cartoon *esperando el milagro* (waiting for the miracle), which appeared in the Mexican newspaper *La Jornada* on July 28, 1993 (Figure 2.1). El TLC hangs among other *milagros*—physical representations of prayers, usually brass and only a few centimeters long, that can be purchased from vendors outside a Catholic church or cathedral and pinned to the clothing of the representations of holy figures inside. The milagros come in shapes specific to particular prayers (Figure 2.2). In Ahumada's cartoon, the leg might represent a prayer for healing arthritis, the heart a prayer for a failing marriage, and the eye a prayer for a relative with glaucoma.

One aspect of visual metaphors is their flexibility to represent different associations, depending on the vantage point of the interpreter. Cartoons can be seen as either outside the realm of the serious or as the unrepressed voice of the people (see Chapter 3 for more discussion of this). The same image can convey many meanings. Ahumada could be telling a story here about NAFTA producing an economic miracle for Mexicans; a story critical of the hopes pinned to the Agreement by the

ESPERANDO EL MILAGRO ■ Ahumada

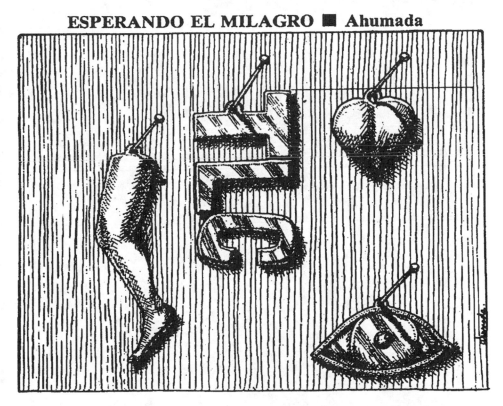

Ill. 2.1 Waiting for the miracle (Ahumada in *La Jornada*, July 28, 1993)

Ill. 2.2 Los milagros [The miracles] (Photo by Ann E. Kingsolver)

national government (demonstrated by the millions spent on promoting the policy); or a story raising a question similar to religious questions about where agency lies in answering a prayer (with the requesting individual or with the petitioned), among other possible ones.

The inaccessibility of the document itself during the 1993 negotiations was the subject of visual metaphorical representation. In a cartoon drawn by Kemchs for the Mexican newspaper *uno más uno* that appeared July 24, 1993, two "bag ladies" are walking along, and in the first conversation bubble is a set of characters unreadable in Spanish. Her companion says, "No entiendo" ["I don't understand"]. In two more panels, the first locutor continues emitting symbolic characters. Finally, the respondent says: "Ya entiendo, que la firma del TLC está en chino." ["Now I understand; the signing/negotiation of NAFTA is in Chinese," or to use an expression familiar to U.S. readers, "It's Greek to me."] As I have said before, a dominant NAFTA story told was about its inaccessibility to those who saw themselves affected by it.

Some speakers used verbal metaphors to convey NAFTA as a threat to the security of the listeners or readers. Ralph Nader, for example, in a speech to the National Press Club on November 4, 1993, said: "NAFTA is a giant Mexican truck in your rear-view mirror as you're driving down the road." And in what may be the most memorable metaphorical allusion made that summer, Ross Perot in numerous speeches and in the book he published with Pat Choate (1993) called NAFTA "a giant sucking sound" [of jobs going from the United States to Mexico].

Robert Reich referred to NAFTA as a "lightning rod" (for anxieties about jobs) in a press conference held [and broadcast on C-SPAN] on September 2, 1993. That notion of NAFTA as a conduit of concerns is similar to a metaphor I, and other interpretive anthropologists, might make of NAFTA as being an empty screen (in lieu of the policy itself) onto which various publics of North America could project their hopes and fears about changes to come in the three nations if the Agreement were to pass later in the year.

The outcome of the NAFTA negotiations, and the national identities of the United States and Mexico, were metaphorically linked to a soccer game by a number of NAFTA storytellers. The Mexican national team beat the U.S. team in a soccer match in July 1993. That victory was seen as symbolically evening the playing field of national identities and fortunes in which the United States had had the upper hand with its power to decide on NAFTA, already long supported by Mexico's PRI government. For example, a political cartoon in the Mexican newspaper

Excelsior (July 26, 1993) shows a long negotiating table with a Mexican negotiator in a sombrero and soccer uniform at one end and a barely discernable U.S. trade representative at the other. In the center is balanced a soccer ball. The Mexican negotiator says, "Y ya en serio: cuándo vamos a firmar?" ["And now, seriously: when are we going to sign?"] On the same day, a political cartoon in *La Jornada* shows a group of fans, still holding their Mexican flag after cheering their team, watching a soccer player with a U.S. flag leave the field with a net of balls, an angry expression, and a bandage on his cheek. One of the Mexican fans, obviously worried, says, "Menos van a querer firmarnos el TLC." ["Now they are going to be less willing to sign the treaty with us."] Transgressive questions about whether the traditional balance of power between the United States and Mexico, as first-world and third-world nations, would continue or be upset, if NAFTA were signed and fully implemented, could be asked through the metaphor of winners and losers in soccer.

As important as the production of these metaphorical representations, of course, is their consumption and distribution.[6] In Mexico that summer, I asked individuals if they were reading the newspaper and what they thought of the political cartoons. For many, they did seem significant not only in releasing tension about confusion over NAFTA but also in framing ways to talk about the issues. On Mexican newsstands, collections of political cartoons were displayed next to financial periodicals and other venues for discussion and assessment of NAFTA. Given what journalists told me about the degree of censorship of the national press, the political cartoons were a tolerated form of dissent journalism, facilitating serious engagement of current issues.

Neoliberal Stories and Counter-stories

The presidential planets were in alignment for a free-trading North America in the early 1990s, as President Bush, Prime Minister Mulroney, and President Salinas de Gortari all favored neoliberal economic policies. Mario Monroy Gómez (1995a; 17) characterizes neoliberalism in these ways: "(1) less intervention of the state in the economy and a larger role for the resultingly unregulated market . . . with more enterprises transferred from the public to the private sector; (2) opening of the economy to business and capital investments from outside the country; and (3) a specific effort to mitigate extreme poverty through social programs like Pronasol or Procampo [meant to encourage labor contributions on the part of the poor to match government or business investments in the community]" (author's translation).[7] Monroy Gómez published the analysis through SIPRO, a popular economics organization, to explain in clear language the history of neoliberal policies in Mexico. He showed that President Salinas de Gortari had been a strong advocate of neoliberal economics as a cabinet member in Miguel de la Madrid's presidency and had thus been part of the neoliberal trends in Mexican national government between 1982 and the 1990s. Specifically, as many I interviewed in 1993 explained, President Salinas de Gortari was a neoliberal "technocrat" winning over more of the opposing "dinosaurs" in the PRI through telling his own persuasive NAFTA stories.

Who were these PRI technocrats advocating neoliberal change through proposing and negotiating el TLC? The DOCEX document I found in Scotland 1992 contained biographies of the Mexican negotiating team for NAFTA,[8] and I learned that most had been trained in neoliberal economics in the same programs as U.S. cabinet members. President Salinas's cabinet of technocrats, or *tecnoburócratas* (technobureaucrats) as Jorge Carrásco Araizaga referred to them in an article about *yupitecas* (Mexican yuppies) and the education of the new elite, held the most higher education degrees in the history of Mexican presidencies, and most of those degrees were from U.S. institutions. Cabinet members in the Salinas administration had M.A. or Ph.D. degrees from the following: Harvard (24), Stanford (18), Columbia (12), Yale (10), MIT, and the Universities of Colorado, Wisconsin, Pennsylvania, South Carolina, and California–Berkeley, as well as Chicago, Cornell, and New York University (Carrásco Araizaga 1993, 7). The Mexican NAFTA negotiating team members were primarily in their thirties and represented a new generation in Mexican politics, having participated fully in transnational conversations about neoliberal reforms with other scholars for years before being appointed by Salinas. Herminio Blanco Mendoza, in charge of the negotiating team, had a Ph.D. in economics from the University of Chicago (former employer of leading neoliberal economist Milton Friedman). Jaime Enrique Zabludovsky Kuper, general coordinator of sectoral negotiating teams, had much experience in the private sector and a Ph.D. in economics from Yale. Guillermo Aguilar Alvarez, the legal advisor to Mexico on trade with the United States, was trained at the University of Montpellier in France and spoke English, French, Portuguese, and Italian, in addition to Spanish. Raúl

Ramos Tercero directed the economic impact studies for NAFTA; his Ph.D. was in economics from Stanford. Israel Gutiérrez Guerrero, director of legislative affairs with links to the private sector, had a Ph.D. in economics from MIT, while José Enrique Espinosa Velasco, coordinator of bilateral commerce, had the same degree from Yale. Juan Gallardo Thurlow, president of COECE or Coordinadora de Organismos Empresariales de Comercio Exterior (Foreign Trade Business Organization), had law degrees from the United States and Belgium. The Mexican cabinet had more transnational ties than the U.S. cabinet, and members of the negotiating teams from both countries had closer intellectual and class ties than the publics they represented in negotiating the document. This is one NAFTA story that was not widely heard in the United States, due to the dominance of stereotypes of Mexico as third world and the resultant perceptions of its leaders as uneducated, parochial, and looking for handouts.

A free-trade treaty between the United States and Mexico in 1993 was only part of the international terrain being discussed by neoliberal politicians and their advisors in the Americas that summer. As one columnist (Bátiz V. 1993, 5) pointed out, the Transit and Trade Treaty between the two countries signed in 1859 had established free trade between them in market sectors specified by the U.S. Congress (Mexico did not have a legislature at that time), so free trade was not exactly a new issue under debate. The neoliberals were more concerned with creating trade bloc areas beyond the United States and Mexico to compete with the solidifying European Union and other large trading entities in the world. Between two meetings of the trinational NAFTA negotiating teams in July 1993, one in Cocoyoc, Mexico, and the other in Ottawa, Canada, President Salinas de Gortari met with Alfredo Cristiani, the president of El Salvador, and made a public statement that "it is necessary to establish through our relations a new point of departure in the construction of a new region, united in its interests, respectful of its sovereignty, joined by its roots, and yet at the same time, recognizing its diversity" (Lomas 1993, 10) [author's translation]. President Salinas was meeting often with leaders of Central American and South American nations that year, promoting ties between existing trade blocs, like the Mercosur, and new trade blocs (e.g., the proposal to incorporate Chile into NAFTA[9]) that brought more and more Latin American nations into a single free-market trading area. The impetus for doing all this quickly, as far as the neoliberals were concerned, was summed up by Mickey Kantor, the U.S. trade representative, in a press conference also held between the two meetings of the NAFTA negotiating teams in July: to strengthen the Americas as a trade area before the negotiations of the Uruguay Round of GATT, to be concluded by December 15 according to the terms of the fast-track legislation. Kantor announced that the North American Free Trade Agreement and the side accords must be approved before that date and that all the world was watching to see how negotiations were going (Notimex 1993, 37).

While some major goals were shared by neoliberal policymakers in the United States and Mexico, there were also some differences fueled by nationalism and the history of U.S. domination of Mexican policy. During the summer of 1993, the Ibero-American summit (Spain and the nations of Latin America) in Brazil rejected the presence of the United States as an observer (Petrich and Gutiérrez 1993, 1). As Kantor stated, while the U.S. government was seeking a free-trade area in the Americas to compete with the European Union's consolidated one, representatives of Latin American nations were talking with their counterparts from Spain at the Ibero-American summit about possibilities for consolidating markets to give Spain (often marginalized in EU debates) economic and political leverage within the EU[10] and to provide Latin American nations with links to the EU as an alternative to U.S. domination of a free-trading American hemisphere.[11] Emilio Zebadúa (1993, 48), in an editorial titled the "Latin American Moment," compared what he saw as the different tones of the recent Group of Seven meeting in Tokyo and the Ibero-American summit in Brazil.[12] He characterized the Group of Seven (G-7) as the richest nations of the world, meeting to discuss coordination of neoliberal macroeconomics policies with the goal of "dominating the capitalist forces of the world." In contrast, he saw the impetus of the Ibero-American summit as understanding the impact of global restructuring on the region. Zebadúa noted that even with the policy changes made to facilitate passage of the North American Free Trade Agreement, and other neoliberal acts in the region, foreign investment in Latin America had been dropping for the last decade. Between 1992 and 1993, capital investment from outside the region dropped from $49 billion (U.S.) to an estimated $41 billion. Zebadúa saw the neoliberal privatization and deregulation policies as a stopgap measure in a growing inequality between the G-7 and the member nations of the Ibero-American summit.

NAFTA stories, then, were only part of a larger set of stories being spun in 1993 about capitalist development, retrenchment, and the fates of various nations in relation to the reconfiguration of the global economic and political landscape. Mexico had only joined the General Agreement on Tariffs and Trade in 1986. In 1993, there were 110 GATT member nations. Hari Shankar Singhania, president of the International Trade Organization, announced that summer that in the rush to complete the Uruguay Round of the GATT negotiations (initiated in 1986), urged on mostly by the G-7 nations, the result would be a war of trade blocs, and developing nations would lose out (Benitez 1993, 1). The NAFTA story I imagine here is that the neoliberal technocrats of President Salinas's cabinet found themselves caught between their training and their nation, so that there were not only divisions (as well as alliances) between G-7 and developing nations in international trade discussions but also class divisions and alliances mirrored *within* nations like Mexico. This was what I heard in the spectrum of NAFTA stories I was told in 1993: class differences between storytellers who saw NAFTA as a promising possibility for demonstrating to wealthy Mexicans that their own country had a stable enough economic climate to bring back their investments or those who saw it as a vehicle for destroying community economic collaboration and creating dependent, underpaid workforces for foreign-owned factories and agricultural corporations.

NAFTA stories also varied tremendously by region. In this book, I mostly describe those told in Mexico City and rural Morelos to the south; different stories were told in the U.S.-Mexican border region. For example, in the summer of 1993, U.S. Secretary of Commerce Ron Brown and Luis Donaldo Colosio Murrieta, a PRI leader who would soon be assassinated (probably due to internal party divisions), led a discussion among more than three hundred representatives of the private and public sector on both sides of the border to discuss the impact of NAFTA on that region. Both Brown and Colosio, neoliberals, assured listeners the treaty would be an instrument for infrastructural development in the region, with a special development fund for the border zone (Hernández and Aponte 1993, 17). In that same region, counter-neoliberal NAFTA stories ranged from white supremacists on the U.S. side protesting what they saw as increasing immigration from Mexico with the passage of NAFTA to artists in Tijuana protesting negative cultural impacts that might come with imposition of U.S. media through NAFTA. Then, in addition, there were networks of organizations cooperating across the North American continent to address environmental, labor, and indigenous sovereignty issues. Each NAFTA story is a reification and not intended here to be representative of a nation or an identity group as a whole. The cacophony of the stories, I think, reveals something interesting about the political goal of *telling* coherent stories about what is in the national interest, for example.

Understanding, then, that this section's organization into neoliberal stories and counterstories is only a heuristic for organizing stories that promote and counter NAFTA for various reasons, I complete the section by discussing neoliberal policies enacted through changes to the Mexican Constitution, interviews about NAFTA, and some alternatives to the Agreement proposed in counter-neoliberal discourse.

President Salinas de Gortari proposed amendments to the Mexican Constitution that were ratified by the Mexican legislature in February 1992. Two major changes in articles of the constitution—Article 4 and especially Article 27—were made that could have a bearing on how decisions were made to transfer land, freeing it up (from a neoliberal perspective) for foreign investment. Article 4 reforms pertained to the recognition of the rights of indigenous communities within the Mexican state, including land rights, but it was not followed up with the necessary implementing legislation that would have granted pueblos indígenas more than symbolic power.[13] Changes in Article 27 were more widely viewed as related directly to preparations for NAFTA. Since 1917, Article 27 had guaranteed ejido lands to those wanting to provide a living to their households through independent cultivation rather than working for others for wages. Changes in Article 27 allowed conversion of these communal lands into private property and purchase of the land titles by investors from outside the community associated with the ejido parcels. Additional articles of the constitution were amended to make way for el TLC.

President Salinas and his PRI government also made legislative changes to privatize what had long been nationalized industries in many sectors of the economy, including banking and communications (areas of investment highly desired by capitalists both in Mexico's private sector and outside of Mexico). These change were seen, in a neoliberal NAFTA story, as necessary to facilitate passage of the Agreement and the investments in the Mexican economy it would encourage. Salinas's cabinet members, however, were often called upon in public appearances around the nation to defend neoliberal policies, which were perceived by many to be putting up Mexican identity itself for sale.[14] For example, Emilio Lozoya Thalmann, the secretary of Energy, Mines, and Parastate Industries (SEMIP), during a ceremony commemorating the death of Mexican President Benito Juárez G., responded to doubts about neoliberal policies and loss of control of the petroleum industry by saying, "Petroleum is and will be the property of Mexican citizens, because it constitutes a natural resource that belongs to the nation. . . . In the free-trade treaty with the United States and Canada, the Mexican state reaffirms its ownership of . . . the oil industry" (*El Economista* 1993, 34) [author's translation]. He went on: "It will not be at the mercy of that which is held most valuable by us, our national sovereignty, that Mexico counts on NAFTA as an additional tool for supporting the growth of the country and promoting job opportunities for Mexicans" (Andonaegui 1993b, 1) [author's translation]. Sovereignty also was cited at the top of Mexican legislators' list of concerns with NAFTA. Senator Carlos Sales Gutiérrez, head of the Mexican Senate's trade commission, announced in July 1993 that NAFTA would not be approved by legislators unless the side agreements under negotiation were favorable in terms of Mexico's national sovereignty and constitution (Rodríguez 1993, 24).

The constitutional changes were still very much under debate–and signal topics in conversations we had about NAFTA—in 1993. In July, Patrocinio González Garrido, Home Office secretary in the Salinas administration, convened a meeting of representatives of sixty indigenous organizations from ten Mexican states in order to discuss rules and regulations associated with the changes in Article 4 (Pérez U. 1993, 7). He was hoping, according to Pérez U., to build consensus among the fifty-six recognized pueblos indígenas within Mexico's borders to unite their cultural values with the legislative future of Mexico as a single nation. He proposed that henceforth October 12 no longer be known in Mexico as the Día de la Raza,[15] which González Garrido said was a negative reminder of the marginalization of indigenous peoples through the imposition of one culture, ideology, and economy on them. He said that instead, from 1993 on, the day would be known as the Día Nacional por el Reconocimiento y Justicia de los Pueblos Indios (National Day of Recognition and Justice for Indigenous Peoples) (Pérez U. 1993, 7). The secretary stated it was necessary for Mexicans to move away from a rhetoric of winners and losers, in terms of identity. "In this country, even though we distinguish ourselves ethnically, socially, and culturally, it has only made sense to be Mexicans above all, and you the indigenous peoples are Mexicans under the law and in the eyes of President Salinas" (Pérez U. 1993, 7) [author's translation]. In Chapter 3, I quote a member of a pueblo indígena who did not experience this promised treatment as a Mexican citizen; he and others were seeking and could not obtain an audience with a representative of the national government, a right guaranteed constitutionally to all Mexican citizens. The EZLN focused its armed protest of NAFTA's imposition on the Mexican people on the neoliberal reforms, including changes made in the constitution. And later in this chapter are statements of campesinos who felt that the changes in Article 27 were the most significant neoliberal policy to address, more than the Agreement itself. National unity obviously was not behind the neoliberal agenda, despite the story President Salinas and his cabinet members were telling representatives of other nations; the same was true of the difference between the national publics of his corollaries and their representatives.

What about neoliberal stories being told in the United States? Unity on the policy was not there in the United States public or government, either. For example, in July 1993, District Judge Charles Richey ordered an environmental impact report to be compiled before NAFTA could be considered for ratification, but an appeal from the Department of Justice questioned Judge Richey's authority to give that order. In response, President Clinton made a statement reassuring the U.S. public that NAFTA would create more jobs than would be lost through investments in the Mexican economy and plant closings. He explained that the goal of NAFTA was to reduce tariffs so that the United States could sell more products to Mexico, not to create conditions for U.S. employers to move to Mexico for lower labor costs (Carreño Figueras 1993, 1, 20). Appearing before the NAACP's Legal Defense and Education Fund representatives in July 1993, Commerce Secretary Ron Brown also announced this as the administration's position: that NAFTA would create jobs and be good for the country. He said that Ross Perot's criticism of NAFTA had been mistaken and that he had lost the presidential election because of it. Secretary Brown stated that the administration was not promoting NAFTA because it would be good for the Canadian or Mexican economy but because it would bring jobs to the United States; for every $1 billion in new exports, nine thousand new jobs would be created (Ferreyra 1993, 1, 20). Secretary Brown went on to explain, according to Ferreyra who attended the NAACP breakfast in Los Angeles at which Brown was speaking,[16] that Mexicans love U.S. products and that the secret to revitalizing the U.S. economy would be access to new markets. NAFTA was only one step; according to Brown, the administration's goal was to extend the trade zone to include the entire hemisphere and to create greater access to U.S. products.

Secretary Brown's position reflected the neoliberal stance taken by

Clinton's administration, concluding negotiations of NAFTA undertaken by the Bush administration. Was the neoliberalism of Bush's administration and that of Clinton's first administration the same? The debates between presidential and vice-presidential candidates had revealed differences, primarily in the state's role in promoting social welfare in a deregulated market. Thus neoliberal policy has been accompanied by increased attention to "civil society"—a notion discussed by Marx in relation to the private sector[17] and in current discussions about the relationship between NGOs and everything from flood relief to supplanting state military forces. It is necessary always to ask questions about specific policies being glossed as neoliberal and about what can amount to very different reasons for supporting the same policies. As an example, an examination follows of some of the discussion of NAFTA and its parallel accord on the environment by representatives of the U.S. government and NGOs.

On September 14, 1993, the leadership of the Sierra Club (one of many U.S.-based environmental NGOs) denounced the North American Free Trade Agreement. The next day in Washington, D.C., a press conference was called in which U.S. Trade Representative Mickey Kantor, Vice President Al Gore, Carol Browner, administrator of the Environmental Protection Agency (EPA), and U.S. legislators and leaders of several environmental NGOs expressed their support of the Agreement. Their NAFTA stories did not all echo one another, since their topics ranged from global modernization (Vice President Gore) to protecting biological diversity (Kathryn Fuller of the World Wildlife Fund), but their particular words can be read as clues to understanding the convergence of neoliberal stories favoring NAFTA during the first year of President Clinton's administration. Mickey Kantor spoke for the administration when he said, "All we need to do is read the document. . . . You will see this is the most protective trade agreement in the history of [protecting] the environment and, frankly, of labor and workers' rights as well."[18] Carol Browner emphasized the uniqueness of citizen participation built into the mechanisms for environmental protection provided for through the NAFTA side agreement, and she also gave voice to another NAFTA metaphor: "When you look at the package in its entirety, it is a home run for the environment; it is a home run for the people who live along the border. And so we are very pleased to be part of this effort to help secure the passage of NAFTA." Although both Browner and Kantor noted the productiveness in the negotiations of environmental activists both for and against NAFTA, in this press conference, only those representatives of environmental NGOs in favor of NAFTA were present. Jay Hair, president of the National Wildlife Federation, said: "NAFTA is proenvironment, and propeople. It should be passed immediately by the United States Congress." Fred Krupp, executive director of the Environmental Defense Fund, stated: "The side accords create avenues for public participation and cooperation to solve real problems that will not be there if we do not pass NAFTA. . . . The question for the environmental community is, 'Will the environment be better off or not if NAFTA is passed?' The answer is clearly yes." Krupp said the side agreement would create a framework for looking at a single geographic air shed in the El Paso/Juarez region, permitting the development of policies to address the worst air pollution along the U.S./Mexican border. The creation of the North American Environmental Commission through NAFTA's side agreement on the environment was also the Natural Resources Defense Council's reason for supporting NAFTA. The National Audubon Society took an official stance in favor of NAFTA as well. Kathryn Fuller, speaking on behalf of the World Wildlife Fund, said, "The environment in North America—the global environment, for that matter—will be better off with NAFTA than without it." She emphasized the structural possibilities for protecting biodiversity. Dr. Russell Millermeier, president of Conservation International, also mentioned Mexico's status as the fourth richest nation in the world in terms of biodiversity, but he took a slightly different rhetorical tack than his colleagues. "The greatest enemy of the environment is poverty," he said, arguing that nations need strong economies to protect their environments and NAFTA was a route toward that strength. Vice President Gore answered questions at the end of the press conference, including one about the split between environmentalists and within the Democratic Party on NAFTA:

It's going to be a hard fight . . . but we will win. . . .When the facts are presented to the American people, the advocates of progress always prevail. . . . It would be absolutely crazy to allow the opponents of NAFTA to prevail. It would hurt the environment. It would hurt jobs. It would hurt our country. It would hurt our relationship with our neighbors—not only Mexico and Canada but throughout Latin America. . . . So for all of those reasons, I predict that we will prevail.

In response to a question about the change from support to opposition by some House Republicans, Gore expressed his confidence that an informed public would be supportive of NAFTA: "The vast majority of Americans are just hearing about NAFTA for the first time now. . . . Now that we are presenting the facts to the people and to the Congress, I am confident that we will prevail." The Clinton administration's NAFTA story, then, was a story of progress for the hemisphere (as Bush's had been), with an emphasis on citizen participation in regulating capital and its effects as the state deregulated markets.

The most powerful support for NAFTA in the United States seemed to come from transnational corporate administrators who would profit from the reduced tariffs, rather than from individual citizens or through NGOs. Christopher Sinclair, president and executive director of PepsiCo International, for example, announced his support on July 20, 1993, in Monterrey, Mexico: "NAFTA represents an important opportunity for all U.S. companies to globalize trade to countries in Latin America, thus the U.S. Congress is obligated to ratify NAFTA" (Chavolla Nava 1993, 3) [author's translation]. At a ceremony marking the opening of a new bottling plant, in which $50 million (U.S.) had been invested and thirteen hundred new jobs had been created, Sinclair said he felt sure that NAFTA would be in effect the following year (Chavolla Nava 1993, 3).

I talked with a U.S. corporate executive about NAFTA in the summer of 1993 who oversaw factories in Canada, Mexico, and the United States. He told me that NAFTA would help him get direct access to land on which to build factories. Earlier, he had relied on connections through his Mexican business partner's family to lease ejido land, but he told me that with the constitutional changes [in Article 27] associated with NAFTA, his company could now purchase the land outright for factory construction. I asked him if he had read any Mexican labor law or if he had seen the proposed NAFTA document. He replied, "No, you get in with the right crowd [in Mexico] and they will steer you straight—they won't let you do anything the way you're not supposed to." His biggest worry with constructing more factories in Mexico, if NAFTA passed, was about transportation: getting trucks carrying products he intended to sell primarily to U.S. consumers across the Mexico-U.S. border on schedule.

What about the workers?

In the summer of 1993, my students and I interviewed an undersecretary in the Mexican Secretariat (parallel to the U.S. Department of Labor) who had helped draft the side agreements on labor. His NAFTA story, an argument for the benefits of implementing the free-trade agreement/treaty, went like this: Internal investment in Mexico was not sufficient for the economy to grow and to create more jobs. Therefore, foreign investment (from Asia and Europe, he specified) had to be sought for growth to take place. In order for that to happen, there had to be very clear and permanent rules governing trade, as in the Agreement, and for Mexico to develop a niche in the world market, the quality of internal production would also have to be clearly regulated. His emphasis on the welfare of the workforce was on training to meet global standards of quality in production in order to compete. The undersecretary stated:

> The most important change is this: NAFTA will open up [the market] and allow free trade, so the national producer *must* lower his prices and modernize himself in order to be able to compete. . . . In the labor market, workers need the concepts of productivity and quality. We will succeed [with NAFTA] in raising salaries and earnings enormously—we could be a model in the world. We [in the Secretariat] are pushing the labor market to do this. NAFTA is an important part of the new economic model of this country. If they don't sign NAFTA, this new model will go on developing anyway. More than with NAFTA, the opening of the market has already started to change labor conditions. [The key is] competition: if they don't reduce accidents—with protection and training—in the workplace, they will lower productivity and be unable to compete. . . . There is a difference between what they pay workers in the U.S. and Mexico, but then the productivity of U.S. workers is more. We want to be more attractive to foreign production, with modern equipment and greater productivity. [author's translation]

The undersecretary stated that the labor side agreement to NAFTA violated national sovereignty in some ways: "Mexico says no, that it is up to Mexico to enforce its own laws." Yet he expressed enthusiasm about the integration of the work of the labor departments in the Mexican and U.S. governments, especially in working out an arrangement for temporary mobility of Mexican workers, citing this example: "A Mexican business gains a contract in the U.S. to wash buildings. They can take Mexican workers into the U.S. more easily to service that contract with [the new agreement on] temporary mobility" (author's translation). This example invokes something between the image of corporate managers and workers from one nation together taking a contract in another and doing that job and the image of stereotypical labor contractors (or *coyotes*) taking independent workers, illegally or legally, across the Mexican/U.S. border for employment by U.S. contractors, an important difference here being who, in the end, is employing the workers. Since the undersecretary was talking about Mexican firms taking a temporary contract in the United States and using Mexican workers to service that contract, he was not referring to anything like the Bracero Program, which established conditions for Mexican workers to enter the United States and take jobs for which their labor had been formally requested by the U.S. government in the mid-twentieth century (specifically, in part, to replace U.S. workers serving in World War II).

I asked the undersecretary—who was seated at the end of a long conference table and who had agreed to a quick conversation—how he would compare the newly formed European Union and the relationship between the three nations of North America that might be forged if NAFTA passed. He replied that there were very strong differences. First of all, the Tratado de Libre Comercio is a commercial agreement—"We are not negotiating social aspects. There are no popular movements reacting to NAFTA."[19] He went on to say that in Europe, there were [transnational] laws regarding the protection of workers[20] and of investments, neither of which was written into the central NAFTA document.

Numerous NAFTA stories about labor were in circulation in 1993. The representatives of national government whose stories I heard generally portrayed NAFTA as being in the best interest of workers in their own nations, through job creation and capital investment that could support wage increases. Alternative stories told by workers, labor union representatives, and labor scholars questioned the benefits of NAFTA for workers. As labor scholar Harley Shaiken (1995, 32–33) put it in retrospect, the most cogent issue facing workers in all of North America at the time NAFTA was being negotiated was not whether there would be a net gain or loss of jobs (which was the main focus of discussion in the news media) but the probability of downward pressure on wages in all three countries because of the "harmonization" of the three national markets. Thus, he was implying, while workers were put in competition with each other through nationalist rhetoric about which labor market might win or lose jobs because of NAFTA, the overall winners would be the owners of capital, whether citizens of Mexico, the United States, Canada, or other countries.

In the summer of 1993, we spoke with a representative of the FAT, or Frente Auténtico de Trabajadores (Authentic Workers' Front), which has a membership of forty thousand workers. "Roberto" met with us in the building used as a headquarters by the Red Mexicana de Acción frente al Libre Comercio, since he served as a FAT representative to the Red or RMALC. In the entryway was a display of publications explaining the North American Free Trade Agreement and neoliberal policies in clear language, including the cartoon book by El Fisgón, *¡Me lleva el TLC!* As we talked in one corner of a large hall, a group of workers was going through newspapers and other print sources in another corner, deciding what to include in a newsletter and calling to Roberto to ask his opinion during the interview. Roberto explained to us that he was an organizer but primarily a worker; he had worked for fifteen years in an auto parts factory, and then he had taken a more active role in his union. Eventually, he started working with the FAT. He told us what that meant:

> I work here in the FAT and find myself, as a result, nearly unemployed because of all the time I have put in trying to organize democratic unions. It is difficult to do, because one can work on the other side [across the U.S. border]. I am responsible for organizing information for the FAT and I take photographs [for the newsletter].
> . . .
> The FAT is an organization that belongs to the Red. The FAT is a national independent, democratic organization. We see ourselves as independent from the government, from *patrones,* from the Church, and from political parties and any organizations not supportive of workers. The FAT has members who are factory workers, campesinos, and members of popular organizations. At the national level, we are in fifteen states and have approximately forty thousand members.
> FAT is uniquely situated as an organization and cannot be compared with any other in Mexico. We are not exclusively a union organization because there are also members of agricultural cooperatives and collectives. Neither are we exclusively a cooperative organization; we are not exclusively urban, nor are we exclusively rural. This is a unique characteristic of our organization. In some states, workers are primarily campesinos [farming ejido lands] and there is hardly any factory work. In others, workers are members of cooperatives. There are places in which there is a little bit of everything.[21]

Roberto described the different situation workers faced in each state of Mexico. For example, in Monterrey, the national army had earlier been called into a factory to disrupt FAT organizing, and the state government had sent police to "sniff out" any trace of the FAT and to use violence to discourage anyone else from joining a union, so in 1993, there was little official membership in Monterrey because of those past events. Similar incidents had occurred in other states.

An important constituency of the FAT, Roberto said, is young workers under twenty-five, like the majority of Mexico's population. He said of these workers:

> In factories, the worst and lowest paying jobs, the most insecure jobs, are given to the young workers. Their point of view is least taken into account [in the factory]. "You're new—we're going to talk with those who have been here a while." "You're new—go do the washing up." If a worker is required to do a dangerous job, the newest worker is given that job. That's the attitude. In the end, democracy means to take everyone into account, doesn't it? In the union, in the nation, wherever one is. So this is one of the demands of the FAT, that young workers be taken into account, that young workers' voices be heard.

We asked Roberto for his sense of how Mexicans were doing in 1993 and what he anticipated as possible effects of NAFTA. He replied:

> What I have noticed is that even though the treaty has not yet been signed, there is already an increase in unemployment. According to those unions affiliated with the FAT, union workers are already being let go. On the other hand, we can talk of salaries. You know, right, that at this moment Mexican wages are approximately the equivalent of $4 U.S. for a workday of eight hours? This is minimum wage, and even at this low wage, factories are implementing policies to increase the quality, the quantity, and—in a word—productivity of work. So that the work that the government is doing toward getting signatures on el TLC has translated [for workers] into unemployment, low salaries, and increasing exploitation.

Of the neoliberal Mexican government, Roberto explained that in preparation for NAFTA, one of the first things done was an attempt to alter Article 123 of the Mexican Constitution, as Article 27 had been changed. He said:

> Article 123, among other things, established a minimum wage and says that minimum wage must satisfy the needs one has for food,

health care, education, clothing, and more. . . . Well, in practice, it
is impossible to satisfy even one of these needs with a salary equivalent to $4 U.S. per day. So the first thing that [the administration]
has to do is comply with the law in the full meaning with which it
was established. Of course it may be convenient or not [for the gov-
ernment], but at this moment they are not complying with the laws,
and there is the very real risk that they will do so less and less in
order to favor the income they want from foreign industries and
new investments to guarantee [their policies]. In order to look more
attractive [to foreign investors], they are looking for more ways to
control us [the workers].

I asked Roberto about resistance within Mexico to NAFTA; he
explained the activities of the RMALC:

The Red is exclusively a network of organizations—more than one
hundred environmental, urban, agricultural, human rights, youth,
and other activist organizations. The principal purpose of the Red is
to focus on the North American Free Trade Agreement. Its function
is to review, analyze, and critique the proposed treaty measures as
they are negotiated by the government and to create alternative proposals. The FAT is one of the member organizations of the Red.

Regarding the FAT's resistance to government policies viewed as hard
on workers, Roberto explained how he saw resistance:

The government permits us to organize in some parts of the country
and not in others. We have a clear idea where we cannot confront
the government and where we are being infiltrated. For example,
there are various unions that form part of the Congreso del Trabajo
(Labor Congress). We call them *oficialistas* because of the government influence, but we also have members participating in those
organizations. They don't go out into the streets with the FAT ban-
ner, but they go to meetings and do what they can to put forward
the proposals and interests of the FAT, inside those official labor
organizations. This is a form of resistance. If the conditions don't
exist for us to have a confrontation with the government—and we
don't just want confrontation for the sake of confrontation—then
we have to keep working for democratization in a form that is func-
tionally democratic, more horizontal, more participatory, and so on.
What we don't want is to disappear. So we keep working, even if it

is under the flag of other labor organizations. Conditions have been very difficult since a while back.

We asked Roberto where he thought conditions for workers were headed in Mexico. He answered that the future looked "gray, if not black." He said that the problem was with the Mexican government offering Mexican labor as a highly controlled, cheap workforce to the rest of the world. He said that the neoliberal changes in labor laws meant that workers were "condemned" to serving as "flexible labor, hourly workers." Roberto explained that labor laws in Mexico were being changed to be more like those in the United States and that Mexican workers had had—"at least in the letter of the law, if not in practice"—more constitutional protection. He said the current government wanted to change all that "for the benefit of investors and at the cost of the welfare and the future of workers."

He said these changes would be dismal not only for Mexican workers but for Canadian and U.S. workers as well:

> For they are going to offer us as cheap labor, and then they are going to say to workers in the U.S., "Well, if you want to keep working, we are going to have to lower your salaries. If you don't accept that, then I will go with peace of mind to Mexico." And the same thing will happen in Canada. It's a downward pressure, working against labor in all three countries.

I asked Roberto if there was coordinated opposition to NAFTA in the three North American nations. He said there was an equivalent of the Red in the United States and in Canada and that they were working together. He also said that similar networks were forming in Chile and Guatemala.

We talked with Roberto about the long-term possible effects of NAFTA and neoliberal policies. He told us about his two teenaged sons, who have Mayan names because their Yucatecan mother wanted to pass along to them her language and culture, and how they loved basketball, especially Magic Johnson and Michael Jordan, and the U.S. rock groups Poison and Guns and Roses. He said the possible long-term effects of NAFTA weren't all bad and saw an increase in technology that might help the country little by little. But he saw NAFTA creating an increasing dependence on the United States and said it presented a mixed bag of opportunities: "Serán integrando a esta cultura de la hamburguesa y la salchicha" ("Hamburger and spicy sausage culture will be integrated").

When I asked Roberto about alternative proposals to the Agreement, especially those advanced by Cárdenas and by Castañeda, he said that their proposals had contributed to the Red position statements on el TLC, which the FAT supported. He told us about attempts Red leaders had made to bring their critiques and alternative proposals to the NAFTA negotiating table. The official negotiators from all three North American nations had been meeting in the Hotel Camino Real (on the *Zôcalo* or central square in Mexico City). The alternative negotiators—the linked networks he had described in all three countries—had met and prepared an alternative proposal for consideration by the official negotiators, but when representatives attempted to take the proposal to the hotel, there was an impressive military response. Helicopters were above them, sharpshooters on top of the hotel, and a line of armed police formed in front of the hotel to prevent their entrance. Roberto's response was, "They'll reap what they sow."

As we left, Roberto gave us literature to study so we could learn more about the FAT and the Red, including the Agenda Social, the set of proposals the alternative negotiators had tried to give to the official negotiators. It presented detailed proposals for democratizing the process of negotiating a trade agreement and for protecting workers' rights, the environment, and human rights in that process. The document acknowledges that the official NAFTA negotiating process has opened up important themes to discuss but states that the Agreement is unacceptable as it stands because it does not contribute to solving North America's serious social problems. Here is an excerpt from the labor section of the alternative proposal:

> Workers and our organizations must participate in national decisions that affect our present and future, and we must be taken into account in this process of discussing, evaluating, and eventually ratifying the North American Free Trade Agreement.
>
> We workers believe that a just trade system is one that considers social, cultural, and environmental aspects as fundamental to itself—not one that leaves to the free market the prospects for improvement and well-being of the population but one that lays out clear accords for reaching those goals.
>
> We want a just trade agreement that attends to the interests of the majority and not exclusively to the needs of transnational capi-

tal. We do not want a treaty that consolidates or promotes development strategies like those that in recent years have brought on
extremes in impoverishment of the population, deterioration of the
environment, and subordination of our economy to the United
States. (Red Mexicana de Acción frente al Libre Comercio 1993, 1)
[author's translation]

The alternative proposals for a free-trade agreement include, in the
labor section, provisions for collective bargaining, contract rights, and
the right to strike, as well as rights to health care, insurance, unemployment benefits and retraining, subsistence, transportation, and an environment free of toxins. The labor provisions call for equal treatment of
workers in all three nations of North America: if workers in the United
States and Canada have unemployment benefits, then Mexican workers
ought to receive the same benefits under the agreement. They also call
for equal protection for agricultural and manufacturing workers and for
protection for migrant workers as laid out in various international
agreements already in place, for example, the United Nations
Agreement on the Protection of the Rights of Migrant Workers and their
Families, signed in 1990. A North American trade commission is proposed as a monitoring entity, comprised of nongovernmental organizations including, for example, the RMALC, the Fair Trade Campaign,
the Canadian Action Network, and the Québec Coalition Against
NAFTA. This commission would consider the harmonization of labor
and environmental standards and advise the national governments on
free trade, bringing the social agenda to their attention.

The RMALC proposal on the environment calls for sustainable
development, which is not fostered by environmental degradation and
economic inequality. One of its principles is the "sovereign right of
each nation to protect its own resources and the responsibility to avoid
doing harm to the environment that affects other nations" (RMALC
1993, 7). The proposal recognizes the unique environmental situation of
each country and calls for harmonization without uniformity in the
environmental regulations attached to free-trade agreements. It calls for
the recycling or disposal of toxic wastes within each country, so that
any one nation does not become a toxic waste dump for others. The proposal lays out mechanisms for environmental regulation and, again, for
the establishment of a commission of NGOs to oversee sustainable
development and to provide a framework for broad dissemination of
information to citizens on environmental matters. Environmental laws,

the means for technology transfer, and financing mechanisms are also specified.

The RMALC proposal on human rights called for the ratification of OAS (Organization of American States) and UN agreements on human rights and acceptance of the rulings of the Interamerican Human Rights Court, with a commission of NGOs to oversee the human rights of migrant workers. It also called for demilitarization of the border and the right of access to information for the families of those killed crossing the border between Mexico and the United States.

In the United States, several months before the RMALC document was published, parallel organizations—through the umbrella Alliance for Responsible Trade and Citizen Trade Campaign—had authored a letter (December 15, 1992) to President-elect Clinton:

> The undersigned environmental, consumer, farm, labor, religious and citizens' organizations applaud your victory and the vision that you have put forward for your administration in *Putting People First*. We believe that one of the greatest challenges you will face early in your administration is the proposed North American Free Trade Agreement. We appreciate your commitment, expressed in your October 4 speech on NAFTA, to improve the agreement's impact on workers and the environment.
>
> In this regard, we believe that many of the provisions in the current NAFTA text would inhibit achievement of many of the domestic policy goals that you and Vice President-elect Gore put forward during the campaign and in *Putting People First*. The following 13 items, culled from more detailed analyses, speak directly to our concerns.
>
> We sincerely doubt that these concerns can be addressed effectively in implementing legislation and supplemental agreements on labor and the environment. We feel that a fundamental recasting of the Bush agenda embodied in the NAFTA is required. Nonetheless, we are encouraged by your determination to seek changes in NAFTA.
>
> We ask that you reconsider the NAFTA in light of the following analysis.
>
> 1. The current NAFTA agreement undermines U.S. food, health, safety, labor and environmental standards.
>
> 2. The agreement provides no means of trade-linked enforcement of environmental, labor, health or safety standards.

3. The agreement undermines U.S. jobs, wages and working conditions and perpetuates the suppression of worker rights in Mexico.

4. The agreement includes an undemocratic dispute resolution mechanism that excludes the public from defending social, environment and labor laws and regulations that may be challenged under the agreement.

5. The agreement threatens the survival of family farmers, farmworkers, and their rural communities.

6. The agreement undermines energy conservation.

7. The agreement ignores the vital issue of immigration except for provisions which allow temporary entry of business and professional persons.

8. The agreement would hamper efforts to lower prescription drug prices.

9. The agreement lacks a commitment of financial resources to pay for environmental clean-up and community infrastructure.

10. Important international environmental treaties will become subject to the interpretation and consent of NAFTA parties.

11. The agreement lacks any meaningful commitment to sustainable development.

12. The agreement promotes trickle-down economics for Mexico, which will perpetuate low wages and an unequal distribution of income.

13. The agreement's accession clause will spread these deficiencies throughout the hemisphere. (Alliance for Responsible Trade/Citizen Trade Campaign 1992, 1–2)

The signatories were fifty-two NGOs,[22] and an appended letter discussed in detail each objection to NAFTA, with reference to the specific articles and paragraphs of the document, indicating that representatives of the NGOs had access to it. In fact, they released the document simultaneously to the public in all three countries before the governments did.

Many NAFTA counterstories were being told and enacted in 1993 prior to the document's ratification, in all three North American nations. The above examples are only some of the collective rejections of the Agreement. In Cuernavaca, Morelos, I saw a group *en plantón,* which literally means undergoing a long wait but refers to a form of social protest in which people occupy a public space continually, as in an encampment, with banners announcing the cause they are bringing to public notice. The organization was called *el movimiento social y democrático*, and like the RMALC, it was opposed to NAFTA. One of the banners read: "México ante el TLC: Morelos ofrece: ecocidio, violación a derechos humanos—asesinatos políticos e impunidad" (Mexico in the face of NAFTA: Morelos offers: ecocide, human rights violations—political assassinations and impunity). Some collective counterstories were being woven plurinationally, some nationally, and some locally. And then there were individually voiced alternatives to NAFTA.

In the United States, three individuals who argued against NAFTA and proposed alternatives to neoliberal policies in 1993 were the Reverend Jesse Jackson, Ralph Nader, and Ross Perot. In a *Today Show* interview on U.S. television on November 7, 1993, Jesse Jackson explained that an anti-NAFTA position need not be interpreted as anti-Mexican. He pointed out that "Mexicans are not taking jobs *from* us; corporations are taking jobs *to* them." His position, much like that of the RMALC, focused on the need to incorporate provisions for social justice into a trade agreement like NAFTA. Ralph Nader called for corporate accountability and democratization of decisionmaking in the face of global trade. In a November 4 press conference, Nader discussed "the secret cabal of big business and big government" making decisions "beyond the reach of voters to affect" and "without global legal accountability." Unlike Reverend Jackson, however, he did use some anti-Mexican language (e.g., the "giant Mexican truck" bearing down on U.S. workers) in his anti-NAFTA speeches, placing him in the nationalist or U.S. protectionist (see, for example, Frank 1999) rather than the internationalist camp of those opposing NAFTA. Another NAFTA counterstory that sometimes drew on xenophobic rhetoric was articulated by Ross Perot, with the assistance of his co-author Pat Choate. While others might see him as a corporate leader (like those Nader was calling to account), Perot often positioned himself rhetorically among the "salt of the earth" who would be harmed by a ratified NAFTA. In their book (Perot and Choate 1993), he and his economist partner argued that NAFTA would be detrimental to the United States because of low-income jobs going to Mexico and Mexican professionals coming north, through NAFTA's provisions for migrant labor, to take jobs from U.S. nationals.[23]

In Mexico, alternatives to the North American Free Trade Agreement were proposed by, among others, Cuauhtémoc Cárdenas, presidential candidate of the PRD (Partido Revolucionario Democrático, or the Democratic Revolutionary Party),[24] and Jorge Castañeda with Carlos Heredia. Cárdenas's proposal stressed building ties with already existing Latin American free-trade areas, instead of increasing dependence on the United States through the proposed NAFTA. Castañeda and Heredia's counterproposal suggested a longer period of adjustment for workers in each country, and transnational funds—similar to those established in what was then the European Community—to facilitate that process (Castañeda 1993, 11–41).

To conclude this section, I think neoliberal stories and counterstories went well beyond NAFTA. One of the major arguments in public space in the early 1990s was about human rights versus capital rights, with plenty of examples of their collision available. The Mexican Constitution of 1917 had been the result of a popular revolution centering on the same conflict. That constitution, Alberto Trueba Urbina (1974, 7) has argued, was more progressive in terms of social justice than any other in the hemisphere, and the provisions on public ownership of natural resources and agricultural subsistence rights (Article 27) and workers' rights (Article 123) were drawn on in drafting the Treaty of Versailles in 1919 and influenced other nations' constitutions. Article 123, for example, states that labor is not a commodity. It enacted as law the eight-hour maximum workday, the right for workers to unionize, one day off in every seven work days, the illegality of hiring children under twelve, and "equal pay for equal work regardless of sex or nationality" (Trueba Urbina 1974, 21). While Roberto of the FAT and many others I talked with in Mexico in 1993 pointed out the discrepancy between labor law and practices, they feared that the neoliberal government would dismantle these constitutional protections, some of which continue to be unavailable to U.S. citizens (e.g., equal pay for equal work). A neoliberal NAFTA story was about international investors' ability to improve the quality of life (and products) for North Americans if they were unfettered by national taxation and some other forms of regulation of capital. A counterstory told of impending losses of rights and wages, and increasing inequalities in all three North American nations, under NAFTA and associated neoliberal policies. At the end of the twentieth century, the welfare of the majority seemed more at risk in the counterstory than in the Mexican constitutional vision in 1917. In the final section of this chapter, I will describe conversations with campesinos, including one elder for whom comparison with the conditions leading to the Mexican Revolution was very real indeed. First, though, I relate NAFTA stories of a nation's prospects in the face of free trade and economic globalization—mostly told by young Mexicans working to envision their future.

Student Stories

How did class position, as well as other markers of identity, affect the telling and interpretation of NAFTA stories? There was so much conflation of nation and class going on in reductionist imagery of Mexico, Canada, and the United States (Mexico often being portrayed as working class and the other two as the capitalists) that it distracted from attention to diversity within nations.

I met a young, middle-class woman in Mexico City who had recently quit a job at one of the new McDonald's restaurants. She told me she had been working six-hour shifts for 2,000 pesos (converted into 2 pesos with the new currency)—under $1 in U.S. currency—for the whole shift; with the expense of getting to the job, she said it was not worth working there. She and her friends despaired about their job prospects. Adriana Sandoval, a Mexican member of our interviewing team who was herself a university student, suggested we interview young, middle-class Mexicans about how included or excluded they felt from talk of national interests and el TLC. I thought this was a good idea, not only because neoliberal discourse anticipated that the middle class would benefit from NAFTA, and it would be interesting to hear whether its young members reflected that view, but also because of the particular cultural position of university students in Mexico City. The national public university has traditionally drawn qualified students for higher education from every state in Mexico, as a service to the national public and at minimal cost to the students. The UNAM has also been a site where the neoliberal national government's policies are publicly contested (as newly imposed fees for an education at UNAM reflected privatization in other sectors); this contestation was demonstrated powerfully later, through both the 1995 student occupation of the rector's tower and then the 1999–2000 student occupation, which closed the entire campus for most of the academic year. In the following interview excerpts, this is what some university students in Morelos and Mexico City (who mostly identified themselves as middle class) had to say in

1993 about NAFTA, national identity, participation in a national public, and their future. Because the future of Mexico rests with the half of its population that is under twenty-five, the positions young people take in relation to the debate about neoliberal reforms should be heeded (I have translated these excerpts from Spanish).

"Clara," a twenty-year-old woman who planned to get a university degree in philosophy, said in response to a question about whether el TLC would affect national identity in Mexico:

> Well, I think [NAFTA] has two faces: one positive and one nega-
> tive. The positive is that probably the economy of Mexico will
> grow because of opening up to other markets and because through
> competition with Canadian and U.S. goods, the quality of Mexican
> goods will go up too. It will probably also benefit Mexico to open
> up to international markets and be part of a bloc as important as the
> one with Canada, the United States, and Mexico will be. This could
> benefit Mexico economically and politically in the future.
>
> But the negative side of NAFTA is that it will Americanize
> Mexico a lot. Already, there are a lot of U.S. companies here for the
> cheap labor, or whatever, and a lot of Mexican products are copies
> of U.S. and European products. This will happen even more with
> NAFTA. And we might even lose some of our national identity.
> Love for what is Mexican will go down little by little . . . that's
> what I think.

To a question about how these changes would affect young people, she answered, "I don't think that young people are a sector of the population on which the treaty is directly focused." Another young person we spoke with in Mexico City said that if he could talk about NAFTA with President Salinas, he would tell him to listen to young Mexicans, or *any* Mexicans for that matter, in making policies like NAFTA.

"Bernardo," an eighteen-year-old architecture student, had a long conversation with Adriana Sandoval about NAFTA. She used questions we had formulated as a group in this semistructured interview. Adriana asked him what he thought of el TLC:

> BERNARDO: Well, it's something that's going to benefit us and affect
> us. That is to say, it is going to benefit us and in addition it is going
> to affect Mexico, especially with the sale of imports at the same
> price as national products.

A.S.: Are you talking about the U.S. products that are sold here?

BERNARDO: Yes, they cost about the same, or the difference in price is very little. But in the United States and Canada they have much more control over the quality of a product—a level of quality control we have not attained here. There will be businesses that will close because people will prefer the imported product. I don't know if it will be because they think it's better or because they know that there is more quality control there. That will affect us because it will cause quality control to be put into practice in a manner that will allow Mexican businesses to compete with any imported product.

A.S.: So is that what has most impressed you about NAFTA?

BERNARDO: No, that's just what I'm seeing right now. . . . Even if a product is of the same quality, people seem to prefer, since they cost about the same, the imported product because they think it's better. So sales of products made in Mexico have dropped. . . . The treaty might motivate Mexican businesses to improve quality control and competitiveness, but some of them are too new to survive the change.

A.S.: And with NAFTA do you think there will be more jobs or fewer jobs here in Mexico?

BERNARDO: It depends on which industries. . . . I think there will be more of about the same kind of work for a lot of people. There is a lot of interest by foreigners in investment here because Mexican labor is very cheap. I think they'll come and establish industries here, and whatever products they make, once they are finished, will be exported back to [where the investors are from]. This has already been happening a lot here in Mexico, with big companies like Ford and General Motors that make products here because of the cheap labor and then take them back there to sell them.

A.S.: How have you heard about NAFTA?

BERNARDO: In magazines, on television, in the newspaper, in school. . . .

A.S.: In school, what do they tell you?

BERNARDO: We have roundtables and debates about various themes, and several times the theme has been NAFTA. . . . There is a lot of interest, and it is clear that a lot are in agreement and others are not in favor of it, but it has to be viewed in terms of how it will benefit us and how it will affect us. [He makes a balancing-scale gesture with his hands.] We have to balance these things to determine if it will make things worse or better than they are now.

A.S.: *And where do you weigh in with this balance yourself?*
BERNARDO: With my profession [architecture], they say things could go very well. I could easily associate myself with North American [Canadian or U.S.] businesses that might pay more than I could make here, but then again there is not a lot of international competition in my field.

A.S.: *So you don't see the change as being very marked. . . ?*
BERNARDO: Not very marked, no. What I can see is that there would be a lot more work if we could work outside the country than only inside the country; for my particular field, that would be good.

A.S.: *And what about technology?*
BERNARDO: Technology? A lot better technology will enter the country with all the foreign investment there is going to be in Mexico. A lot of businesses already well established here in Mexico will receive foreign capital to invest in equipment that will be more labor-efficient or will improve quality control.

A.S.: *Do you think that as a sector of the population, young people have been taken into account by the treaty?*
BERNARDO: Looking to the future—not directly in the present. Young people are going to be the consumers of the products that will be most greatly affected by the treaty: the electronics industry, CDs, some kinds of food products. Young people are going to be the largest percentage of consumers in those markets. They're not taken into account at the moment, but they figure into the treaty as future consumers. They are going to be the "X" consumers.

A.S.: *Do you think the government is interested in the welfare of young people in thinking about NAFTA?*
BERNARDO: Yes, for the same reason that they are the future of the country. Like a lot of things, this runs under the surface. . . . If the government wants young people to be in favor of NAFTA, then it

will put it in place as a system of education to create a good image of NAFTA within the population through primary school, secondary school, and even in the universities.

A.S.: *And what about other sectors of the population?*
BERNARDO: I don't think the worker and campesino sectors will be changed very much. That is to say, the farmer will be on his parcel of land, or work on a ranch, or drive a truck that comes around daily or once a week for the produce and takes it to market. If the farmer does this type of work and does not work for a cooperative, for example, one that sells beans to a supermarket, then he will not be affected by the treaty because he will go on working in the same way. But those who work in cooperatives will definitely be affected. There's new equipment to think about and all that. If a business is not going to be affected by NAFTA, then the worker will go on working in the same way. As they say, it's relative. If the business is affected, then it's like a pyramid: if NAFTA affects it at the top, then NAFTA will make everything at the bottom work differently.

A.S.: *So are you saying that for the worker and the farmer, things will go on about the same?*
BERNARDO: It depends on if they work for an individual or a company. If the boss decides to invest in modernization, things might change a little, more for the worker than the farmer.

A.S.: *How informed do you think you are about NAFTA?*
BERNARDO: Well, we could say about 20 percent. I don't know exactly how it's going to work, but it's easy to figure out that in the end, it's going to have an effect on the country. One knows more about how it will affect the country than about how it will function exactly.

A.S.: *Why do you think you only understand about 20 percent?*
BERNARDO: Because the media doesn't tell us everything, and because as young people we don't understand diplomatic language very well.

A.S.: *If you had the opportunity to speak with the president about NAFTA right now, what would you say?*
BERNARDO: That he demand improvements in quality control for

those businesses that are on the verge of collapsing, that's what I'd say.

A.S.: What do you think about the environment and the treaty?
BERNARDO: This will depend a lot on what happens. If a lot more factories come to Mexico, it will matter where they are. If they are built in a zone that is already saturated, then there is going to be a lot more pollution. I imagine that NAFTA will mean a lot more contamination for Mexico City, because as the capital, there will be more business and more traffic here—not vehicular traffic, I mean more people coming and going through the city than there are already. And that increase in traffic will be in foreigners, not in nationals.

A.S.: And do you see this increase only in the big cities?
BERNARDO: In the capital and in other important cities, especially industrial centers like Monterrey and Guadalajara, more or less, and with Cuernavaca too.

A.S.: Do you know if NAFTA has any regulations that have to do with the environment?
BERNARDO: The truth is I don't know that there are any yet, but there must be measures authorized by SECOFI that regulate the use of machines to make their products.

A.S.: Are you an optimist or a pessimist about NAFTA?
BERNARDO: An optimist, because it is going to raise the consciousness we have about work and lessen the attitude of "Oh, well, it doesn't matter" or "Leave it until tomorrow." The manner of approaching work is going to change totally.

A.S.: Do you think that change will come easily?
BERNARDO: No, it's not going to be easy. If one is going to work for an American business, they're not going to want someone of this style, who takes things easy. There is going to be a lot of competition in the labor force. . . .

A.S.: Have you seen interest expressed by the government in asking what young people think?
BERNARDO: From time to time they interview young people on the television or on the radio, but they are superficial interviews—they

don't touch on things with a lot of depth. Right now, young people are only instrumental, a market. Young people are a market, children are a market, women who don't work are a market, and so forth. It is the businessmen who are going to decide how to manage this; workers and farmers will go on about the same as before.
[author's translation]

One way Mexican students envisioned changes in their nation with NAFTA, then, was to tell stories about nations as collections of workers, all already competitive or all needing urging toward more competitive attitudes in the inevitable global factory.[25] Another kind of nation story Bernardo was telling here was about a nation as sets of consumers—young ones, old ones, gendered ones, and so on. As a consumer of information himself, it seemed that he was tuned in to what the news reporter had said was one of the issues the Mexican government gave out through the press that summer to promote NAFTA: a concern with quality control and the story that Mexico needed foreign investment and also an infusion of capitalist ideology, both seen as coming with NAFTA.[26]

"Gustavo," another university student who was eighteen, told Adriana Sandoval that he thought Mexican youth were better informed about NAFTA than those in the United States because of the extensive daily press coverage of NAFTA in Mexico. But he said young people might be *less* inclined to demonstrate against government policies because of residual fear from the 1968 government massacre of young protestors in Tlatelolco. The interview continued:

A.S.: *And will NAFTA affect Mexican identity?*
GUSTAVO: This depends on Mexicans. . . . If we adopt this type of consciousness, of mentality, adapted to free trade or not. We could continue feeling "Viva México!" and all that, being traditionalists, but look at it from a new point of view. We could look at our national identity in terms of how NAFTA might allow us to develop and amplify this identity even more. We could restrict ourselves from adopting new customs that could be bad or that might look good but could harm our national identity.

A.S.: *How do you think it could be harmed?*
GUSTAVO: If we come to value foreign things over Mexican things, because Mexican goods can be of very high quality and yet we

Mexicans might not appreciate that because we want to buy for-
eign-made things—even if they are of lower quality.

A.S.: *Why do you think that is?*
GUSTAVO: *Malinchismo.*[27] [author's translation]

Such caricatures of national identity—whether Mexican *malinchismo* or U.S. puritanical efficiency—made it more difficult to articulate
the distinctions within national publics and how different sectors
(young people, for example) might be affected by the Agreement under
negotiation. From the stories these and other middle-class young people
told us in 1993, they did not agree with President Salinas that they
would be wholly served by NAFTA's passage, and they were unanimous in their sense of being disregarded as a population sector in the
negotiations. Some young people in Mexico City expressed their views
through "zines" (individually produced publications, either circulated in
print or on the Internet), while some shared Gustavo's sense of futility
or fear about public expression and others joined political organizations. In the next section, I take up the strand of NAFTA stories told in
and about the agricultural sector in North America.

Farm Stories

There was a circle of fears expressed by farmers in all three North
American nations in a NAFTA story that said each country's farmers
would lose out to those in one of the other nations because of perceived
advantages that NAFTA would give to other nations' agricultural production through a combination of changes in technology, labor, price
regulation, and tariffs.

The North American Free Trade Agreement, which was under
debate leading up to ratification in 1993, contained specific provisions
that—from a neoliberal prospective—provided time for agricultural
sectors to become competitive in crop production over the fifteen years
of the Agreement's implementation. For example, sorghum, Christmas
trees, and garlic (not central staple crops) could be imported into
Mexico without tariffs in 1994. But corn, beans, and powdered milk
could not be imported from the United States and Canada into Mexico
without tariffs until 2009. Indicating similar sectoral concerns in the
United States and Canada, broccoli, tomatoes, and flowers may be

imported without tariffs into Canada from Mexico until 2004, and only in 2009 will peanuts, orange juice, and melons be allowed into the United States from Mexico without tariffs.[28]

Before the U.S. Congress ratified the Agreement, I interviewed a farming couple in rural Kentucky about both NAFTA and GATT. "Dot and Tommy" had two young children and were trying to inform themselves about how these policies would affect the future of small-scale farmers in the United States. Like most farmers in the area, Dot and Tommy had off-farm jobs to support the farm, and tobacco was their main cash crop at that time. They belonged to an organization started through Willy Nelson's FARM-AID concerts, and through that organization they were seeking information about transnational policy and lobbying against NAFTA. Dot and Tommy were opposed to NAFTA, partly due to fears about Argentinian burley tobacco[29] coming into the country through Mexico—with NAFTA opening a gateway for all Latin American agricultural products to flood U.S. markets, as they saw it. This view of Mexico as a floodgate for competing products paralleled a Mexican view of GATT providing an opening for competitive, less expensive Asian products like shoes to enter Mexico through South America. Both perspectives bring to mind Robert Reich's reference to NAFTA as a lightning rod for anxieties about the future of livelihoods in a global economy.

Dot got out her folder on NAFTA to show me letters she had written to and received from congressmen about the policies. She was concerned about fast-track legislation and had written information sheets to give out in her community about the "banana issue": what she saw as less regulation of pesticide use on imported food crops through NAFTA and GATT. Dot said most people around her did not have time to get information on these policies and with the new baby, she was going to have to cut back herself. She said this about NAFTA:

> I guess basically what I'm saying is that we, as farmers, in our organization basically are against everything that NAFTA stands for at this point. There isn't anything that is going to benefit me or anybody like me and it's totally not to my advantage, totally to my disadvantage and even to my entire community. . . . This entire community is just going to be wiped off the map. Basically, people are just going to straggle along if they happen to have some type of means of support, and I see no good anyways in its structure right now, and I'm gonna fight it tooth and nail.

Farming families in the state of Morelos were also thinking about what NAFTA, especially the constitutional changes made to facilitate it, might mean for the future of their families and communities. For many Mexican farmers, 1993 was a difficult year, for different reasons depending on where they were located in the country.[30] In Morelos, campesinos were facing the third year of a severe drought, and its effects were compounded by the constitutional changes made in preparation for NAFTA. When I use the term *campesino* here, I do not intend to bring along the baggage of the translated word *peasant,* with assumptions of isolation and pre-modernity; campesinos are as much global citizens as anyone else (Kearney 1995, 77). According to Miguel Morayta M., the anthropologist who has been interviewing rural residents of Morelos since the mid-1970s, the privatization of the banks had a powerful effect on rural agricultural workers, whether members of cooperatives, contract workers, or those working family subsistence plots. The banks froze credit and increased interest rates sharply on existing mortgages and loans. The state government, involved in its own credit problems from the privatization, imposed such high taxes that many Morelos residents were forced to abandon their homes.[31] Some found contract work through Canadian agribusiness firms; others went to Mexico City.[32] Inflation caused as much as a 400 percent increase in some agricultural costs, and Morelos farmers attributed to GATT the entrance of rice from Asia and peanuts from Argentina into the Mexican market, decreasing demand for their products, which were more and more costly to produce under neoliberal policies (Kingsolver and Morayta M. 1995). Miguel Morayta M. summed up the effects, in rural Morelos, of the changes in Article 27 (altering ownership of ejido lands, among other provisions):

> The changes pertaining to land tenure in Article 27 of the Mexican Constitution, which were made in 1992, created concepts and expectations a bit far from reality. For some, this change generated a clearer sense of ownership of their land—no longer the state's land, but theirs. For others, it gave them hope to sell the land because for one reason or another they were no longer working the land. In 1992, I interviewed a farmer about his feelings toward the land. He spoke to me about the love of the land and the respect for the land that his parents had instilled in him. In the interviews of 1993, the same farmer told us, "If someone wants to build a factory that will secure employment for my children, I'll give it to them

gladly." In one of the communities, ejido land has already been sold, designated as a rest home for the people of Mexico City, under conjecture about the new modifications in the laws, although legal procedures were not followed. But the purchase of lands for agriculture was not happening in 1993. (Kingsolver and Morayta M. 1995) [author's translation]

Morelos had been a sugar-producing center during the colonial period, with haciendas (agricultural estates) so large that their former areas were now the sites of multiple agricultural communities. Now, as one travels across the state, with its wide, fertile valleys and mountainous regions, it is possible to see both large-scale production of corn, cotton, and flowers (in the lowlands) and ejido subsistence production, which has often been pushed into the rockier highlands. In 1993, much agricultural land in Morelos looked dusty and cracked, with crops that came up unevenly and often did not survive long enough for a harvest. Families organized themselves to carry water from sources closest to their fields, but one problem described in their NAFTA stories was the shortage of labor, since working-age children often had migrated to find employment that would provide cash for the families' phenomenally increasing debts. Unemployment was increasing in Morelos, along with violence, indicating an increase in state repression. Those we interviewed in small agricultural communities in western, central, and eastern Morelos told us that members of the state police force were carrying out acts of random violence, in some cases killing several teenaged boys every weekend with impunity, as mentioned earlier. When the townspeople of Jonacátepec rounded up the police force and put them in the town jail, and the governor came to negotiate their release, the townspeople took the attorney general of Morelos into custody as well. They said they had had enough. While this solution to the violence was not a long-lasting one, it demonstrated that the undersecretary of labor had perhaps underestimated the potential for resistance to neoliberal policies as they went into effect.[33]

The rest of this chapter is dedicated to NAFTA stories told by Morelos farmers. I do not name the communities because of possible consequences for those interviewed. The communities and the narrators are sometimes placed[34] as indígena and sometimes as campesino, by themselves and by others. I have translated the interviews from Spanish.

"Claudio," the leader of a union of ejido farmers in a small community, sat outside his house drinking orange Fanta with us as he described conditions for farmers in Morelos and what he thought of NAFTA:

> Well, we think it will be even harder, farming [after NAFTA is ratified], because it is very difficult for Mexicans to compete with those in the United States. Farmers here are behind, especially since they are totally mechanized there in all their work. It's going to be very difficult for us to compete. Our production is always lower in comparison with theirs. Their prices are lower, but they can recover the costs through their high production. . . . They have said that [NAFTA will bring] agribusiness from the United States interested in becoming partners with us, but I feel that that will be very unlikely, especially if this drought continues. The main point is that we don't have water; that would be what we would need to improve crop production. . . .
>
> It seems like they're still not sure how the treaty is going to function, but if it goes into effect and if it affects us, it will not be for the better. There could be some advantages—I don't know; they say that we could associate ourselves [with agribusiness partners], but I feel that would be difficult.

One of us asked Claudio how he was getting information about the free-trade agreement. He said:

> We certainly lack a lot of information. We don't really know what might happen, because we lack a lot of knowledge about it. They've only come to talk with us [the cooperative] about it one or two times. Since this has never happened before here, as it has in other countries, we don't know what it will be like to industrialize in this area. Canada has had this type of treaty before, but Mexico is a lot poorer. It's poorer, and it had more difficulty competing. . . .
>
> Right now, everything here is lost because of the drought. The corn plants are in sad shape; it's going to be very hard on us here. How could we compete? . . . It's going to be very difficult to remain in farming here. We are thinking about looking for alternatives. In [he named the specific union of ejidatarios to which he belonged], we are thinking about forming a business. We only have fifteen members, and no one here knows how it would work with so few of us. The business would buy seeds, for example, and resell them,

looking for a market in which we could earn more. We're looking for a way to make income—maybe a corral in which to fatten some beef cattle. . . .

Miguel Morayta M. asked, "Without middlemen?" and Claudio replied:

> Yes, this would be a way to sell directly, ending our dealings with middlemen, because it is they who take the majority. It would cost more to be a member of such a cooperative business—we are thinking of charging 109 pesos for someone to join—and some say it is too much. Already, we hardly have any way to survive.
>
> We don't know what will happen at the end of this year; it will be the third year in which we have lost harvests [due to the drought]. The prices that crops bring have been dropping; in 1992, they were lower than in 1991. And agrochemical prices went up, so it costs too much to try to grow crops to earn something from. We just plant to try to harvest something to eat.
>
> A lot of people have already left, and more are leaving. In past years, when they got bad or no harvests, they left and went to Mexico City or to the United States. The majority of residents of the community have left, so there are only a few left here who are able to work. If those who have moved away come back, it's only temporarily. Some go to other states to work and come back every weekend. . . . I've been selling off my things in order to try to stay in farming, but I'm looking at having to get out of it.

We asked Claudio about the changes in Article 27 and what he thought would happen to the ejido lands. He said he'd been told that factories would come, but there were already a lot of factories around Mexico City, and they came with their own problems. He continued:

> I say, if they are going to open more factories, who is going to consume what they make? I don't know what kind of factories they would be, but why would we want factories if no one here can buy what they would be making?
>
> We're still hanging in there, but in coming years, if we stop farming, I don't know what will happen to us. If agricultural investors did come [through NAFTA], they would logically want to

earn something, and without rain, it's very risky to think they could earn anything. They're not going to want to take the risk here.

Claudio talked about the opportunity to sell lands through the changes in Article 27. He said that nobody would want to buy them for farming, because they would have the same problem with farming that the ejidatarios were having—water. He talked of the need for more secure sources of water and of credit. There used to be a state fund, he said, for ejido producers to receive loans in order to plant the year's crop, but that had dried up. They had had to turn to other sources of credit, and with the drought, each year a farmer might only recover 30 or at most 40 percent of a loan through the meager harvests, so everyone was getting more and more in debt.

We helped carry lunch up the hill to "Leonardo and Diana," who were working in their ejido plot. Their older children were doing agricultural contract work in Canada, and their youngest two had walked down to what water was left running in the river, to fish with a casting net.

Leonardo had this to say in response to our question about what might happen with NAFTA:[35]

> I don't understand the treaty very well; I don't understand what will happen. There is a lot of talk here in the community. Some say that it will go badly with us if the treaty is in place, because we will be forced to produce more and better. They talk about competition, and here in Mexico we are very behind—not very competitive. That's why I don't understand; I think that it's going to go badly for us campesinos.
>
> It has to do with trade, but the other part is the change in Article 27. I think that that is a good change, because our ejido plot will now be recognized as ours. According to Article 27, we are now the owners of the land—it is converted into property. That's good on the one hand and bad on the other. On the one hand, it makes the hold on the agricultural land more valid; if one wants to sell the land, one can. Before, you couldn't sell ejido land. One can now sell the land without fear of anybody; one can sell it freely. On the other hand, if ejido land becomes property, then it makes more sense to sell it, because one has to pay taxes on it. This is convenient for the government. Paying taxes is a disadvantage for us. They say we are now owners of the land, and maybe we are, but in reality

the government owns the land because we are being charged high taxes.

Leonardo got into a discussion with Miguel Morayta about the history of paying taxes on ejido lands. When he was a boy, Leonardo remembered his father paying minimal taxes on them, but for the past thirty or so years, he said, ejido lands had not been taxed—only property, and it had been increasingly taxed.[36]

> With my house, I have about 1450 square meters in the community. Four years ago, I paid about 8,000 pesos a year. Now [my taxes] have gotten to be 400,000 pesos.[37] It is not just, and I have not paid it. I have gone two years without paying [property taxes]. They are too high.
>
> Now one has to play a game of whether to plant and whether to harvest. We have to go so far to sell the crop.

Leonardo explained they just didn't have the money. He and Diana were pulling water from a small pump on top of a hill, and they had a few rows of cucumbers that were nearly ripe. Leonardo took us through the scenario of their decisionmaking about whether to sell the crop or leave it in the field:

> They say that cucumbers are bringing 4,000 or 5,000 pesos a crate in the market. The pickup truck to take it to market costs 3,000 pesos. What's left? Maybe 2,000 pesos. And the labor to help pick? That could be 15 or 20 thousand pesos.
>
> Something might be left out, but at 5,000 pesos, it's better to leave them here in the field. I would have to hire workers. There's only us left to pick here. . . . Maybe something will come of the tomatoes. The price has been good, but now it's falling. We've had bad luck. We haven't been able to hit it right.

We asked about the sale of ejido lands. Leonardo said that two farmers were thinking of selling their land to buyers from Mexico City who wanted to build vacation homes in their community, but at an assembly, the ejidatarios were told they could not sell their plots until their titles arrived. No one knew when that might be.

About NAFTA, Leonardo said that representatives of the government agricultural ministry had come to assemblies in the community to explain free trade. He and others also got information about NAFTA from television and newspapers; from what he understood, NAFTA would go into effect the next January. He said:

> This is what they tell us. That people [from outside Mexico] are going to come, and they are going to say, "I'll put up the land and you plant the seeds and do the harvest." And they say that if we are not going to be absolute owners of the land, they are going to send us away, right? They're going to make deals with farmers and they will bring better technology than we have here and they will send us off the land, some say. But I say that here in Mexico we are very behind in technology, and that's why we can't advance. We don't produce as well as more advanced countries—they are saying that too. I think it would be good if they came to teach us what we don't know. We are going to learn a lot from them. They'll show us, if we are behind. I think that would be good. It's only that if they try to send us away, we are not going to give up our lands.

Leonardo explained that some ejidatarios were trying to get a loan to build a hog farm: "They say that they are going to send hogs from Canada, where my children are, to raise here. We will shift [from growing crops] to hog production." He looked down the hill at the bridge that crossed the river, now hardly running for the drought. Wasn't it beautiful? he asked us. He said the community members had built the bridge themselves; the government had only helped out with the concrete.[38] He told stories of how they had crossed the river to get to the ejido lands before they built the bridge. There was a cable stretching across, and during the rainy season many tried to cross with donkeys loaded with seeds and fertilizer. They had some scares, with people nearly drowned and many donkeys losing their cargo.

Leonardo was reflecting on the last fifteen years of farming in his community. They had been hard years because all the costs had been going up and harvests had been going down. Overall, the cost of living had gone up. He explained that one by one, ejidatarios had gone outside the community to find work: some to Cuautla or Cuernavaca [cities in Morelos] and some to Mexico City. Some friends had gotten jobs as policemen and gardeners, and they worked in those jobs January through April, then returned to the community in May to prepare their ejido plots for planting in June, when the rains would come. If there was no harvest, they would go to the cities in search of work again.

I asked if only men went to the cities to seek work, or if women went as well. He said that girls and widowed women went, but if they were married, their husbands usually went. A lot of women work as maids, and children help out their families this way. Women get paid well, Leonardo said, for cooking and cleaning jobs in the city, but daughters return to their families on their days off. He thought that after NAFTA people would leave the community to find work in about the same numbers, but then, he said, he didn't understand the treaty that well.

In answer to a question about whether anyone was saying that factories might come to the community, Leonardo replied, "They say yes, that possibly a factory might come. Someone said they might want to buy my land. If I see that my crop comes to nothing, listen . . . [he gestured that he would consider it]." He said that a factory would mean work for his children in the community, with a weekly paycheck, instead of his passing along to them the risk that comes with planting crops. He thought it would be good for them to farm, but not as their primary way of making a living. He said that it was hardly worth planting crops any more; one couldn't get loans, and if one did, the interest rate was 20 percent compounded monthly. He himself was out of money. They would not be able to get the cucumbers or tomatoes to market if they did decide to harvest them. Although he was ashamed to do so, he was going to ask his sister for a loan; they had already sold a lot of their things to pay for the planting, but there was no other way to finance the crop. A friend who mortgaged his house to pay for seeds and fertilizer the year before (also a drought year) had lost his house and everything, ending up a drug addict, Leonardo said.

We ended the interview with a discussion of the plants in their field, which had various diseases because of the drought. As we walked through the field, Leonardo and Diana told us that their sons in Canada were being treated well; that their work included airfare to Canada, good housing and food; and that they had returned to the same farm for several seasons. They stated again their willingness to sell the ejido plot if anyone wanted to build a factory on it. Considering how few members of the family were left to farm, as well as the drought, they were ready to get out of farming.

On the other side of the state, I asked a member of an earlier farming generation, "Don Hugo,"[39] how he viewed conditions for farmers in Morelos and the recent changes made by Salinas's administration. Don Hugo and I sat on the roots of a tree probably surpassing his ninety or so years, with a turkey hopping onto and off our laps, in the midst of a household where women were outside preparing the cooking fire and an injured man rested inside the house. This is the NAFTA story Don Hugo told, excerpted from the interview.[40] I will end this chapter with his words and say that he taught me the importance of considering the North American Free Trade Agreement in the perspective of a century spanning from the administration of President Porfirio Díaz[41] to the neoliberalism of the 1990s.

Well, according to anyone, maybe the government has finished with Mexico. Because where are we headed? The crisis in basic foods has already begun, mostly because of the drought. Those who have a little corn won't sell it. They don't want to sell any more because they say they have to eat, so those who don't have corn have to buy it. Or else not eat—I don't know what they do. They eat only bread maybe. I don't know.

All of us older people think that people are going to start selling their ejido lands in order to have anything, to sustain themselves, to buy something to eat. So I myself do not understand why the government has applied [the changes in] Article 27. According to what our ancestors have told us, around the year 1878, people came from someplace else—nobody knew where they came from or what nation they belonged to—and they bought a plot of land and the neighbors had to sign for the sale of that land and they received, too, the rate they had signed for. It was a robbery, then. And that's where we are headed again with the changes in Article 27 because the government says that now it has the right to sell land at the price it wants, to whoever it wants.

That is a bad step, because that has happened already; it's what happened with our ancestors. The hacienda appropriated . . . that is to say, the Spaniards came with the power accorded by Spain to buy [land] at perhaps a high price, what do I know, but the worst is what happened: the neighbors had to sign away lands and collect for them also, and if all the land was not bought [from those who actually owned it], it was robbery.

According to the government, the change in Article 27 goes along with the adjustment in the currency and to the currency exchange. How is that going to benefit the poor? If today he is earning 25-30 thousand pesos, the worker is not going to have a better standard of living [with 25–30 pesos], and how is it possible that 1,000 pesos drop to 1 peso? If a person can't make a living with 25,000 pesos, how is he going to make a living with 25 pesos? How is he going to survive at all?

I understand it this way: according to what the government says, free trade means that one country can bring trade to another. And from that country, they can bring trade to the other. All that goes on for free. And I don't understand that; if that multimillionaire is going to profit by that business, what's going to be free or how is he going to be affected? That's where competition comes from—if they make it better and sell it for a quarter of the price, that's what is going to sell. It's like finding out who is the stupidest; in the end, the one that wins, loses, and I say no, thank you. It's a question of the poorest of the poor. There will be war.

Our president tells us that he is going to help the community with the changes in Article 27 and in the currency. But it's a lie. A lie. It's a big lie.

Like in the Porfiriato. Because this is how it was: the poor people here in Morelos had to work in sugar cane and carry the cane until someone called Zapata came along who wanted to take the yoke off of the poor. . . . My father (and uncle) were revolutionaries.

Well, if agriculture goes the way I think it's going, we'll have to take a stand because it is a basic resource. Agriculture provides the means for life. If you take, for example, a home with five or six children, a family of eight with the mother and father, and four go away to work and two stay to work the land, then they can sustain themselves. [Without agricultural land] how will the parents survive? If everybody goes away, are the parents supposed to eat air? One would have to be a balloon!

Notes

1. This passage is from page 31037 of the *Congressional Record*–Senate, 103rd Cong., 1st sess., 139, part 22, 20 November 1993. On page 31040, the vote on the North American Free Trade Agreement Implementation Act (H.R. 3450) is recorded. There were 61 yeas: Baucus, Bennett, Biden, Bingaman, Bond, Boren, Bradley, Breaux, Brown, Bumpers, Chafee, Coats, Cochran, Coverdell, Danforth, Daschle, DeConcini, Dodd, Dole, Domenici, Durenberger, Gorton, Graham, Gramm, Grassley, Gregg, Harkin, Hatch, Hatfield, Hutchinson, Jeffords, Johnston, Kassebaum, Kennedy, Kerrey, Kerry, Leahy, Lieberman, Lott, Lugar, Mack, Mathews, McCain, McConnell, Mitchell, Moseley-Braun, Murkowski, Murray, Nickles, Nunn, Packwood, Pell, Pressler,

Pryor, Robb, Roth, Simon, Simpson, Specter, Wallop, and Warner. There were 38 nays: Akaka, Boxer, Bryan, Burns, Byrd, Campbell, Cohen, Conrad, Craig, D'Amato, Exon, Faircloth, Feingold, Feinstein, Ford, Glenn, Heflin, Helms, Hollings, Inouye, Kempthorne, Kohl, Lautenberg, Levin, Metzenbaum, Mikulski, Moynihan, Reid, Riegle, Rockefeller, Sarbanes, Sasser, Shelby, Smith, Stevens, Thurmond, Wellstone, and Wofford. Senator Dorgan did not vote.

2. Of course, I do not spend all my days observing congressional proceedings. It is more likely that this is the "real" and what is surreal is my expectation of public decisionmaking.

3. Mateo Zapata is a leader among agrarian groups and communities in Morelos. One of his colleagues told us that the collective was unable to view the documents relating to the proposed changes in agricultural provisions of Article 27 of the 1917 Mexican Constitution (which Mateo Zapata's father, leader of a similar farmers' organization, had died for), but that nonetheless President Salinas de Gortari had asked for Zapata's support—with all the symbolic support it would bring—of the constitutional changes and, later, of NAFTA.

4. An ejidatario is one who produces on ejido lands—those lands held by the community in trust from generation to generation for agricultural use, according to the 1917 constitution. The changes being discussed by campesinos working (at least in part) ejido lands in 1993 were those made in Article 27 of the constitution, which would give titles to those who had been the stewards of ejido plots. As described in the last section of this chapter, advantages and disadvantages to this arrangement were voiced in community discussions. One advantage was the ability to sell the land, since one would actually hold a title to the formerly communal lands, and a disadvantage to that titleholding was the taxation of the newly created property holders.

5. See Pierre Bourdieu (1977) for a discussion of symbolic capital.

6. An ethnographer who has paid close attention to the distribution and consumption of representations of national identity, as well as their production, is Néstor García Canclini (1993, 28).

7. Those familiar with recent Mexican history and policy will remember the Salinas campaign, Solidaridad (perhaps symbolically borrowing the prolabor overtones from the Polish movement), a development policy giving communities building materials, for example, if community members would donate their own labor time to construct schools bridges, and so on. The program, Programa Nacional de Solidaridad, is also referred to by its expanded acronym PRONASOL. Monroy Gómez referes readers to an article on this topic by Julio Boltvinik.

8. As noted in Chapter 1, even a journalist covering the presidential administration did not have access to this information. After more than sixty years in power, the PRI as a whole did not seem to find it necessary to explain the currents of internal differences and responsibilities to the national public.

9. The governments of Chile and Mexico had negotiated a free-trade agreement in 1990. The negotiators of the North American Free Trade Agreement were discussing fast-tracking the consideration of bringing Chile into NAFTA as the next partner nation.

10. While EU is the abbreviation for European Union in English, EU or EEUU is the abbreviation for the United States in Spanish.

11. The Mexican commerce secretary, Jaime Serra Puche, and the Spanish minister of trade and tourism, Javier Gómez Navarro, met in July 1993 to discuss their mutual interests. Gómez Navarro said that NAFTA would present Spain with an opportunity to reach North American markets through Mexico, and Spain could in turn be Mexico's port of entry into European Union markets. Mexico and Spain already had at that time significant trade with one another. "In 1992, Spain exported to Mexico $88 million U.S. dollars' worth of goods, and imported primarily oil from Mexico valued at $1,350,000,000 (U.S.)" (*La Jornada,* July 1993, 24) [author's translation].

12. The Group of Seven nations began meeting in 1985. The member nations are Canada, the United States, France, Germany, Italy, Japan, and the United Kingdom.

13. In part to conform with the International Labour Organization's (ILO) Convention 169, which recognized plural cultures within nations rather than promoting cultural assimilation, and in part because as the Quincentenary (of Latin American Conquest) scrutinized conditions for indigenous peoples in the Americas, Mexico was behind other Latin American nations in recognizing their rights, the national government amended Article 4 to recognize Mexico's pluriculturality and the rights of pueblos indígenas, but the latter's language was so abstract as to be more cosmetic than a guarantee of sovereignty for those communities (Hindley 1996). Article 4 was mentioned in many EZLN documents but mostly to reference the fact that the Mexican state did not go far enough in recognizing the rights of pueblos indígenas to control their land and make their own decisions.

14. One example of the Mexican administration's assertion of its separate status as a nation from the United States, and its ability to reject requests strongly made by the United States, was the case of 659 undocumented Chinese migrants in the summer of 1993 who were refused U.S. entry and were sent to Mexico. There were complaints in Mexico against the Mexican government that, because of the desire to have the NAFTA signed, Mexico might become a sort of migration service agency for the United States. Perhaps in response to these criticisms, the Mexican government flew all the Chinese citizens back to China. Andrés Rozental, Salinas's undersecretary of *Relaciones Exteriores* (foreign relations), stated that Mexico did not intend to be a third-party nation dealing with undocumented migrants and that the underground trafficking of human beings had to be addressed. The Chinese migrants had been promised passage by boat to the United States, and then were refused entry and could not afford passage back to China. One source on this situation is Andonaegui (1993a, 1, 8).

15. *La raza* (the race, but not a simple translation to English), like *mestizaje,* has a double face as an identity term: it can carry pride associated with a distinct ethnic identity, as it has been used in the Chicano political movement in the United States, for example; the term also connotes the history of forced Spanish conquest of indigenous peoples in Mexico expressed through mixed physical heritages.

16. Mexican reporter Carlos Ferreyra asked the head of the NAACP Legal

Defense Fund, Elaine R. Jones, at the event whether the NAACP had taken a position on NAFTA. She replied that it had not, stating that the NAACP's struggle remained focused on reducing conditions of injustice and poverty in which many U.S. residents live and improving education, voter participation, employment, and the justice system (Ferreyra 1993, 20).

17. Karl Marx said this about civil society in "The German Ideology" (Marx 1978, 163):

> Civil society embraces the whole intercourse of individuals within a definite stage of the development of productive forces. It embraces the whole commercial and industrial life of a given stage and, insofar, transcends the State and the nation, though, on the other hand again, it must assert itself in its foreign relations as nationality, and inwardly must organize itself as State. The term "civil society" (*bürgerliche Gesellschaft*) emerged in the eighteenth century, when property relationships had already extricated themselves from the ancient and medieval communal society. Civil society as such only develops with the bourgeoisie; the social organisation evolving directly out of production and commerce, which in all ages forms the basis of the State and of the rest of the idealistic superstructure, has, however, always been designated by the same name.

18. I recorded this press conference on September 15, 1993, from its broadcast on C-SPAN; all quotes in this paragraph are taken from that broadcast.

19. Of course, there were indeed popular movements reacting to NAFTA on the day of its implementation, January 1, 1994, when the EZLN made its statements in Chiapas in protest of NAFTA and neoliberal policies (e.g., the constitutional changes), which the EZLN viewed as affecting the lives of many Mexicans detrimentally.

20. The details of the difference between European Union labor law and the provisions of the NAFTA came up in a conversation I had in 1995 with Bertha Luján, a labor activist with the RMALC (see Chapter 4).

21. I have translated "Roberto's" words from the 1993 interview in which he responded to questions by the students, myself, and Jorge Carrásco Araizaga.

22. The signatories to the December 15, 1992, letter to President-Elect Clinton included: the Amalgamated Clothing and Textile Workers Union (AFL-CIO); the American Agriculture Movement; the American Federation of State, County, and Municipal Employees (AFL-CIO); the Americans for Democratic Action; the Animal Welfare Institute; the Association of Farmworker Opportunity Programs; the Child Labor Coalition; the Committee for Humane Legislation; the Communication Workers of America (AFL-CIO); the Community Nutrition Institute; the Development Group for Alternative Policies; the Economic Policy Institute; Environmental Action; the Fair Trade Campaign; Friends of Animals; Friends of the Earth; the Government Accountability Project; Greenpeace USA; the Institute for Agriculture and Trade Policy; the Institute for Food and Development Policy; the Institute for

Policy Studies; Interfaith IMPACT; the International Brotherhood of Electrical Workers (AFL-CIO); the International Brotherhood of Teamsters (AFL-CIO); the International Labor Rights Education and Research Fund; the International Ladies Garment Workers Union (AFL-CIO); the International Union of Electronic, Electrical, Technical, Salaried, and Machine Workers (AFL-CIO); the International Union of Food and Allied Workers, North American Region; the International Wildlife Coalition; the Jewish Labor Committee; Labor Notes; the Maryknoll Society Justice and Peace Office; the Missionary Society of St. Columban, U.S. Region; the National Coalition Against the Misuse of Pesticides; the National Consumers League; the National Family Farm Coalition; the National Farmers Union; the National Lawyers Guild; the National Rainbow Coalition; the National Toxics Campaign; the North American Worker-to-Worker Network; the Presbyterian Church (USA) Washington Office; Public Citizen; the Sheet Metal Workers' International Association; the Sierra Club; the Society for Animal Protective Legislation; the United Church of Christ Network for Environmental and Economic Responsibility; the United Electrical, Radio, and Machine Workers of America (UE); the United Food and Commercial Workers Union (AFL-CIO); the United Methodist Church, General Board of Church and Society; Witness for Peace; and Zero Population Growth.

23. Perot and Choate (1993, 91) reproduced a page of the North American Free Trade Agreement, yet to be ratified, that listed sixty-three professional occupations that might be entered by temporary workers from Mexico. I read that passage of their book as intimating those jobs rightfully belonged to Anglos. In Chapter 3, I discuss the book in the context of xenophobic NAFTA stories.

24. The PRD is considered to be to the left of the long-governing PRI, and the PAN (National Action Party) is considered to the right of it. Cuauhtémoc Cárdenas had popular support in a number of Mexican states; his father was Lázaro Cárdenas, who had been president of Mexico. In the late 1990s, Cuauhtémoc Cárdenas was elected mayor of Mexico City. This was interpreted by those I spoke with as indicative of some movement away from the PRI monopoly in national government, but there was some question as to whether the police force and other official bodies would really answer to Cárdenas or whether de facto PRI governance of arguably the largest city in the world would continue despite Cárdenas's election.

25. Of course, Mexico had already been competing in the global market-place for some time. So the rhetoric used in NAFTA stories told by the Mexican government, of Mexico as insular and unable to compete, really reflected an argument within the PRI, the ruling party for most of the twentieth century, between the neoliberal "technocrats" favoring privatization and encouraging foreign investment and the "dinosaurs" who had governed the large national-ized industries like PEMEX.

26. That would mean capitalist ideology most suited to management's goals, which Weber (1980) saw as Calvinism. Although I do not discuss it at length, Protestant religious movements as well as evangelical Catholic ones grew tremendously during the period NAFTA was being discussed and first

implemented, and anthropologists have documented (Annis 1989) the ideological parallels between newly spreading religious logics and the rationalization of what Bernardo characterized as the virtues of North American workers, including efficiency and competitiveness.

27. Malinchismo invokes a nation story particular to Mexico: the tale of La Malinche, the *indígena* woman who was impregnated by Cortes and gave birth to the first Mexican *mestizo*. Much has been written about Mexican national self-image and mestizaje by force of conquest, Octavio Paz's *El Laberinto de la Soledad* (*Labyrinth of Solitude*) (1950) being one famous example. *Malinchismo* is a term that can be used with layers of pride and self-deprecation (according to the stereotype) and also as an ironic reference to the just-so story about Mexican identity it presents. See Lomnitz-Adler (1992a, 83) for a discussion of not only the traditional meaning of mestizaje but also his own concept of how it is used to separate individuals from and subordinate them to elite regional culture. J. Jorge Klor de Alva (1999, 174) describes the strategic possibilities of mestizaje for countering ethnoracial marking and discrimination—attributing the origin of discriminatory practices to dominant European ideologies in Latin America, especially in the 1800s.

28. These examples are taken from a Mexican summary of the Agreement (SECOFI 1992). Similar documents for distribution in Canada and the United States might have emphasized different examples of agricultural products causing the most concern regarding the lifting of tariffs.

29. This is the kind of tobacco grown by Dot and Tommy and other Kentucky tobacco farmers. Tobacco companies require many different kinds of tobacco to make one cigarette; for example, burley tobacco is added to cigarettes to hold flavorings. Dot and Tommy had been told that tobacco companies were going to Latin America to build tobacco barns and teach Argentinians, for example, to raise burley tobacco. Their sense of being flooded out by Argentinian tobacco was a position I found supported in a farm-magazine article from that period (Bickers 1993, 60), so it was a shared view in their economic sector. While it would seem to reflect the kind of general xenophobia discussed in Chapter 3, this fear of Argentinian tobacco did not extend to fear of an influx of Latin American workers into the United States. In the same interview, Dot and Tommy told me they depended on Mexican laborers, newly come to Kentucky as seasonal farm workers, to plant, cut, and prepare their burley tobacco crop for market.

30. I heard a lot of NAFTA stories about hardship in other parts of the country, although I can only write about what I saw in Mexico City and Morelos, the sites of my conversations with people about NAFTA. An example of the stories I heard about other areas was told by a construction materials salesman in Morelos, who said that an indígena community in a northern state was starving because they were forced to give away their timber rights under the neoliberal legislation and were left with no land, and no farming base. He told me that unless the government began to address human rights, poverty, and the growing disparity between rich and poor, whatever changes might be brought by passing NAFTA would not be worth the trouble. For more historical background on conditions in the state of Morelos in particular, see de la Peña (1981) and Lomnitz-Adler (1992b).

31. Property taxes were increased by the governor of Morelos by 50 percent during the drought of 1993, according to the people with whom we spoke. Since the harvests were failing and credit was nearly unavailable, especially for small loans but also to agricultural cooperatives, these taxes were seen by many as unrealistic, and popular resentment was expressed en plantón and in graffiti around the state. Similar conditions were occurring in surrounding states.

32. According to Miguel Morayta M., many rural residents left Morelos and settled in Mexico City during a severe drought in 1983; this was a permanent migration for many of them. In turn, agricultural labor—especially for the least desirable jobs—was provided in Morelos by migrants from the states of Guerrero, Mexico, and Puebla, and many of those migrant workers settled there (Kingsolver and Morayta M. 1995).

33. This is, in part, why I do not discuss extensively the EZLN and its actions contesting the imposed NAFTA story at the moment it unfolded in January 1994. I did not go to Chiapas to interview participants. What I witnessed, however, was international interest in the EZLN and especially in the words and ski-masked image of Subcomandante Marcos, who was often its spokesperson. The EZLN's symbolic force, in representing an alternative route to neoliberal policies for Mexico and for the world, surpassed its military force. I think that questions need to be asked, in analyses of the many strands of agency in relation to neoliberal stories and counterstories, about why the EZLN came to be viewed by many as the only popular movement countering NAFTA and why Subcomandante Marcos (with his awareness) became the face, albeit masked, of resistance. Many acts of resistance to NAFTA occurred before its passage and after, and I have included the story of the townspeople of Jonacátepec to show just one of them *prior* to the EZLN's more organized resistance with Internet reports and video broadcasts. Popular responses to long-term police and paramilitary repression and worsening conditions under neoliberal policies (and I speak not only of Mexico here) were more chaotic and varied than can be gleaned from a simple reading. I have simplified much in conveying these NAFTA stories, but I leave the story of the EZLN to other writers, including the analyses written by some of its members.

34. See Kingsolver (1992) for a theoretical discussion of "placing" and identity, and Kingsolver and Morayta M. (1995) for Miguel Morayta M.'s discussion of his long-term project on identity in Morelos. His research has focused on the ways identity has shifted back and forth between indígena and campesino for many rural Morelos residents and how that shift is related to, for example, changes in government policy, including the changes to Articles 4 and 27 of the Mexican constitution.

35. Leonardo spoke during this recorded interview, and Diana did not. In a follow-up interview during another agricultural season, Diana did the speaking.

36. This distinction Leonardo drew between ejido lands and property, and their conversion into property, is indicative of the difference between the logic of the Mexican Constitution of 1917 and the neoliberal logic of the Salinas administration. Commodification of all land meant opening it to the market, with subsistence being at the mercy of that market, rather than placing the public's subsistence as a priority before the welfare of the market.

37. One of the changes made by the Mexican government to accommo-

date the NAFTA negotiations was a change in the currency. The peso was devalued, so that 1,000 pesos became one *nuevo peso* (new peso). In addition to the periodic devaluation that takes place in Mexico, I believe that President Salinas was symbolically moving to synchronize the peso with the U.S. dollar in anticipation of better times. The exchange rate in 1993 was about 3 pesos per U.S. dollar, but that exchange rate would worsen as the financial crisis (the one recognized in the world banking industry) neared. In the rural areas of Morelos especially, those we talked with in the summer of 1993 continued to refer to pesos in the thousands rather than in terms of converted pesos. Indeed, one interviewee expressed—as noted later in this chapter—that the conversion from old to new pesos had been experienced as an actual loss in money.

38. This bridge was built at the beginning of the Salinas administration, through the Solidaridad campaign that provided construction materials to communities who, in turn, provided the labor to build schools, roads, and other public works. This policy is consistent with neoliberal thought as described earlier in this chapter.

39. *Don*, like *Doña*, is a term of respect for the elderly. I should also explain here that I am using first-name-only pseudonyms not out of disrespect, but to make it clear when I am using a pseudonym and when I am not.

40. As with all the interviews in this section, the words are translated from the original Spanish. In the parts of the interview not included here, Don Hugo talked of the police violence aimed at young men in the community and fear and anger about that, and of moving the ejido crops up into the hills, which he remembered people had done during another severe drought in the 1930s.

41. The Porfiriato, the period of Díaz's presidency, was a time when Mexico's government encouraged capital investment by inviting foreign companies to Mexico for the cheap land and labor; the resulting conditions were so bad that the Mexican Revolution started in the state of Morelos over access to subsistence lands. For a discussion of some parallels between the liberalism of Porfirio Díaz and the neoliberalism of Carlos Salinas, see Beaucage (1998).

3

1994: NAFTA
and National Identities—
Stories of Racialized Difference

There are many NAFTA stories to tell for the first year of its implementation. I have chosen to focus on stories of xenophobia[1] to explain some of the connections between perceptions of NAFTA and the debates about a policy that would block undocumented immigrants from access to health and educational services—California Proposition 187.[2] Those stories are followed in the racializing stories below. Public protests in both Mexico and the United States—specifically, California—against neoliberal and anti-immigrant policies are described in the final section on stories of public protest. There were complex strands of protest to follow; President Salinas himself made an official protest against the United States regarding Proposition 187 and associated sentiments against Mexican immigrants, even as he ignored hunger strikers protesting the neoliberal reforms he had promoted to facilitate the Agreement, for example. In the United States, white supremacists protested the wave of undocumented Mexican immigrants they believed NAFTA had encouraged—acting with Lights on the Border, a type of citizen vigilante system along the U.S. side of the U.S.-Mexican border—and students, health workers, teachers, and others took to the streets across California to protest the passage of Propositions 187 and 184, the "three strikes" initiative.[3]

Don Hugo was right when he said there would be a war soon, in Mexico. The EZLN took up arms in Chiapas in a well-publicized conflict with the Mexican national military, when NAFTA went into effect at the beginning of 1994, and it posted (in forms ranging from handbills to web pages) a platform against neoliberal policies and for basic human rights, including indigenous sovereignty. One of the human rights issues raised was the treatment of undocumented immigrants coming over the border from Guatemala into Mexico. In so many NAFTA stories, that border and the Canadian-U.S. border were obscured by the singular, symbolic focus on "the border" as the line demarcating the United States of America from the United Mexican States (and in some symbolic systems, the first world from the third world). This chapter considers the magnification of attention on the Mexican-U.S. border as part of the strategic alterity necessary to capitalist logic and practice.

Strategic alterity is the term I use for the practice of shifting between strategic assertions of inclusion and exclusion (or the marking and unmarking of "selves" and "others") to both devalue a set of people and to mask that very process of strategic devalorization. For example, the text of California Proposition 187 actually blamed so-called illegal aliens for Californians' experiences of economic hardship. I argue that, rhetorically, both the text of the proposition and the arguments of its supporters symbolically "whitened" the identity of "true" Californians and selectively marked undocumented immigrants as "Mexican," thus unmarking all other immigrants to the state through the silent process of racialization. Despite the long history of Mexican-American identity in California, in the symbolic language of Proposition 187, the identities of all immigrants to the state from many countries were filtered and reduced to the term "Mexican," and the distinction was made between that racialized (dark-skinned), gendered (male), Spanish-speaking, national (Mexican), imaginary "other" and a Californian "self" assumed to be "white," "American," and economically threatened (Vila 2000; Zavella 1997). This distinction was used, in the "geography of blame," as Paul Farmer (1993) put it, to create an explanatory, scapegoating framework for economic difficulties in what were supposed to be good times in an ever more free-trading and globalized economy.[4]

Why is this a NAFTA story? Because the story of neoliberal free-trade policies like NAFTA, creating a free-trade area in North America, is a story about free-trading capitalists, all equally positioned to make a profit and support themselves through the free market. The silent or unmarked story of neoliberal capitalist policy is that those free-marketeers, or citizens of the free market, are most often benefiting (whether they see it or not—the rhetoric of "freedom" here can be blinding) from the unfree labor of a strategically altered group of people that is helping them produce what the free-market citizens are selling.[5] I would consider undocumented workers, for example, upon whose labor California agribusiness very much depends (as a storyteller in this chapter points out), to be unfree laborers sustaining free-marketeers, because the threat of deportation may keep them from leaving jobs in which they are ill paid or ill treated. Neoliberal reforms, like "welfare-to-work" policies in the United States, Solidaridad in Mexico, and the encouragement of economic growth through tariff removal as in NAFTA, use language that indicates increasing freedom and democratization of well-being through free-market capitalism, but they do not account for full living wages for everyone in the economic arena. How vital a role, then, do immigrants from one state to another (as from Guerrero to Morelos) or from Central America to Mexico, or from Mexico and China to the United States, working at subminimum wages, play in the economic success of the neoliberal agenda, even as they are marked as the "problem" in xenophobic rhetoric like that of California Proposition 187? NAFTA negotiators, already skittish about discussing national citizenship and immigration in North America, certainly did not discuss the distinctions between *national* citizenship, *market* citizenship (as I call the right to participate fully in free-market capitalism as a free-trader of goods or services), or *cultural* citizenship (Rosaldo 1999, 257), which became significant distinctions in the symbolic wars over who actually was entitled to participate in the economic democratization of North America. In the aftermath of the NAFTA debates, with such notably xenophobic phrases as Perot's "giant sucking sound" emanating from Mexico, the way was open for more overtly racializing and xenophobic discussions of policies like Proposition 187 and the English-only initiatives to follow.

Racializing Stories

In following the story of racialization as it pertains to Mexican-U.S. relations, I want to make clear I am not talking about a Mexican race, an "other" race, or an "immigrant" race, as though any of those labels could refer to people. I am talking specifically about a strategy of racialization implemented by white supremacists, most overtly, and more widely in subtler ways. In understanding this strategic racialization—which arbitrarily collapses diverse identities into its binary, white/nonwhite logic—I find useful Omi and Winant's (1994, 55) definition of "*racial formation* as the sociohistorical process by which racial categories are created, inhabited, transformed, and destroyed."[6]

Also helpful—in understanding the way in which "white American" is empowered through Proposition 187 rhetoric, for example, as the unmarked but "default" Californian and U.S. identity—is Charles W. Mills's writing on the "racial contract." Mills discusses the racial contract, through which privilege is rationalized in terms of race, asserting that privilege is least visible to those who benefit most by the racial contract. He states that "the whole point of establishing a moral hierarchy and juridically partitioning the polity according to race is to secure and legitimate the privileging of those individuals designated as white/persons and the exploitation of those individuals designated as nonwhite/subpersons" (Mills 1997, 32–33).

Thus the racial contract is considered by those defining themselves as white to grant particular privileges, including economic privileges. Anti-immigrant or xenophobic language used to discuss the potential influx of Mexican laborers (and the outpouring of U.S. jobs to Mexico) because of NAFTA and to promote California Proposition 187 focused on the threat that racialized *Mexicans* presented to this unwritten but often assumed contract guaranteeing preferential employment access to white U.S. citizens. Patricia Zavella contextualized Proposition 187 amidst other recent policies in relation to this racial project based on such a perceived threat to U.S. white supremacy:

> The new nativism we see in California—expressed through the attempt to pass the English-Only proposition, and more recently the passage of Proposition 187 and the introduction of the California Civil Rights Initiative [Proposition 209, which would eliminate affirmative action policies in California]—reflects a sense of loss of white control over the affairs of state. . . . What is new about the fin de siècle nativism is that white supremacy has been undermined by global economic restructuring, which has created tremendous wealth while increasing the vulnerability of white citizens. (Zavella 1997, 136–137)

Support for the "Save Our State" (S.O.S.) initiative, another name for Proposition 187, although by no means coming only from white Californians,[7] was perhaps encouraged by a dawning realization that the "other," as bell hooks (1992, 165) writes, is white.

On October 21, 1994, just before the election in which Proposition 187 was passed by California voters, a photograph appeared in the *Santa Cruz Sentinel* of a political supporter reaching up to a bus window to shake the hand of candidate Michael Huffington, who had just voiced his strong support for Proposition 187. The supporter shook Huffington's hand with one hand and with the other she held up a hand-lettered sign that read, "Is this really *America?*" I read her sign to mean that the racial contract she took for granted, supporting white privilege in the United States both legally and culturally, was—as Zavella has said—perceived as being threatened by undocumented immigrants and global economic change. This between-the-lines, larger-than-NAFTA story was about who *isn't* considered American by this white woman and many other people, even if they have U.S. citizenship. It reveals a story within a story, usually unmarked, about whiteness (see Almaguer 1994, Blee 1991, and Dyson 1999 on white supremacy in the United States, and Hartigan 1999, Bonnett 1999, and Hurtado 1999 on whiteness).

The racial contract has been governing labor relations in the United States for centuries. For California, for example, Tomás Almaguer (1994) documents the history of white entitlement and supremacy strategies beginning with the "free labor" ideology of Andrew Jackson and the doctrine of manifest destiny that guided the state logic of oppression (including genocide) of American Indians, Mexicans, African Americans, and Asian immigrants.[8] These groups were strategically altered, in turn, to provide low-wage labor in a California economy, and that arrangement supported the ideology—largely unarticulated but powerfully assumed—of white entitlement, or *real* citizenship, in California. Almaguer (1994, 14–15) wrote about the long history behind divisive stereotypes that support white supremacist logic in California:

> White antipathy toward Mexicans, Native Americans, and Chinese and Japanese immigrants was typically couched within the rubric of this "free white labor"/"unfree nonwhite labor" dichotomy: Mexicans became inimically associated with the "unproductive," semi-feudal rancho economy that European Americans rapidly undermined after statehood; Indians with a "primitive" communal mode of existence that white settlers ruthlessly eradicated through violence and forced segregations; and Asian immigrants with a "degraded" unfree labor system unfairly competing with and fettering white labor. The class-specific nature of contention between these racialized groups and the European-American populations were all cast in terms of these symbolic associations.

Claims about who were the true (white) citizens of California were subtly and not so subtly made through the wording of Proposition 187 and support for it. Renato Rosaldo has made the distinction between national and cultural citizenship, and those lines were definitely drawn in the debates about the proposition. Rosaldo (1999, 257) said that "in California statewide initiatives provide citizens with an occasion for voting their prejudices. Proposition 187 was arguably in large measure an expression of white supremacy." By denying health care and educational services to undocumented immigrants and by asking service workers to report "illegal aliens" to the INS, the proposition was designed to create a racializing atmosphere. The language of its supporters selectively marked and racialized "Mexicans," calling citizenship into question for all those who looked Mexican, whether citizens or not. The proposition may have sounded reasonable to some. As Richard Delgado (1999, 251) has said, "Efforts to limit citizenship are efforts to maintain a system of white supremacy and to give that system the veneer of fairness and principle." But the stereotypes promoted through the support and passage of Proposition 187 were more than misleading: they could be very dangerous. Hate crimes against Latinos increased sharply after its passage (Finnigan 1995, 6); the perpetrators did not stop to inquire whether the Latinos they discriminated against, turned away from hospitals, beat, or killed had citizenship papers or not. Such acts, especially when sanctioned or carried out by police officers, seemed to support a white supremacist notion of who constituted the real public of, or who was entitled to citizenship in, California and the United States.[9]

Oppression of Latinos/Latinas in the United States has not only been in the form of white supremacist violence. Martha Menchaca, for example, documents the history of persecution of Mexican Americans by Anglo-Americans in California not only through formal organizations like the Ku Klux Klan but also through what she calls *social apartness*—the enforcement by Anglo-Americans (no longer through segregationist laws but through more subtle forms of oppression) of the social distancing of nonwhites from respect and resources in their own communities (Menchaca 1995, 172–173). Menchaca sees the current enforcement of social apartness as linked to the history of racialization and white privilege that has manifested in different communities in different forms (1995, 172).

The authors included in Rodríguez O. and Vincent (1997) also examine white privilege historically, but in the context of Mexican-U.S.

relations. In their introductory essay, the editors point out the long-standing confusion of racialized rhetoric with transnational policy:

> Although both the United States and Mexico have suffered from internal conflicts over the question of race, they persist in their race-based distrust of each other as nations. Moreover, the important distinctions between race and culture often are blurred as both people tend to interpret cultural differences in racial terms. Intellectuals and writers in both countries have frequently contributed to such misunderstandings. (Rodríguez O. and Vincent 1997, 12)

There is, then, a much more complex tapestry of identities and strategies in Mexican-U.S. relations than I present here. While framing this discussion in terms of white supremacy, I do not mean to say that only those voters racialized as white supported California Proposition 187 or that all white voters voted *for* the ballot initiative. As stated earlier, the voting record and the politics were more complex than that. A Mexican-American government worker I interviewed in California, for example, expressed anti-immigrant sentiments.[10] What I am talking about is a more general process of racialization of U.S. identity as symbolically white and Mexican identity as symbolically nonwhite in discussions of internal and transnational policy in 1993 and 1994. With the analytical framework for discussing this racialization process in place, I now discuss how I see it being implemented in discussions of NAFTA and California Proposition 187.

One of the visual and verbal NAFTA stories told prior to its passage in 1993 summarized the economic nationalist view in the United States that NAFTA would cause factories and jobs to go to Mexico and—in a related conclusion—both Mexican-made goods and Mexican workers to flood the United States. Behind many of these representations of NAFTA were assumptions that collapsed and even racialized national identities in the three countries, with the United States and Canada portrayed as white (especially in political cartoons, which typically use individual figures to portray nations), and Mexico portrayed as mestizo or indígena. While these stereotypes associated with NAFTA were remarkably racialized, there were also curious absences: I saw no portrayals of African-American or Asian-American identity in these images. The representations seemed to draw from a Euro-American framing of light skin equated with owners of capital and dark skin as laborers for capital. These nationalized stereotypes overrode, as the television news director pointed out in his interview, the complexities of class, ethnicity, and racialization *within* each North American country. Two opposing sets of NAFTA stories were told about identity: one was a strategic story collapsing national identities into racialized and class-marked identities in order to describe what would happen with NAFTA's implementation; the other set of stories emphasized the plurality of identities within and across political boundaries within North America, as in the example of indigenous nations (or First Nations, the term used in Canada) organizing for economic and political sovereignty across the continent.[11] The second set of stories is discussed in Chapter 4.

As one narrator in Mexico told me in 1993, "Cada país tiene miedo de cada país" ("Each country is afraid of the others"). The degree of xenophobia invoked in discussions of NAFTA before its passage could perhaps be measured by the strength of disclaimers regarding such fears and acts of othering. Then-presidential candidate Ross Perot, for example, said in his book:

> The quickest way to discredit a critic, discount an argument, or intimidate an opponent in U.S. politics is to label that person a "racist." It happens time and again because it works. Once a prominent official makes the smear, it is repeated by the media, and the victims are then forced to prove they are not bigots. The accusers are rarely criticized by the media.
>
> The "racist" card is already being played by the pro-NAFTA advocates. High-level administration officials are telling reporters in "off the record" interviews that NAFTA opponents are racists. Several Members of Congress are making similar slurs in public. It is, of course, all planned and coordinated. Politicians who claim otherwise should be asked to explain such demagoguery to their consultants.
>
> The fact that American workers don't want their jobs moved to Mexico is not "racist." (Perot and Choate 1993, 65–66)

Despite this statement, if Perot did not originate the notion that Mexicans would somehow pollute the other two North American nations through NAFTA—most specifically through pulling down wages or standards of living— he certainly did not dispel it. I wondered about Perot and Choate's intended audience as they hinted at a Spanish-speaking invasion of the workforce and Mexican theft of U.S. jobs. Perot used class stereotypes in various ways in his contestation of NAFTA, sometimes appealing to white-collar workers and at other times saying that he stood for the interests of the working class, as in a November 4, 1993, announcement that he spoke "for millions of ordinary, hard-working Americans" when he asserted that "plumbers, electricians, the salt of the earth have read the big document, and they're against it."

I wondered who "ordinary" Americans might be, in other terms. What was being codified in the language (not just by Ross Perot but in many NAFTA stories) of normalcy, American-ness, difference, and the border? The U.S.-Mexican border figured often in NAFTA stories (made in the United States) as a dangerous membrane—its porosity considered with renewed attention, often with biomedical allusions to breakdowns in the immune defenses (see, for example, Martin 1994) of supposedly coherent nations. Xenophobia regarding transnational migration was focused on the Rio Grande in many political cartoons and in the social movement Lights on the Border, which was comprised of U.S. citizen-volunteers assisting the INS in patrolling the U.S.-Mexican border on the U.S. side by parking their cars and aiming the headlights at the fence. Symbolically, one could see this as another invocation of lightness and darkness in stereotyping U.S./Mexican identities in a "racially" codified economic nationalism.

In 1994, NAFTA stories seemed to emphasize difference. This began, of course, with the EZLN and Salinas administration's armed conflict over neoliberal policies. The differences within and not just between national publics were being discussed more. Economic inequalities within and between North American nations continued to grow, which in turn supported xenophobia (in this case, the fear of others taking jobs). A key NAFTA story that year was California Proposition 187, since it linked NAFTA-related xenophobia with an opportunity for California's registered voters to act on those fears. The week before the vote in November 1994, I was in Mexico City as well as central California, following political cartoons and textual accounts of Proposition 187 and interviewing individuals in both settings about that policy and life with NAFTA in its first year of implementation. The political cartoonists in Mexico were visually linking white supremacists and Proposition 187.[12] I took this seriously as a NAFTA story containing an argument about the funding of public policy and researched that argument.[13] What follows below is an in-depth discussion of border stories, Proposition 187, and arguments about difference, as well as a description of events surrounding the final annual address to the nation by President Salinas, which happened within a week of the California vote.

The border between Mexico and the United States came to represent, in NAFTA stories, contested and transgressed national identity even as it represented a hyperassertion of each nation's identity, especially as it became more militarized. Some political cartoons and editorials compared the U.S.-based proposal to construct a wall between the two nations to the Berlin Wall. See Figure 3.1 for an argument-by-metaphor that California Proposition 187 was such a wall in relations between the United States and Mexico, as national states and as fluid populations. The wall put an image with the xenophobia expressed in the United States in terms of the fear of waves of migrants crossing the Rio Grande.[14] I heard no NAFTA stories in the United States about a fear of Mexican migrant workers leaving the United States and the construction of a wall to contain a low-wage labor force, but just how much Mexican labor contributed to California's agricultural and microelectronics industries' wealth was noted in a NAFTA story told by an indígena activist (see below).

I look to Mexican scholars to tell a story of how the border figures in the imagination and practice of Mexican-U.S. relations. Eduardo Huchim (1992, 22) argued that it was because of historic mistrust of the United States (due to its having taken more than half of Mexico's lands in the nineteenth century) that some Mexicans rejected NAFTA. Juan Gómez-Quiñones (1994, 333) articulated why there was such a preoccupation with the cultural and national future of those on both sides of the border in discussions of NAFTA:

> In a border region, issues or practices of social identity, nationality, and culture are particularly significant, since they are consequences of fundamental economic relations. On the border, aspects of nationality include the recognition of national identities and perceptions of distinct cultural identities, a greater national sensitivity and demonstrations of antagonism, as well as emulation of the other nationality. In some cases this perception embraces ethnocentrism as a component of national sensitivity, and a general consciousness of the historical master in the relations between the nationalities, including past victories and losses. The cultural aspects of language, traditions, and social behavior on the border represent a

Ill. 3.1 187: The Wall (Kemchs. *Los Caricaturistas [Periodismo Gráfica de Actualidad]*, 4th week of October 1994)

range of local and national expressions of transculturation. [author's translation]

José Manuel Valenzuela Arce (1994, 430) has said:

> Identities can refer to traditional cultural elements, which are fundamental referents of group identity strongly anchored in the social practices of a group, but they can also be derived from shared interests or in answer to new conditions—which can give rise to new nexes of identity. [author's translation]

Various new "nexes of identity" came along with NAFTA. Anti-Latino and anti-immigrant views had been expressed at other moments in the United States (Perea 1997; Almaguer 1994), but with the xenophobic rhetoric associated with NAFTA came new opportunities for mobilizing support for such anti-immigrant policies as California Proposition 187. Supporters of the proposition specifically blamed the most recent Mexican immigrants for job losses, in the year NAFTA went into effect, even though researchers monitoring immigration with Jorge Bustamante at the Colegio de la Frontera Norte found that Mexican immigration to the United States decreased after NAFTA (personal communication to author 1996). In part, this could have been due to increased INS and civilian surveillance of the border on the U.S. side. The U.S.-Mexican border, with its long history of problematic (Flores 1995) and transformative (Klahn 1994) cultural representations, once again became a significant symbolic reference point, or nexus of identity, in relation to NAFTA and Proposition 187.

The sombrero was used as a summarizing symbol to represent Mexico in many political cartoons, as in one appearing in the *Nation* (1993: 256[23], 827) that portrayed American Express, General Electric, the Brock Group, Shearman and Sterling, Burson-Marsteller, and Kodak as happy white men dancing in circles around a large sombrero labeled "Mexico." Symbols and metaphors can have different meanings according to the perspective of the viewer or listener. Such flexibility in the interpretation of metaphors is particularly useful to politicians trying simultaneously to invoke agreement, disagreement, inclusion, exclusion, specificity, and generality in every articulation of a position. As Canadian columnist Charles Gordon (1986, 27) said, "Remember, what the politicians say is always based on what they think we are thinking." The trick (for both the listener and the politician) is to figure out who constitutes the "we" and how many forms of "we" can be invoked simultaneously (and often in contradiction). One NAFTA story may be read in how political actors President Salinas and Governor Wilson shifted articulations of who constituted their publics during the negotiation and implementation of NAFTA.

On November 2, 1994, President Salinas de Gortari gave his *sexto informe* (his sixth and final annual national address, a presidential term in Mexico being six years). Within a week, on November 8, the registered voters of California had the option to vote on Proposition 187 and passed it. The relationship between Mexico and the United States was very much mirrored in these two events. Both Salinas and Wilson, while having earlier applauded the multicultural qualities of the bodies they govern, negated the pluralism of their polities strongly in the fall of 1994.[15] While President Salinas did mention the earlier violence in Chiapas in his address, saying that he promoted negotiation rather than annihilation in response to such an internationally visible post–Cold War conflict (Salinas 1994, 2–3), he avoided direct reference to the pueblos indígenas movement for autonomous regional governance in Chiapas and throughout Mexico. Instead, he invoked the more unicultural term *campesinos* in referring to rural Mexico:

> In the countryside, through dialogue and joint efforts, we have made far-reaching reforms to reactivate production with greater freedom and justice. Peasants now have full rights over their lands through amendments to Article 27 of the Constitution. . . . Peasants have become the engineers of their own transformation. (Salinas de Gortari 1994)

The president did not say how much agency he thought campesinos had accrued. But he did find it necessary to have the national military throw indígena activists (also identifying themselves as campesinos) out of the central square on the very day he gave his speech there.

Governor Wilson had similarly used state force to address the Los Angeles riots/rebellion, although the racializing lens of U.S. culture makes it difficult for many to focus on events in Los Angeles and those in Chiapas in the same frame.[16] Both President Salinas and Governor Wilson, as violence related to resources and identity increased, talked less about the multicultural nature of their publics. In 1994, Governor Wilson, in speeches supporting Proposition 187, held immigrants from the unspecified south (invoking nonverbally the dangerous and militarized membrane of the border) responsible for a panoply of problems in California, ranging from depleted funds for education and health care to the incidence of crime. Yet to a more restricted audience of Pacific Rim capitalists, with reference to NAFTA and GATT, Governor Wilson had earlier invoked Latin Americans' presence in California as positive proof of California's plural society and economy. The 1992 speech to the Pacific Economic Cooperation Council included this excerpt:

> As our nation's gateway to the Pacific, California itself is something of a Golden Gate, opening America to the extraordinary opportunities of the Pacific Rim. In fact, in the 1980s America's trade with the Pacific Rim surpassed that with Atlantic basin countries.
>
> Recent figures from California's World Trade Commission show that despite the sluggish economy at home, last year in California exports grew by $4.7 billion, creating nearly 50,000 new jobs. Whether it's selling Central Valley fruit in Japan or Silicon Valley technology in Mexico, California is competing around the world by offering quality products at competitive prices.
>
> Our people are no less diversified than our economy. The 32 million citizens of California constitute the most diverse society in the history of man. To paraphrase Churchill, "Never before have so many come from so far away to live so closely together. . . ."
>
> Parents from the highlands of Guatemala and Laos, from the cities of the Phillipines and Nigeria, are sending their children to the same schools in Los Angeles, in Modesto and Marin. (I like to say that only in California can you order and actually get a kosher burrito, with a side order of kimchee.)
>
> This diversity is one of California's greatest assets in what is becoming an increasingly global market. For all these reasons, I like to say that California borders the world. (Wilson 1992)

While, obviously, different representations of national and cultural identities are made to different audiences, it is interesting to pay close attention to the choices made in emphasizing or silencing aspects of those representations as intended audiences shift. For example, in Wilson's 1992 speech, the diversity he invokes is constituted through recent transnational migration rather than domestic diversity based on far older migrations with different histories, as with African-American and Asian-American diasporas. Perhaps this was a strategic choice in a speech to potential investors made just months after the Los Angeles riots, which had been widely covered in international news accounts. Another set of silences, not only in Governor Wilson's speeches but in many U.S. references to the Pacific Rim, is reflected in the fact that Mexico and Canada are seldom mentioned as Pacific Rim nations. I believe this contributed to (and stemmed from) separate discussions of NAFTA, GATT, and Pacific Rim trade initiatives, rather than facilitating a general discussion of reconfiguration in global capital and labor flows.[17]

The inclusiveness of Governor Wilson's rhetoric in the speech cited above contrasts with the position he took two years later in support of the ballot initiative most commonly referred to as "Prop. 187," which begins:

> The People of California find and declare as follows:
> That they have suffered and are suffering economic hardship caused by the presence of illegal aliens in this state.
> That they have suffered and are suffering personal injury and damage caused by the criminal conduct of illegal aliens in this state.
> That they have a right to the protection of their government from any person or persons entering this country unlawfully.[18]

The text of Proposition 187 goes on, as stated earlier, to require reporting to the INS those people suspected of being undocumented, including teachers reporting schoolchildren suspected of being in the United States illegally, and to deny public health care and education of any kind to a person of any age living in the United States without legal documentation. Proposition 187 galvanized public debate about who constituted "the public" in California, and it ran counter to the state constitution, which guarantees the right to an education for all residents of California. U.S. District Court Judge Mariana Pfaelzer ruled the bulk of the proposition unconstitutional in March 1998, and injunctions prevented its going into effect between its passage and when it was struck down. All along, its primary purpose seemed to be symbolic, even to a principal proponent, Governor Wilson (who was running for reelection on the same ballot offering Proposition 187). In his only debate with gubernatorial challenger Kathleen Brown, Wilson said that if and when it passed, Proposition 187 would be challenged by a lawsuit and taken to the U.S. Supreme Court. Kevin Johnson (1997, 178) provides strong evidence that Proposition 187 was advanced to support nativist ideology rather than to save money for the state (as purported), since it would cost the state more to implement than it would save by cutting social services to the targeted population. Its power seemed to be, then, as a summarizing symbol in what Paul Farmer (1992) has called the geography of blame.

Mexican political cartoonists, in the weeks before the vote on Proposition 187, compared Governor Wilson's proposal of the ballot initiative to the eugenicist actions of Hitler and the Ku Klux Klan (see Figures 3.2 and 3.3). The argument that eugenicist perspectives lay behind the proposition was less accessible in California than in Mexico due, I think, to the obfuscating power of the racial contract (Mills 1997). Taking the Mexican political cartoonists' NAFTA/187 story seriously,[19] I researched the link between white supremacists and California Proposition 187. Omi and Winant document that white supremacists became much more active in the 1980s in reaction to what they saw as a threat to and a need to define whiteness, and that the whiteness was usually defined in contrast to an "other," which could be defined as "across the border" in many senses. Eduardo Barrera (1996, 190–191), drawing on the work of José Manuel Valenzuela Arce, documents how the U.S.-Mexican border has served as a U.S. media trope for not only distinguishing an other but at the same time imagining that other as subordinate to what is reputed to be the dominant social collective. Omi and Winant (1994, 118) describe how Tom Metzger, "a television repairman from San Diego, California, won nomination as the Democratic candidate for Congress in the 43rd Congressional District" and then was revealed as having once been "Grand Dragon of the California branch of the Ku Klux Klan." Metzger "first garnered public attention when he offered to help the U.S. Border Patrol hunt down 'illegal aliens.'" This volunteerism, in Omi and Winant's argument, assisted Metzger in defining and securing his whiteness. This racialization project to serve the joint purposes of the state and white supremacists through patrolling literal and figurative borders can be seen as continuous with the backing of California Proposition 187.

The two cartoons included here (Figures 3.2 and 3.3) appeared in one of several cartoon weeklies that became popular in response to the latest round of neoliberal policies in Mexico. They exemplify the themes of rejection, expulsion, and racialization in analyses in the Mexican press of California's (read U.S. national) policy toward undocumented immigrants from Mexico and elsewhere. Like these examples,

Ill. 3.2 Similarity: 1940, Hitler; 1994, Pete Wilson (Rruizte, *Los Caricaturistas [Periodismo Gráfico de Actualidad]*, 4th week of October 1994)

Ill. 3.3 "We are also getting ready for a rally in support of 187." (Terrazas, *El Día*, October 19, 1944, p. 1)

some made metaphorical connections between Governor Wilson and famous eugenicists from the past such as Adolf Hitler. One account mentioned the Pioneer Fund, a white supremacist organization, as the major financial backer of the S.O.S. ("Save Our State") Initiative, or Proposition 187.[20] Jean Stefancic (1997) has researched and verified the funding connection between the Pioneer Fund, FAIR (the Federation for American Immigration Reform), and California Proposition 187. The Pioneer Fund is a U.S. eugenicist organization (a kind of NGO not usually conjured up by that term) with a long history; not surprisingly, it is difficult to trace. Bill Blakemore, an ABC news reporter, attempted to find a spokesperson for the Pioneer Fund at the time *The Bell Curve* was published (Herrnstein and Murray 1994),[21] but he found that the multimillion-dollar foundation, with tax-exempt status, operates from a mailbox service in Manhattan and that the officers refused to be interviewed (ABC News Investigative Unit 1994). FAIR has a website, www.fairus.org, and I find both its statements and its silences interesting: on the page listing terrorist attacks in the United States, for example, meant to encourage anti-immigrant sentiments, the attack with the most fatalities—the bombing in Oklahoma City by a white U.S. citizen—is noticeably not mentioned.

Anthropologist Virginia Domínguez (1986) has written about a cultural and legal fixation on "blood" identity and racialization in the United States. Eugenicist emphases on purity of the national blood, however oddly imagined, have found their way metaphorically into U.S. discourse in more and less subtle ways. Sheila Croucher (1997, 82) documents that a member of the U.S. Congress used the phrase "a hemorrhage of people" in referring to undocumented immigration from Mexico to the United States. While the legislator may have used the phrase in reference to stopping the flow, I think it could also be read to signify (although this meaning has not been claimed or marked) the tainting of U.S. (white) blood, drawing applause from eugenicist supporters of anti-immigrant policies like Proposition 187, which some saw at the time as a template for national legislation. Pioneer Fund monies had been used earlier to promote voluntary, paid sterilization for welfare recipients with IQs (intelligence quotients) deemed low ($1,000 for every point below the white mean of 100) (Miller 1994, 112) and to cut the Head Start preschool program, since in the view of those controlling the Pioneer Fund, the majority of recipients were black and their academic performance was "the result of irreversible genetic deficiencies [not economic inequality] and government funding for remedial programs was consequently a waste of taxpayers' money" (Fischel 1995, 17). Therefore, cutting social services to undocumented immigrants, as proposed in the 1994 ballot initiative, was in keeping with the Pioneer Fund's eugenicist and meritocratic agenda. The fund had directly entered the political arena before. Bob Herbert traced the relationship between Pioneer Fund officer Thomas Ellis and North Carolina Senator Jesse Helms's campaigns, which Ellis advised. Herbert reports (1996, A15) that:

> In 1990 Mr. Ellis was one of the architects of Senator Helms's vicious, racially polarizing re-election campaign against Harvey Gantt, the first black mayor of Charlotte. When polls showed Mr. Gantt ahead late in the race, Mr. Ellis and his colleagues came up with the now notorious "white hands" television ad. The hands of a white man were shown crumpling a rejection letter while the voice-over said a less-qualified "minority" got the job because of a racial quota.

In short, then, the Mexican political cartoonists' links between eugenicists and California Proposition 187 were not far-fetched; they were perhaps more honest in making that connection than many in the United States were able to be. Through FAIR, the Pioneer Fund supported the Proposition 187 campaign. FAIR brought together eugenicists with anti-immigration activists and zero-population-growth environmentalists, and with over a million dollars from the Pioneer Fund, it succeeded—at least symbolically, until the proposition was overturned—in its aim to stop delivery of social services to undocumented immigrants in California (Rosenthal 1995, 54).[22]

In the next section, I turn from stories of racialization to those of public protest against that racialization and associated experiences of inequality on both sides of the Mexican-U.S. border.

Stories of Public Protest

On the Day of the Dead, November 2, 1994, in Mexico City, drummers stood on the Plaza de la Constitución or *Zócalo*—the central plaza constructed by the Spanish colonizers over Aztec temples—and beat out the rhythm to the familiar political chant, "El pueblo, unido, jamás será vencido" ("The people, united, will never be defeated"), as I watched

with other passersby. Dancers joined the growing circle from the surrounding crowd. No one was singing the words, so no words could be
silenced. Just a day earlier in the same spot, indígena solidarity activists
and the altars for the Day of the Dead had been removed forcibly by
federal soldiers and the metropolitan police. Hunger strikers, vendors of
EZLN newsmagazines, T-shirts, and buttons, and PRD supporters who
had registered votes under a picture of Cuauhtémoc Cárdenas the day
before, had all been chased with clubs at 1:00 A.M. to another part of the
Federal District.

The plaza or Zócalo had been cleared because of President
Salinas's official address to all Mexicans to sum up his administration—the *sexto informe* or *sexenio*. On that morning, truckloads and
buses of metropolitan police from other parts of the city arrived in the
Zócalo, and those police workers stood shoulder to shoulder with soldiers from the National Palace, surrounding the entire empty plaza.
Gates were erected to prevent free entry into it, except for those with
credentials stating they were members of the PRI. Inside the barricades,
PRI hats and banners were distributed, and the loyal stood for three
hours awaiting the president as he journeyed from the Casa de
Diputados (House of Representatives), where he gave his address,[23] to
the National Palace on the Zócalo.

Members of unions supporting and supported by President Salinas
and the PRI were allowed into the Zócalo; members of the shoemaking
union, who work in one of the sectors hard hit by NAFTA, were not. I
saw them being turned away at the gates and, just beyond them, their
march being broken up by soldiers. On streets surrounding the plaza,
there were PRD (Democratic Revolutionary Party), CND (Convención
Nacional Democrática), and Zapatista rallies contesting the PRI display
of popular support. In the Marcha de marchas (March of marches),
coffins bearing the PRD insignia were carried toward the Zócalo, representing the hundreds of assassinated PRD members, and the coffins
were broken into pieces by the police (*La Jornada* 11/2/94).

During these graphic demonstrations of division over political control of the Mexican nation, there was agreement across party lines in
Mexico on one issue: condemnation of Governor Wilson of California
and Proposition 187. President Salinas de Gortari, one of three finalists
in a worldwide search for a leader of the World Trade Organization,
presented his final national address very much to a world audience.
While he tended to portray Mexicans as supportive of ongoing economic ties with the United States and as united behind the NAFTA that

his administration had negotiated, President Salinas said this in his address:

> Local political interests in California tend to blame Mexican workers for that society's problems. Mexico affirms its rejection of this xenophobic campaign and will continue to act in defense of the labor and human rights of our migrant workers.
>
> The existence of 50 Mexican consulates in the United States makes it possible to provide systematic legal support to Mexicans to an unprecedented degree. We are also intensifying the dialogue between our two countries through the Bilateral Working Group on Migration and Consular Affairs, the Binational Commission, and the High-Level Meetings on Border Violence, in order to prevent incidents. We have seen that there is room for respect, cooperation and mutual benefit in the complex, and historically sometimes traumatic, relationship with the United States. While developing our relations with the United States, we are also launching new initiatives aimed at other regions, because when the decision is made to intensify relations with such a powerful nation, an effort must also be made to bring your faraway friends closer. Through this strategy, we are diversifying our international relations. (Salinas de Gortari 1994, 5–6)

Salinas went on to discuss strengthened ties with Canada after the passage of NAFTA, a policy he described as successful.[24]

In diplomatic letters sent to the U.S. State Department, the Mexican government was even more forthright about its position on California Proposition 187:

> The government of Mexico believes that the hostile climate, and the growing incidence of abuse and harassment of Mexican nationals, is at the risk of affecting economic and commercial interchanges, and affects negatively bilateral relations between Mexico and the U.S.
>
> Mexico considers such anti-immigrant attitudes, including anti-Mexican attitudes, to be encouraged by the arguments embodied in Proposition 187. They are in every way contrary to the spirit of cooperation and bilateral exchange. (*El Día* 1994, 3) [author's translation]

This letter was sent during the same period Mexican political cartoonists were comparing California's governor to white supremacists. Also during the week before the vote on Proposition 187, a boycott by Mexicans of U.S. companies—including McDonald's—in California and Mexico was reported in many Mexican press accounts to have been responsible for an 80 percent drop in California sales.

Several groups were en plantón in the Zócalo. On November 2, 1994, members of the EZLN and the CNPI (Coordinadora Nacional de Pueblos Indios) had been hunger striking for twenty days, returning even after being removed by soldiers to another square. The military had ejected members of three communities in Chiapas from their land in order, they said, to give it to a California-based agribusiness. The hunger strikers were protesting that action along with others associated with the constitutional changes preceding NAFTA. They took up their position, visible from the National Palace, in order to challenge the government on Article 8 of the constitution, which guarantees the right to petition. By the time of the Day of the Dead, they still had not received an audience, and although physically weakened by the hunger strike, they were planning to continue. Their spokesperson agreed to be interviewed, and I asked about his perceptions of Mexican-U.S. relations nearly a year into the implementation of NAFTA. Here is his response:

> We are from the National Committee of Indian Peoples, from Veracruz, from Chiapas, from Oaxaca, and from Guerrero. We come from those states because right now, that is where the most problems are. . . . Some of us have been hunger striking for more than twenty days. . . .
>
> We say that the constitution of the United Mexican States gives us the right to demonstrate publicly, without hurting anyone. And when we go without food, we demand with our hunger that there be justice, that the corruption end, that the abuses of power end, and that there be security in our country. We make this demand legally and reasonably. And our demand is supreme because there is no gift that matters more than life itself. And with our lives we demand justice. We demand liberty. We demand our right to govern ourselves according to the decision of our peoples. We will not conform to decisions that are imposed on us by some government, only to those made by our own peoples. . . .

In the Imperial Valley of California, all the modern agriculture is mechanized, and they only want Indians to go pick cotton and harvest tomatoes and vegetables in the north. Mechanized agriculture is to make food for the gringos, because the gringos want good, pretty, cheap things. They come to rent our land and they take the produce, but they pay the laborers very badly. . . .

The majority of Indians work the land. There are Indians who are lawyers and engineers and everything, but they are acculturated.[25] What I was talking about does not only happen in Mexico. It also happens in Canada and in the United States. I attended a congress in Canada in which they said, "Here, we Canadian Indians are in institutions." And we said, "What is an institution?" And they said, "It is a jail." . . . There has been a lot that has happened here in Mexico that has lowered the standard of living since the changes in Article 27. . . . We do not need to sign treaties like the gringo government signed with the tribes of the United States—treaties which they have never respected. . . .

If the gringos respect us, there will be peace. If the gringos want to rob us of our oil and rob us of our land like they have already robbed us of our labor, there will always be war. War breaks out when those who have money abuse those who do not. And the governor of California is abusing his power. Yes, with Proposition 187, because the Californians will turn around and elect him governor again. He says we are going to get rid of the nasty Mexicans. We are no longer going to give education or other services to Latin Americans. But they do not know that they have wealth thanks to those nasty migrant workers.

There will be war, because we are not going to allow them to kill us with hunger. We will fight. Those of us here choose to fight with our lives, for all to see. But there are others that do not think the same way . . . they have formed the Zapatista National Liberation Army, and they are armed. They say, "We prefer to die fighting against those who are killing us with hunger." [author's translation]

Visual reminders of death, either by hunger or war, and of persistent connections to the land and those who lived on it before were all around us in the skull decorations for the Day of the Dead. After that interview, I walked through the city to meet with one of my collaborators in this research, financial journalist Jorge Carrásco Araizaga, to ask him how he saw conditions in Mexico nearly a year after NAFTA's implementation. On the way, I saw the skulls, special bread, and paper art prepared for the holiday and also the faces of plastic jack-o'-lanterns familiar to me from Halloween celebrations in the United States.[26] I asked Carrásco to comment on this in the interview. Here is how he summed up 1994: "Like in the film, this has been the year in which we have been living dangerously. Whatever positive effects NAFTA might have had have been cancelled out by the political situation" (author's translation).

By that, he meant the assassination of presidential candidate Luis Donaldo Colosio in Tijuana and others within the PRI. He explained that he thought NAFTA should not be satanized as a policy in itself but that one would have to pay careful attention to how it was interpreted over time and the effects it was having on the country. He went on:

Nationalism has not been overflowing in this past Mexican presidential administration, nor do I think we will hear nationalism as a word used very much by the next administration. Which brings us back to the subject of [class] divisions. There are those who have the information and the access to become part of this globalization, and they are the ones for whom there is a change in national culture, because they are the consumers of [global] culture. For example, they can afford to go to McDonald's in Mexico City.[27] And on TV, we now have the U.S. National Basketball Association. Some are consuming these things in Mexico, but then we still have the Day of the Dead. [With NAFTA], there are more Halloween products being sold, but we still make our Day of the Dead offerings. . . . So consumption of other cultures goes up, but there are aspects of this culture that are never going to go away. . . . Those with money [and he explained that the division between rich and poor was greater in 1994 than at any other time in the twentieth century] will buy modernity here or will go to California or Texas shopping. But those who don't have money are in the majority.

The same is true of the United States, and sometimes there is political mobilization in the interests of that nonelite majority. One week later, I stood on an overpass doing interviews in Spanish and English with some of the hundreds of protestors who had marched up the ramp and stopped traffic on Highways 1 and 17 in Capitola, California. We were there to protest the positive votes on Propositions 187 and 184 the day before.[28] Capitola police workers in full riot gear stood shoulder to shoulder on the entrance ramps to prevent other protestors from joining those already on the overpass and to break up the protest. Traffic was stopped for two hours. I thought about the transnational Mexican political community as the refrain was taken up on the overpass, just as it had been drummed out in the Zócalo: "El pueblo, unido, jamás será vencido" ("The people, united, will never be defeated"). Among those contesting Proposition 187 were teachers wondering if their students would be allowed to continue coming to school and health workers wondering if their clinics would close. A student said this about Proposition 187:

> I think it's just a racist proposition that they are trying to pass, trying to stop the problem of immigrants coming in; they're saying that we're paying too much in taxes for them. But they don't know that the immigrants who have a fake social security number are paying taxes, but they never get that money back. They're also paying taxes, those immigrants who are here [without legal status]; they do have a fake social security and most come to work. They don't come to take welfare. They don't come to take social services.
>
> Everybody needs medical attention. Everybody needs an education. It's not fair to target just the immigrants by saying that they are taking all the services. I'm saying this is racist because they're not gonna be targeting people that have blonde hair and blue eyes. Of course it's going to be targeting dark people, with dark hair and dark eyes. And that's the way it's becoming more racist. All my friends and my family are not citizens. Most of the ones affected could not vote. That's why they brought up this immigrant issue, because they knew that the people that they were gonna target were the people that couldn't vote.

Her point about undocumented immigrants paying social security and taxes that would not benefit them was a challenge I heard often in response to Proposition 187 supporters' portrayals of "illegal aliens" as parasites on the U.S. citizen population. One set of stories in 1994, then, challenged increasing racialization in the representation of "Mexicans" in the United States following the passage of the North American Free Trade Agreement. After the collapse of the Mexican currency in December 1994, another set of NAFTA stories came into circulation. Those are followed in Chapter 4.

Notes

1. Alterity, or the positing of an "other" different from one's self and one's own group, is a process usually infused with power distinctions. The process of creating an other, considered to be inferior to, or to have less agency than, a self, has been described by Simone de Beauvoir (1999, 337–339); postcolonial theorists Albert Memmi (1991), Frantz Fanon (1991), and Aimé Césaire (1972); and anthropologists Brackette Williams (1991, 1996) and Michael Taussig (1993, 144–161), among many others.

2. The ballot initiative proposed and passed in California in 1994 is reproduced in the appendix. The law denied access to public services (e.g., schooling for children and public health care) for "illegal aliens." It was struck down (many parts of it for being unconstitutional) by U.S. District Court Judge Mariana Pfaelzer in March 1998. Its purpose seems to have been primarily political, since it was always too unwieldy to implement, and in public discussions of Proposition 187, only Latino immigrants without INS papers were targeted in public representations of the ballot initiative as those for whom services would be cut—never undocumented immigrants from, for example, Ireland, Israel, or Russia.

3. Proposition 184, the "three strikes" ballot initiative, promoted mandatory life sentencing for anyone who had had three felony convictions. Those who contested the initiative felt it further linked criminalization with racialization processes in the state, since felony convictions occurred in disproportionately smaller numbers for white Californians, in part because of the racial profiling in police departments that has since been under public scrutiny. Guillermo Rojas (1998, 89) put it this way: "Fear of illegals was translated into the rhetoric of Proposition 187 and fear of criminals was translated into Proposition 184." Both propositions garnered support by capitalizing on prejudices.

4. Rojas (1998, 88) argues that the loss of 730,000 jobs since just before Governor Pete Wilson's last election were actually due to the cutback in defense contracts, a point on which Wilson was markedly silent during his reelection campaign; he focused instead on blaming undocumented immigrants (from Mexico, it was always intimated) for economic hard times.

5. As Patricia Hill Collins says (2000, 227–228), the *matrix of domination* "describes this overall social organization within which intersecting oppressions originate, develop, and are contained." Here I am only talking about some forms of alterity and oppression within capitalist logic and practice. Karen Brodkin (1998, 63) more fully describes the ways U.S. capitalism has always relied on fluid "race making" practices, linking "job degradation and racial darkening" with the production of gender identities in different ways over time, depending on the least-desirable occupational niches that needed to be filled by persons marked by racialized or gendered identities (see also Brodkin 2000).

Many times, individuals may be situated in the matrix of domination as both oppressed and oppressors. Maxine Baca Zinn and Bonnie Thornton Dill (1999, 108) point out that "intersecting forms of domination produce *both* oppression *and* opportunity." Karen Hossfeld (1990, 150) describes how what I would call the strategic alterity of managers can be used against them by their workers. Workforces have been divided in many ways from identifying with one another's experience—see Eric Wolf (1982, 380) on "ethnic segmentation of the labor force" and Gustavo Lins Ribeiro (1995, 343) on the dehumaniza-tion/decontextualization of transnational migrant workers. The possibilities of seeing around the thought styles (Fleck, as used by Douglas 1986) or ideologies that strategically divide us have been raised by the plurinational organizing efforts described in Chapter 4. See Gayatri Spivak's (1990, 93) discussion of "strategic essentialism" for an analysis of the way identities are caricatured or simplified for purposes of collective action. I bring this up here to say that strategic alterity is happening in many directions, not just from the top down or on the part of white supremacists. Capitalist logic relies on strategic alterity; how much does counterpractice also rely on that logic, since most of us in the world today have been schooled in the logic of capitalism one way or another?

6. Michael Omi and Howard Winant (1994, 55) define race as *"a concept which signifies and symbolizes social conflicts and interests by referring to different types of human bodies."* They discuss each racial project as *"simultaneously an interpretation, representation, or explanation of racial dynamics, and an effort to reorganize and redistribute resources along particular racial lines"* (Omi and Winant 1994, 56). (Italics in original)

Faye Harrison (1995) traces the history of the ways moral, political economic, nationalist, anthropological, advancing, and transformative arguments about racialization have been made. Her definition of racism is useful, as is Omi and Winant's, for seeing race as a category that refers to power relations rather than essential biological identity. Harrison (1995, 65) says: "Racism must be understood to be a nexus of material relations within which social and discursive practices perpetuate oppressive power relations between populations presumed to be essentially different." The distinctions drawn between forms of racism discussed by the authors collected in Goldberg (1990) are helpful, too, in understanding this kind of racialization project.

7. See R. Michael Alvarez and Tara L. Butterfield's (2000) analysis of why 59 percent of California's voters (of many identities) passed Proposition 187. They concluded that its passage was linked with "cyclical nativism" related to a poor economy and to the endorsement of political candidates who used stereotypical images of immigrants in their campaign ads.

8. "Free-labor adherents believed that social mobility and economic independence were only achievable in a capitalist society unthreatened by non-white populations and the degrading labor systems associated with them. European Americans repeatedly associated nonwhite people with various unfree labor systems that ostensibly threatened their superordinate social standing and class prerogatives in California" (Almaguer 1994, 13). It was part of the westward expansion ideology that made white landholders feel they were true citizens and the mainstay of the U.S. economy, without marking for notice the role that unfree labor played in the national economy, making that white privilege possible.

9. Not only those who carried out physical acts of violence against

Latinos/Latinas contributed to anti-immigrant sentiments; symbolic violence was also promoted through the dehumanization of Mexican immigrants, for example, in press accounts (Fleischmann 1992, 65–67).

10. See Bonilla et al. (1998) for excellent discussions of U.S. Latino/Latin American identity formation and political relations.

11. This plurinational organizing was strengthened in response to both the constitutional change in Mexico and events in Chiapas, as representatives from many indígena nations conferred about those situations and others in North America. A sociologist in Mexico (who asked for the same anonymity given to other narrators in the book) explained one of the plurinational responses to the EZLN's initiative:

> When the Chiapas rebellion began, a commission of Canadian Indian nations came to Mexico. They observed the situation and concluded that the Indian peoples of Chiapas were right in their actions. A new [plurinational] commission was created to fight for more respect for Indian peoples in Mexico. They have made joint declarations. Here in Mexico, the government "took the natives for granted" [for this phrase, he switched to English]. "They're here, they'll follow us, they're Mexicans," and so on. [The government] wants a passive Indian population. That is what the government counted on with respect to NAFTA, in accordance with the fatalism myth, that [the Mexican people] would believe that there was no other option and accept it. [author's translation]

12. White supremacists are understood here to be those who see race in biological terms, with a white race superior to all others and thus more deserving to control physical and social resources. White supremacy and eugenicist thinking are closely linked, since eugenicists advocate that those classified as inferior or unfit in their racializing model should not be allowed to reproduce (i.e., forced sterilization) or to live (i.e., genocide).

13. As indicated in Chapter 2, I agree with those who believe political cartoonists can sometimes articulate arguments in public space that are otherwise repressed. I also believe, as stated in the introduction, that everyone makes theories and that academic research needs to be more broadly informed by sources of argument—including political cartoons. In academic contexts, we have access to information resources to do background research that might complement or counter assertions of those working in other contexts, but I do not see them as totally disparate knowledge domains (e.g., the ivory tower and the public sphere).

14. I am thinking here particularly of anthropologist Emily Martin's (1994, 25–33) discussion of immune system metaphors as castle walls and the construction of "safety" from disease and the Cold War through that flexible metaphor. The fortress metaphor, when invoked in NAFTA stories told by some situated in the United States, was used to racialize notions of dominant national identity by asserting protection for white citizens and white economic and political dominance in a similarly flexible (and unmarked) manner.

15. In President Salinas's case, he was laudatory of *pueblos indios* at the

time of the reforms made in Article 4 of the Mexican constitution—two years before NAFTA went into effect and the EZLN demanded that indígena sovereignty over resources to meet basic needs be respected by the national government.

16. The rioting in Los Angeles following the police beating of Rodney King in 1992 is referred to as riots or as a rebellion, depending on the speaker.

17. Such a discussion *was* organized through plurinational NGOs and events associated with NAFTA's negotiation and passage (see Chapter 4).

18. The full text of California Proposition 187 is included in the appendix.

19. The play with symbolic meanings in political cartoons makes it possible to articulate the unspoken in public discourse. John Johnson (1980), discussing the formation of racialized attitudes toward Latin America by U.S. residents and the association of this process with U.S. political cartoons, examines in detail the debate over whether cartoons *shape* or *reflect* public opinion. I see them as doing both, just as arguments in journalism and academic contexts do, but political cartoons are broadly accessible and—as stated earlier—capable because of how they insert arguments into public space that can otherwise be dangerous or unacceptable to articulate. George Black (1988) also took political cartoons seriously, in his analysis of U.S. representations of Central America and the Caribbean. For a close study of the history and political impact of Mexican political cartoons, see an article by El Fisgón, himself, in which he writes:

> Linked to specific political movements, those artists of irony contributed through their art to political and social change in Mexico. Their cartoons offered tools of analysis laced with irony that, by translating the complex and often abstract world of politics into simple and tangible images, made them accessible to most Mexican citizens. (Barajas 2000, 13)

20. The Pioneer Fund connection with Proposition 187 was also reported by Catherine Clayton and Michael Schallenberger in a student project in the Anthropology Board of Studies at the University of California–Santa Cruz. They attempted to contact a representative of the Pioneer Fund directly to confirm or discount this connection but were unsuccessful. I did not try to do this myself, but ties have been established between the Pioneer Fund and the Save Our State initiative by several authors (Stefancic 1997). Apparently, the Pioneer Fund gave financial support to FAIR, a major backer of Proposition 187. The Pioneer Fund has a long history of supporting white supremacist research and activism (ABC News Investigative Unit 1994; Fischel 1995; Herbert 1996; Lane 1994; Mehler 1988; Miller 1994; S. Rosenthal 1995; Sedgwick 1994; and Short 1991). In 1894, the Immigration Restriction League was formed by Harvard alumni to "restructure immigration policy solely on racial grounds" (Smedley 1993, 269). The Pioneer Fund kept such eugenicist activity going throughout the second half of the twentieth century and continues to do so.

21. Chapters 13 and 14 of *The Bell Curve* (Herrnstein and Murray 1994) provide supporting evidence (through the perspective of scientific racism, as many in the discipline of anthropology label it) for dismissing affirmative

action policies, articulated directly on the California ballot as Proposition 209, or the "California Civil Rights Initiative." They state that such policies as Head Start and affirmative action are ineffective because accomplishment is due to the inherited "g" factor of intelligence, which the authors arranged on a racialized "bell curve," justifying a white meritocracy biologically. Their argument has been amply countered by Stephen Jay Gould and others collected in Fraser (1995).

22. Note Faye Harrison's (1995, 65) statement that "unintended actions—even those intended to be antiracist—can have racist and racializing effects." By focusing on the story of racialization in this section, I have not intended to promote the *process* of racialization or to further empower the Pioneer Fund. Wetherell and Potter (1992, 219) argue for a place in a larger antiracist project for "identifying the forms legitimation takes, and charting also the fragmented and dilemmatic nature of everyday discourse, because it is at those points of fracture and contradiction that there is scope for change and the redirection of argument." One form of legitimation much in need of reform is scientific discourse itself, as pointed out by the Third World Network (1993, 485): "Science is closely correlated with the existing, dominant and unjust, political, economic, and social order of the world." That not only includes the kind of scientific racist projects supported by the Pioneer Fund but also projects in social science like this one, and I understand that while I am critical of racializing projects, I am also participating in the institutions that in part sustain them.

23. The president's annual address opens the legislative session.

24. This address was made one month before the crash of the peso in December 1994, which led many in Mexico who supported NAFTA to question it. From the vantage point of early November, though, this is how President Salinas saw NAFTA and related neoliberal trade policies in his summary address:

> In the current times of increasing globalization, a broad interrelationship with the world economy is necessary to fully benefit from Mexico's competitive advantages and thereby ensure the profitability of investment, the creation of jobs and steady improvement in the standard of living. Protectionism unquestionably favors capital and concentrates income, while greater openness favors employment and the redistribution of income.
>
> Macroeconomic stability, trade opening, agreements promoted by the government to open up markets abroad and deregulate the domestic market, have increased the country's export capacity. Thus, exports rose from slightly more than 30 billion dollars in 1988 to nearly 52 billion in 1993, and during the first eight months of 1994, they amounted to 39 billion dollars. Imports also grew significantly from 28 billion dollars in 1988 to 65 billion in 1993, and amounted to almost 51 billion dollars as of August 1994. Imports of intermediate and capital goods account for nearly 90 percent of import invoices.
>
> We have advanced toward creating a new export culture, based on the outstanding growth in manufacturing. The share of manufactured goods in

total exports grew from 56 percent in 1988 to nearly 70 percent during the first half of 1994. Petroleum exports account for only 12 percent. The Mexican economy has been depetrolized.

In these years, we have established clearer and more transparent rules for international trade. Nearly all prior import permits have been replaced by tariffs. We have reduced the tariff spread. We have also strengthened export promotion instruments and mechanisms for protection against unfair practices in international trade. In 1994, the National Foreign Trade Bank will grant a total of nearly 16 billion dollars to incorporate more than 20,000 new companies into export activities. The Joint Commission for Export Promotion was consolidated as a legal entity for coordinating and reaching concerted agreement between authorities and the export community.

Free trade agreements have enabled us to diversify markets, attract capital and gain access to advanced technology. From the very outset, we clearly established that we would not negotiate a common market, but a free trade agreement which, on the one hand, would fully preserve the sovereignty of the country and strictly observe the provisions of the Constitution and, on the other, would create stable and lasting conditions for the access of Mexican products to such markets.

During the period covered by this report, the legislative bodies of Mexico, Canada and the United States approved and ratified the North American Free Trade Agreement, signed in 1992 by the Heads of State of the three countries, as well as the side agreements signed in 1993. As a result, the NAFTA entered into force on January 1, 1994.

The NAFTA has created unprecedented conditions for the growth of our exports. Initial data confirm this: between January and August 1994, total Mexican sales to the United States grew 22 percent over the same period in the previous year; nonpetroleum exports grew 25 percent, and the greatest increase was in the export of manufactured goods, which rose 27 percent. This growth rate is more than double that of exports to the United States from the rest of the world. Exports to Canada, in turn, grew 36 percent during the first half of the year. Foreign investment also increased substantially; between January and September 1994, more than 10 billion dollars in foreign investment entered the country.

These promising results show, on the one hand, that Mexico is successfully meeting the challenges of greater openness to trade and, on the other, that it has made good use of the advantages offered by the NAFTA to attract capital and technology, to increase its productivity and successfully compete in the markets of North America. The NAFTA has thus become a powerful tool for attracting new investment, creating productive jobs and enhancing the well-being of Mexicans.

Within the country, over the past six years we have emphatically applied a set of reforms to the framework for regulating economic activity. From 1989 to 1994, approximately 60 areas of economic activity were deregulated. The New Federal Law on Economic Competition supplemented the deregulation program by including diverse provisions that allow corrective action to be taken by the government to prevent monopolistic practices. (Salinas 1994, 10–11)

25. The hunger-striking spokesperson was himself a lawyer and aligned himself very much with the concerns of fellow members of indígena nations. His analysis of class, indígena identity, and strategic positioning, then, was more complex than it would appear in this interview.

26. An anonymous reviewer of this manuscript pointed out that Day of the Dead and Halloween symbols have long been mixed in celebrations of the Day of the Dead on both sides of the U.S.-Mexican border. The presence of plastic jack-o'-lanterns should not be attributed simply to economic policy but also to important cultural practices among those who move back and forth across the border. See Brandes (1988) for an anthropological discussion of commercialization of the Day of the Dead, and Carmichael and Sayer (1992) for comparison of elements in both celebrations.

27. In Mexico, McDonald's caters to middle- and upper-class consumers. I am told a "Big Mac" sandwich costs nearly ten times more in U.S. currency than it would in the United States, so going to McDonald's in Mexico City is a sit-down, "fancy" dining experience.

28. California Proposition 184 made changes in the mandatory sentencing legislation and became known as the "three strikes, you're out" bill because it linked a third conviction to a mandatory life sentence. Since Proposition 187 made it a felony to use or produce false nationality papers, for example, even as it increased the likelihood that papers would be checked and that individuals would feel pressured to use false credentials—including schoolchildren wanting to attend public school—one reason for protesting the two propositions together was that both were seen as particularly targeting Mexican undocumented immigrants. Another was to protest the disproportionate numbers of California residents marked as other-than-white who live in prisons and in poverty.

4

1995: Stories of
Crisis, Critique, and Change

In December 1994, a financial crisis in Mexico mirrored the political crisis that had begun the year. The relationship between the United States and Mexico was examined once again by both publics one year into NAFTA, with talk of dependency as just one interpretation of the financial assistance provided to Mexico by the U.S. government following the fall of the peso.[1] In this chapter, I follow NAFTA stories I heard in 1995: stories of crisis and critique, of plurinational action, and circulation stories. In the first section, the economic crisis, analyses of changing Mexican national identity, and the first annual national address of President Ernesto Zedillo Ponce de León are discussed. The second set of stories includes changes envisioned by the EZLN as articulated by Subcomandante Marcos and others, as well as interviews with a member of the Alianza Cívica (the Civic Alliance, which administered an independent balloting process among Mexicans in 1995), teenagers who voted in the Consulta Nacional Juvenil, and a leader in the plurinational movement to negotiate alternatives to neoliberal economic policies. The last section, "Circulation Stories," relates the accounts of farmers I revisited in Morelos and Kentucky and a member of the Mexican secretariat of the treasury, regarding their perceptions of the circulation of opportunities and commodities two years into NAFTA, and follows the story of transnational migration for Mexicans after California Proposition 187.

In August, September, and October 1995, I was a researcher in the CISAN (Center for Research on North America) at UNAM. In addition to semistructured interviews, the information in this chapter comes from observations as a participant in public rituals (e.g., la Noche

Mexicana—the celebration of Mexican Independence); written materials from those *en plantón,* newsstands, the CISAN reference staff, or handouts; and casual conversations in the course of everyday life.[2]

Just as with the plastic jack-o'-lanterns I had seen on the Day of the Dead in 1994,[3] one more year into NAFTA I saw more commodities being sold in Mexico that resembled U.S. products or carried their trademarks. These were the surface changes that reflected deeper effects of neoliberal policies. In 1995, Hershey bars were being sold in the Metro subway tunnels, and there were Barbie doll stalls in the mercado;[4] even U.S. news stories seemed to be sold in the Mexican market more vigorously, like the daily reports from the O. J. Simpson trial that fall. Labeling provided some indication of who were the intended consumers for products in the North American market. Kellogg cereal boxes on Mexican grocery shelves, for example, had no translation from English into Spanish, while Quaker boxes had some. The text on Nestlé cereal packages was completely in Spanish. This did not necessarily mean, however, that the Kellogg cereals had been produced in the United States.

The main worry for many Mexican consumers, however, was not the language the ingredients were listed in but how to pay for subsistence goods. Some observations based on personal experience were made to me by middle-class Mexicans living in apartments in Mexico City. "Serena," who had retired from a profession in public relations and the arts, said that retirement incomes had not been adjusted for inflation, so many elderly people who thought they would have a secure retirement income were living with hunger every day. A university professor, "Marta," told me she thought minibus taxi drivers earned more than she did, and—articulating the major problem for many—with the monthly credit card interest rate over 100 percent, "debtors could not pay back the debt even if they wanted to."[5] Another professional, "Daniel," living in the newly fashionable neighborhood of La Condesa, told me that recently privatized (under Salinas) monopolies like the phone company were impossible to deal with. He said he had been waiting three months to have a telephone installed in his apartment, and then he received a bill for those three months for 300 pesos. He was also worried about his retirement income.[6] For all the years he had worked and had been supposedly paying into a retirement fund, there was suddenly nothing to show for it: the funds had not been managed well and had disappeared. Daniel said that with the economic crisis, the Mexican people had lost their spark and had become very tired. He was impatient with the political system—specifically, the labor office in charge of the retirement system—and asked me, "How can we enter the twenty-first century with a country that is politically in the nineteenth century?" He talked about the "dinosaurs" (the old guard of the PRI), corruption, and the in-fighting at the recent PRD conference, and he said that the conservative PAN administrator of Guadalajara had recently outlawed the wearing of miniskirts by women there, just one sign of censorship in civil society.

The mobilization of such middle-class[7] concerns into *el barzón* (the debtors' movement that began in Guadalajara)[8] was one of the changes resulting from the economic crisis, which many I spoke with attributed to NAFTA. In 1995, there was still police repression in Mexico City and in many Mexican states, but there was also an obvious rise in popular movements critical of government policies. The murders of prominent PRI members José Francisco Ruíz Massieu and Luis Donaldo Colosio,[9] rumored to have been ordered within their own party, and the very public confrontation of the Mexican national administration by members of the EZLN, seemed to have caused the PRI to back down and allow, for example, more critical public commentary in the Zócalo in Mexico City; between 1994 and 1995, critical periodicals sold at newsstalls, including *Boletín Mexicano de la Crisis* (*Mexican Bulletin of the Crisis*), had proliferated. In the coming section, I discuss more evidence of increased public contestation of the neoliberal policies of the Mexican administration, which I read and heard in NAFTA stories about the economic crisis.

Stories of Crisis and Critique

The economic crisis of December 1994 signified the greatest recent change in Mexico for those I interviewed in 1995, whether they attributed it to NAFTA or not. In impact, it was compared by many with the Great Depression of the 1930s in the United States. Some saw the "bailout plan"—as a U.S. loan package to Mexico was called in the U.S. national press[10]—as confirmation (1) of some Mexican citizens' worries that their country would lose at least economic, if not political sovereignty through NAFTA, and (2) of plurinational labor alliances' fears that NAFTA would eventually pull wages down in all three countries rather than bringing Mexican wages up to equal those in the United States and Canada.

According to figures from the Economics Department of the

UNAM, reported over Radio Red in Mexico City on October 4, 1995, minimum wage in Mexico was the lowest it had been since President Lázaro Cardenas established one a generation before, and the nation's unemployment was the highest it had been in fifty years. I heard different stories about long-term changes associated with NAFTA. The miracle some had anticipated in 1993 had definitely not arrived by 1995. Neoliberals told me it was just a matter of time—that small enterprises unable to compete were going under as a matter of course and that by the time the Agreement had been fully implemented in 2009, Mexico would have the same wages and standard of living as the other two North American nations. Others told me that by 2000, NAFTA would be broken, and the PRI (the party of De la Madrid, Salinas, and Zedillo,[11] the Mexican presidents who have most fostered free trade and privatization of industries) would be out of power. This proved to be true, with the election that year of President Vicente Fox Quesada—from the PAN, a party to the right of the PRI.

The Mexican administration's political future was not the only one linked to neoliberal free-trade policies, of course. María Cristina Rosas (1995) observed that a U.S. Congress "dominated by a conservative and isolationist Republican majority wants to capitalize on Mexico's problems" as ammunition against President Clinton's reelection campaign. Rosas discussed "the NAFTA effect," which European Union investors and politicians, as well as those throughout the Latin American markets, were tracking closely. By the NAFTA effect, she meant the crisis resulting from the Mexican administration's attempt to reduce a runaway deficit and inflation rate by combining an austerity program with monetary devaluation; this resulted in lower consumer demand for products from the United States and Canada, which had been some supporters' rationale for the neoliberal policy in the first place. Rosas documented the rise and fall in consumption of Canadian and U.S. products in Mexico after NAFTA went into effect. In January 1994, she said, fifteen hundred trucks loaded with various products were leaving Laredo for Mexico daily. U.S. Trade Representative Mickey Kantor had predicted that two hundred thousand jobs associated with exporting goods to Mexico would be created in the United States. Instead, because of the NAFTA effect, according to Rosas, by the end of 1994, thirty-five thousand U.S. workers had requested retraining because of jobs due to NAFTA, and the unemployment rate in Laredo was 13.8 percent. By that time, U.S. exports to Mexico had fallen 11.9 percent while Mexican exports to the United States had increased by 29 percent (according to figures from the U.S. Trade Department). Despite their perky smiles, those Barbie dolls in the *mercados* may have been suffering from the NAFTA effect.

On September 25, 1995, an economic reporter on Radio Red anticipated that in 1996, the peso would be worth fifteen to the dollar. He said that Mexicans needed to take control of the situation, not just watch it and lament. One person who was doing something about the situation was Mario Monroy Gómez, a member of the RMALC and director of an NGO called Servicios Informativos Procesados (SIPRO), which gathers and publishes, in a clear and affordable form, economic and policy information for Mexican readers.[12] Monroy trained with participatory researchers Paulo Freire and Myles Horton[13] and had worked with other workers for many years, he told Lucy Luccisano and me,[14] and he felt that in analyzing current issues in civil society—such as neoliberal trade policy and its effects—a key was the availability of concise, readable information on the national economy and policies that affected everyone in Mexico. In 1993, for example, SIPRO published *¿Socios? ¿Asociados? ¿En sociedad? Asimetrias entre Canada, EEUU, México (Partners? Associates? In Society? Asymmetries Between Canada, the U.S.A., and Mexico)*. That book showed, with clear graphics, the differences between the three North American nations in income, debt, education levels, health care, inflation rates, imports and exports by sector, wages, consumption of information, and so on. The book's argument, expressed in the preface by Bertha Luján U. (a spokesperson for the RMALC), was that the asymmetries between the three nations were not taken into account in the NAFTA negotiations and should have been. In 1995, Monroy wrote another book (*Los saldos de la crisis*)—distributed with the assistance of other NGOs in Mexico—that explained clearly the financial crisis of 1994 and its context, going back to the introduction of neoliberal policies several administrations earlier. Monroy (1995b) demonstrated the concentration of wealth under the neoliberal administration of President Salinas: twenty-four Mexican multimillionaires earned the equivalent of the earnings of 40 percent of the Mexican population in one year. Public analyses of neoliberalism, rather than leaving such decisions up to the national government because of their complexity, seemed to be widespread in Mexico in 1995, and again, I think that was facilitated by the work of the EZLN in creating alternative pathways for critical social analysis. In fact, one of the many new publications available in Mexico City was called *Forum (periodismo de análisis y reflexión)*, and it was sold at a Zócalo stall staffed by individuals who said they were interested in democracy.[15] The long-term effects of structural adjustment policies encouraged by the World Bank and the International Monetary Fund had failed in Mexico, according to Heredia and Purcell (1995, 24), precisely *because* they did not take people's well-being into account, only corporate profits:

> What has been missing in the process of [structural] adjustment in Mexico is an economic and social policy that truly puts people first. The government of Mexico and the multilateral development banks have all supported policies that have more to do with satisfying the demands of the commercial banks than with attending to the needs of the people. It is urgent that a balance be found between efficiency, on the one hand, and social justice, on the other, in order to promote the well-being of [Mexican] society. [author's translation]

This was the story of the crisis I heard over and over again in Mexico: that it was time to pay attention to the well-being of all Mexicans rather than tailoring policies to those profiting from neoliberal privatization.[16]

As a taxi driver told me in September 1995, *something* had to happen, times were so hard. One thing that happened in Mexico that year was a tremendous increase in public demonstrations. The barzón movement accounted for many of those, and it was not only a middle-class movement. On October 2, 1995, I heard on the news that in Jalisco, demonstrators converged on Guadalajara from all around the state on tractors, on burros, in cars, and on foot to register their frustration at the level of interest rates on debts and the impossibility of paying off debts or obtaining more credit at such incredibly high rates. An analysis written by Millán Núñez and Pérez Vences (1995, 46) traced the origin of the debt crisis to NAFTA, which they saw as giving more government support to speculative rather than productive activity in Mexico, thereby disadvantaging those who are not only debtors but productive workers. They said that official members of El Barzón (la Unión Nacional de Productores Agropecuarios, Comerciantes Industriales y Prestadores de Servicios A.C.) numbered 1,100,000 nationally in Mexico, and that the majority of debtors were indebted for small but still insurmountable amounts of money. Juan José Quirinos Salas, the national president of El Barzón in 1995, according to Millán Núñez and Pérez Vences (1995, 45–46), found the debt alleviation programs proposed by banks and the Office of the Exchequer and Secretary of Public Credit to be limited to a strictly financial perspective; he proposed that the banks and the government negotiate with El Barzón representatives to include a broader perspective on the problem. For example, even if the interest rate were reduced to 25 percent, debtors could not pay that rate given what was happening to real wages after the financial crisis. Added to that was the problem I heard about from workers—including government workers—who were not receiving their paychecks on time (sometimes they were delayed for months), while credit card bills doubled, tripled, or more.

On August 31, El Barzón mobilized a march of twenty-five hundred people in the capital, and Quirinos Salas said at that time, according to Terrazas (1995): "If the debtors do not receive a definite answer, congruent with our demands, we will ask for the president to step down. The abuses have already brought us close to social breakdown" (author's translation). There were other debtors' organizations mobilized as well, for example, the Asemblea Ciudadana de Deudores de la Banca (Citizens' Assembly of Debtors to the Bank), led by Gerardo Fernández Noroña (Terrazas 1995, 39). A weekly publication called *El Barzón* was started in November 1995, published in the San Luis Potosí offices of *El Ciudadano*, which had gone out of business due to the economic crisis. *El Barzón* advertised the support of prominent cultural critics, among them Carlos Monsiváis (Carrizales et al. 1995).

Retired people also formed a social movement. An organization called the Movimiento Unificado Nacional de Jubilados y Pensionados (Unified National Movement of Retirees and Pensioners) had five hundred local branches across Mexico. Three thousand members of the organization demonstrated in the capital on September 8, 1995, with these demands: (1) that Social Security not be privatized; (2) that retirement incomes be increased to keep up with the 40 to 80 percent increase in subsistence goods; (3) that a 50 percent discount on water, gas, and electricity rates be given to retirees; and (4) that cigarettes, wine, and beer be taxed and the revenue invested in social security funds. A spokesperson for the organization said that retirees' income did not amount to the equivalent of the national minimum wage (Amigón 1995). As Serena had told me, older people were going hungry. Many blamed neoliberal policies for the dramatic redistribution of income in Mexico and for the lack of accountability of investment fund managers to those whose money had been invested over the years in retirement funds, since many rules regulating banking, for example, had been changed to accommodate the NAFTA. On the day of the demonstration, a PRI legislator, Rosa Márquez, publicly received the document of demands from the retirees' organization; she promised that IMSS (the national social security organization) would not be privatized and that she would work to make sure the standard of living for the elderly improved (Amigón 1995).

The saying painted on many walls throughout Mexico in 1994–1995, *Todos somos Marcos* (We are all Marcos) (see Figure 4.1), appeared to reflect a growing sense of agency in civil society: the notion that anyone could speak up, take action, and contribute to social change as Mexico experienced crisis as a nation.[17] In 1995, 7.7 registered demonstrations per day occurred in the national capital alone. More than a million Mexican citizens demonstrated in the 2,094 officially acknowledged protests between January and September 1995, and they focused on topics including (but not restricted to) Ruta 100 (a transportation strike), street vending, land use rights, education, housing, and public services (Ballinas 1995). Elsewhere in the nation, some citizens took social justice into their own hands, as the EZLN had claimed to do, with complaints that state government officials were oppressing (even killing with impunity) citizens rather than serving them. In Cuautla, Morelos, so many citizens were abducted in 1995 that a civic organization was formed, as a network of ejido, human rights, business, service, and intellectual organizations, to demand and work for increased public safety (Guerrero 1995). In Tepoztlán, Morelos, citizens closed off roads around the town,[18] formed a protest network called the Comité de Unidad Tepozteca (Committee of Tepoztecan Unity) with international support, and eventually succeeded in halting construction of a golf club in a zone that had been declared a national park in 1937 and a protected ecological zone in 1988 (Montero 1995). The golf club, and the popular coalition of subsistence farmers, environmental activists, and others that halted its construction, came to signify in 1995—as the EZLN had done in 1994—the possibility of using actions in civil society to counter neoliberal government policies, in this case, the changes made in Article 27 of the constitution to facilitate NAFTA, which allowed the national government to privatize lands that had been held communally.

Connections were made in public discourse (including civil actions) between social movements in 1995, at the intersection of economic and political crises, and earlier moments of cultural contestation. Twenty-seven years after demonstrating students were killed by the Mexican government in the plaza of Tlatelolco on October 2, 1968, events were held throughout the nation: marches took place with calls for "clean

Ill. 4.1 We are all Marcos (photo by Ann E. Kingsolver)

elections all around the country"; removal of the governor of Guerrero; schooling for children of workers and campesinos; support for the EZLN; a 50 percent discount in transportation costs; support for the students excluded from the UNAM (who were occupying the rector's tower at the time); freedom for political prisoners; and an antiviolence rock concert was held in Veracruz (Morquecho et al. 1995). In the capital, hundreds participated in a march that ended with the burning of eight buses in the Zócalo by Ruta 100 strikers[19] and the arrests of two hundred people (Chávez, Leñero, y Gonzáles 1995); the action was connected to the commemoration of the students' deaths perhaps only through a high level of frustration with current conditions. As Ifigenia Martínez (director of the UNAM Economics Department in 1968) put it: "In 1968, it was the big movement against authoritarianism and government repression. The movement of today, in 1995, stems from the economic crisis and from the imposition of the neoliberal model" (author's translation) (Morales 1995, 11).

The public demonstrations I have been describing were not without risk to the participants. On the morning of October 2, 1995, I spoke with a man in Mexico City who had been in Tlatelolco in 1968 when the students were killed by the soldiers. He said he felt sure that the rector of UNAM had ordered the killings then. (Students later demanded that the rector resign.) The man I spoke with wanted to participate in the commemorating march twenty-seven years later, but he said it was too difficult—and "difficult" seemed to have several layers of meaning. It was as though he could see that the march would end in violence and arrests, as it did, and also as though the memories of 1968 were difficult to relive in the current crisis. Soldiers and arrests were frequently the national government's answer to public demonstrations in 1995. An advisor to the Movement of 400 Pueblos,[20] César del Angel Fuentes, had been arrested by more than ninety police officers (more than they would send to arrest a major drug dealer, one member of the Movement said), and a march of more than a thousand women of the movement on May 18, 1995, was broken up by the military (Pérez 1995). The national and state military used force against not only those considered left of the PRI government but also to the right politically, as in the use of tear gas against PAN demonstrators in Oxkutzcab, Yucatán, on August 31, 1995 (Boffil Gómez 1995).

I have been following here the stories linking NAFTA and neoliberal policies with the economic and political crises in Mexico from the perspective of social movements, but what about the national government's perspective? In the midst of his own political crisis (with conflicts, to the death, within the long-governing PRI), President Ernesto Zedillo Ponce de León delivered his first "State of the Nation" address (*primer informe*) on September 1, 1995, in the Casa de Diputados in Mexico City. That morning, I asked a taxi driver if he knew what time the speech would be; he said no and he was not interested. "Mentiras, puras mentiras" ("Lies, nothing but lies"). Then I asked him if he was interested in the Consulta Nacional.[21] He replied, "Sí, con esa, hay que salga *algo*." ("Yes, with that one, *something* will come of it"). I mention this individual's attitude toward the president's speech because Zedillo faced hostility even in the chamber as he gave the address—several legislators protested with signs or shouts.

I watched the primer informe that morning on Televisión Azteca, with colleagues at the university. Jaime González Graff, a political analyst, explained before the speech that according to the Constitution, the president is obligated to give this annual address, but that society this year was actually demanding his accountability to the Republic through the speech. *The News,* an English-language newspaper published in Mexico City,[22] published the entire address in English. Since that translation was authorized by the administration, I cite it here.

President Zedillo began by saying he had submitted the written annual report to the Congress as mandated by the Constitution but that he wanted to use the address to "speak about the three subjects that most concern the Mexican people today: our economic situation, justice and the progress of democracy in Mexico" (Zedillo 1995, 2). He attributed the economic crisis to no "single act nor to any one economic policy decision" but to these factors: capital flows that were more speculative than long-term, a lack of domestic savings in Mexico, and a massive withdrawal of investments from Mexico after the devaluation of the peso (Zedillo 1995, 2). The president justified the cuts in public spending (and other austerity measures) as necessary to save jobs and correct the balance of payments internationally. He attributed the negotiation of the $50 billion "financial backing" package from the United States and partners in multilateral organizations to the framework afforded by the North American Free Trade Agreement. Zedillo said:

> Negotiation of all the loans that comprise the financial package, as in all cases, were conducted under the principles of respect for national sovereignty and the dignity of Mexicans. Nothing was ever

negotiated behind the back of the Mexican people. (Zedillo
1995, 3)[23]

To demonstrate the solution to the economic crisis, the president
announced that the balance of the Mexican debt in treasury bills (which
he stressed could be bought by individual small investors, who—unlike
governments—were impossible to negotiate with in a time of financial
crisis) had dropped from $29,206,000,000 in December 1994 to
$3,173,000,000 at the time of his address. "The threat of financial col-
lapse that existed during the initial months of the year has clearly van-
ished. . . . The costs of the crisis have been very great and very painful,
but they would have been much worse if the economic adjustment plan
had not been adopted. Moreover, we would not now have the prospect
of recovery before us" (Zedillo 1995, 3).[24] He detailed new support programs to help those most affected by the economic crisis, including an
expanded school breakfast program, a tortilla consumption subsidy program, and a family food and nutrition program, and he reiterated his
"commitment to Mexico's rural areas. We will progress toward a com-
prehensive policy for rural development that will stimulate employment, foster production, strengthen marketing, and modernize farm
infrastructure" (Zedillo 1995, 4). He also announced improvements in
school drop-out rates and teacher training, and compensation for the
neediest children attending schools.

The president outlined the future steps in the economic adjustment
program, saying there would be "legal reforms aimed at encouraging
public and private investment in railways, telecommunications, civil
aviation," and natural gas (Zedillo 1995, 4); deregulation to promote
private enterprise; public investment in infrastructure to attract private
investment; and debt relief. As a nod, no doubt, to El Barzón, he
announced that "the Federal Government has committed part of its
financial capacity to easing the burden of most of the country's debtors,
particularly those with the least means" (Zedillo 1995, 4). He said that
economic recovery was based, to a great extent, on stimulating the
export sector, and therefore: "We will continue negotiating free-trade
agreements with other countries and regions" (Zedillo 1995, 5). He
announced tax reforms to encourage domestic savings and said that
housing construction and plant modernization would be two areas of
domestic investment encouraged by the government.

In the transition to the third section of his speech, democratic
reforms, President Zedillo acknowledged the outrage of the Mexican

public over the difference between the law and its administration and the deficiencies in the public safety and justice systems. To address this, he announced constitutional changes before the congress that would reform the justice system; one major change was that the federal judicial branch would be independent of the executive branch—elected by the congress rather than appointed.[25] Zedillo announced the coordination of local, state, and national police training and administration through the new National Public Safety System, meant to address corruption, and a bill against organized crime. On democracy, he said:

> Community life ruled by law and civic participation is the basis for economic growth and true democracy. When I took the oath of office as President of the Republic, free of prior agreements or pressures, I called for the thorough democratization of the Nation, based on the reform of the State. A reform that would strengthen the balance between the branches of government, construct a new federalism, and promote definitive electoral regulations. (Zedillo 1995, 6)

These reforms in governing Mexico were being called for, of course, by those nations and multilateral organizations advising political as well as economic structural adjustment as part of the recent loan packages, in addition to calls for democratization inside Mexico. After more than a half-century of PRI power, President Zedillo talked of increasing the representation of multiple parties in the legislative branch, as well as the strength of the legislature in governing the nation. He called for reform of the State:

> The federalist ideal has deep roots in our history, roots entwined with our first aspirations for independence and original struggle for national sovereignty. The organization of the Republic as a federation inspired heroic acts and demanded the finest talents of great Mexicans.
>
> We must recognize that a century and a half later, the reality of our federalism is not yet in harmony with that ideal, with those deeds, with those Mexicans. To a great extent, the states and municipalities—and the men and women who live in them—continue suffering the consequences of centralism.
>
> We must propose clear and immediate initiatives to build a new federalism that can strengthen democracy, fuel the unity of the

Nation with our diversity, and promote a more balanced and more just development. (Zedillo 1995, 7)[26]

President Zedillo went on to propose a number of new policies that would decentralize government and give states and municipalities more authority. At this point, he mentioned Chiapas:

All Mexicans have recognized the lags and the contrasts, and the conditions of injustice and poverty that prevail in Chiapas.

On taking office as President, I stated that peace with justice and dignity can only be reached in Chiapas through dialogue and negotiation, within the framework of the law, without resorting to violence and without allowing the conflict to spread. (Zedillo 1995, 7)

He said that violence in Chiapas had decreased and that government assistance programs had increased there, and he thanked the legislators who had participated in the Concord and Peace Commission and who had supported the passage of the Law for Dialogue, Conciliation, and a Dignified Peace in Chiapas. The president called for further dialogue to resolve agrarian problems and proposed

that the Legislative and Executive branches use the experience gained from dialogue and negotiation to draft a Law on Indian Rights to provide regulations for Article 4 of the Constitution. The time has come to redefine the relationship between the Mexican State and indigenous communities, to enable the latter to play a leading role in their own development within the framework of our Constitution. (Zedillo 1995, 8)

President Zedillo went on to express his commitment to electoral reform and ended the speech by acknowledging the crisis and calling for unity: "United let us reaffirm the will of all Mexicans to enhance our sovereignty, by defending our identity and culture, our pluralism and institutions. . . . Through effort, dedication, peace and union, we will endow Mexico's development with strength and certainty" (Zedillo 1995, 8).

Televised commentaries from members of different political parties followed the address, and by the next day, there were numerous analyses in the press.[27] But I wanted to see and hear the public's immediate responses, so I made my way to the Zócalo via the Metro, with members of the Mexican public President Zedillo had just addressed, at least in principle. What was the relationship between the democracy he called for and that envisioned by other citizens of Mexico?

On the Zócalo, I stopped and talked with a member of the CND. They had been en plantón there for seventeen months, handing out information to those passing by. Their work was inspired by the opening of a national dialogue about democratization through the EZLN's actions. Later that afternoon, I interviewed a member of the Alianza Cívica, the group administering the Consulta Nacional por la Paz y la Democrácia, the independent political referendum called for by the EZLN (that interview is discussed below). In the center of the Zócalo, a growing crowd gathered around a small stage where a performer was singing and talking, openly making fun of President Zedillo and that morning's ceremony. He told jokes about ex-President Salinas and about the police, and he said that those in the National Palace (housing the administration) had Colosio killed. The performer talked about events in Chiapas and the war he said was inevitable within Mexico before the year 2000. He announced to the crowd that if he had to move from the Zócalo, he would be near the statue of Benito Juárez—the one in which the ex-president was sitting down. He told us that when the police came to his house, he told them, "I'm a singer—how could I be a guerrilla?" He said that power rested with the people, and he figured it was better to take a knife in the front than in the back for saying so.

The street performer spoke of ex-President Salinas, said to be living in Ottawa at that moment, and asked the crowd if we knew why Salinas was accepted in Canada and why he had been invited to New York and Washington. He answered himself: "Because he gave them NAFTA!"

At this event, two CND periodicals were being circulated: *Corre la voz (People are saying* or *The word is)* and *El Desperta Ciudadano (The Awake Citizen)*. It was indicative of the crisis in Mexican political identity that this event, which was broken up by national police the year before when President Salinas had given his final address, was at least momentarily tolerated by the police whose abuses of power had been pointed out by the president that morning. And yet, multiple meanings of democracy and sovereignty were circulating and that circulation was agitated by the crisis.

Another time I observed public responses in the Zócalo to the crisis (in the ability to make a living, in political representation, and in national identity) was during *La Noche Mexicana,* the celebration of Mexican

Independence on September 15. I joined the crowds there for the late-night observance, but similar gatherings took place in neighborhoods all over the city and the nation.

A joint concert was given that night, a few blocks from the National Plaza, by Paquita, La del Barrio, and Astrid Hadad, representing two generations and styles of cultural criticism; they included in their songs and exchanges with the audience comments on the "Americanization" of Mexico through NAFTA, ironically noted on this patriotic night for Mexico.

The streets were barricaded off for blocks around the Zócalo, with civil guards frisking streams of people on their way in, but this time the crowd was full of good will, with people carrying babies, buying masks for older children (Bart Simpson and the bratty baby working-class dinosaur from U.S. television series were popular that year), eating at food booths, or buying plastic bags or eggshells full of flour from roving vendors to throw at strangers, whitening the crowd in a different sense than I wrote about earlier; the vendors themselves, defenseless with both hands on their cart handles, were hit often. My friends and I got to the central square at a quarter to eleven, and the Zócalo was packed with celebrators. The military band was playing, and a video screen showed the televised broadcast that Serena, the retiree mentioned earlier, was watching at home. People were tooting horns, throwing confetti, and setting off firecrackers. Through the haze, I saw President Zedillo and his wife step out onto the balcony of the National Palace, and he raised his arm to initiate the *grito,* the traditional shout of Hidalgo celebrating Mexican Independence, won from Spain in a long struggle that began in 1810 and ended in 1821. Those around me commented that he had cut short the grito this year. From *Uno más uno,* here is a partial transcript of what he said from the balcony:

> "¡Mexicanos! . . . Viva nuestra Independencia . . . Viva Hidalgo . . . Vivan los Héroes que nos dieron patria . . . Viva nuestra libertad . . . Viva México . . . Viva México . . . Viva México."
>
> "Mexicans! Hurrah for our Independence . . . Hurrah for Hidalgo . . . Hurrah for the Heroes who gave us our nation . . . Hurrah for our liberty . . . Hurrah for Mexico . . . Hurrah for Mexico . . . Hurrah for Mexico." (Monroy Aguirre 1995)[28]

President Zedillo held out a Mexican flag toward the gathering of people, and, united, thousands of voices shouted, "¡Viva!" The grito could be heard internationally, too, as Mexicans honored the Noche Mexicana at just before midnight, *Distrito Federal* time, at parties or alone in the Mexican transnational community.

Usually, those around me explained, the president would raise a cheer not only for Hidalgo but for Morelos and the other heroes of the war for Mexican Independence in the nineteenth century,[29] and additional cheers would be added for Zapata, a hero from another Mexican war (for independence from some of the same conditions reemerging under neoliberal governance). Many noted that President Zedillo made no mention of Zapata—in this time of Zapata's revival as the EZLN's namesake. Emiliano Zapata stood for a populist notion of Mexican independence—agrarian self-sufficiency and freedom from low-paid work for international capitalists—and Ernesto Zedillo stood for a notion of independence related more to balancing debt payments by what he saw necessary means than to protecting communal lands and workers' rights. The distance between these two views of democracy and sovereignty was noticeable in the silence as Zedillo left Zapata and others out of the grito, making it (like the national address two weeks before) the shortest in history.

After the grito, the band played the national hymn, the president rang the same bell Hidalgo had rung 185 years before, and cannons began shooting red, white, and green fireworks over the square. Still-burning embers fell into the dancing crowd. As though it were Carnival, people formed dancing lines to move out through the barricades and toward the closest Metro stations that were open. In this Noche Mexicana, perhaps an extra sense of collective relief was being celebrated—despite the crisis since the last one—because (as a friend put it) it was a focus to gather around and because—in Mexico City—people were glad to have survived the earthquake a few days earlier, which was so strong it brought back nightmares about the devastating one a decade before.

Numerous commentaries around the time of La Noche Mexicana linked NAFTA, increasing economic and cultural dependence of Mexico on the United States, and a decrease in Mexican national sovereignty. For example, on September 11, 1995, the front cover of *el chahuistle*,[30] a critical commentary and political cartoon magazine, had a drawing of the bell rung by Hidalgo to announce Mexican Independence with a "For Sale" sign tied to it and a note above the bell saying: "¡Que viva México! (lo que queda, pues)" ("Long live Mexico! [or what's left of it]"). In an interview with Magú, the political cartoonist and commentator (Sosa 1995, 7), Magú said this about the grito:

Mexican society, awake and critical, sees in the ceremony of the grito a farce, a theatrical performance: a president, a governor who comes out to shout praise for independence and the next day it seems that he is incapable of making any real effort toward that independence. For many, this is like a lie.

As I see it, it is a caricature, even as I find it offensive that he waves the flag, puts himself on a balcony, and shouts phrases that any other day he would be unable in any form to carry through on.

We are not Puerto Rico, nor are we a star in the U.S. flag, but neither can we speak of ourselves as independent if we consider the application of a national project determined by treasury bonds and international capital; not determined by the need to create jobs or the need to see that everyone has an opportunity to go to university.[31] [author's translation]

The grito has come to represent more generally allegiance to Mexican interests, and it figured in a discussion of neoliberalism as directly countering growth with equity (Semo 1995a, 6) in this way:

There is unprecedented international support for the Mexican government's [neoliberal] policy. Presidents Bush and Clinton have supported it [in the face of opposition], and in its last meeting, the Group of Seven endorsed it explicitly. The International Monetary Fund and the World Bank continue to recommend it as an example and minimize the importance of the crisis. For their part, Mexican industrialists, in terms introduced by Albert Hirschman, have preferred to leave rather than to *gritar* [express nationalist allegiance]. That is to say, when the storm clouds gather, they tend to take their money, associate themselves with foreign capital, . . . [and] speculate with exchange rates instead of looking for ways to defend their productive interests. [author's translation]

Thus there were discourses and counterdiscourses regarding what was in the national interest and what constituted supporting sovereignty, in circulation in Mexico in 1995. The president was obligated to put sovereignty at the top of his agenda. In fact, the Plan Nacional de Desarrollo, 1995–2000 (National Development Plan), which his administration was constitutionally obligated to produce, began with a section on "Sovereignty at the end of the twentieth century" cited in the introduction to this book. The Federal Executive Power (officially authoring the text) asserted that defense and strengthening of national sovereignty constituted its primary goal. The neoliberal development policies laid out in the plan, however, were critiqued in a counterdiscourse as not contributing to a people-centered notion of Mexican sovereignty and development. José Luis Calva, for example, in an article entitled (in translation) "The National Development Plan 1995–2000; ends, means, and alternatives," claims that the administration's long-term development plan actually would undermine sustained economic growth (necessary for economic sovereignty), and he advocated abandoning neoliberal policies and adopting an alternative development plan, which would emphasize "sustainable growth with equity." The plan would include renegotiating Mexico's external debt to payment levels that would allow for internal investment; using NAFTA provisions to safeguard wage levels for Mexicans so they are not so distant from those of U.S. and Canadian workers; and coming up with real incentives for production in the agricultural and other sectors, with attention to the needs of small- and medium-sized enterprises (Calva 1995, 50–53).

The story told through the debate on sovereignty, of course, was a more encompassing crisis story. As Georgina Sánchez L. (1995, 43) put it, in a very clear analysis of the relationship between globalization and discussions of sovereignty, "Political, technological, cultural and social—especially with migration" permeability of national borders increases with international economic integration, and just as nation-states are called on to come up with stabilizing solutions to economic crises brought about by globalization, there is "a growing uncertainty about the future of nation-states, governments, and political regimes." She said that the real question to ask is why sovereignty survives at all in this climate. I think it survives, in part, as a way to conceptualize the need for some accountability for the movements of international capital and to counter the submission of whole nations of humans to other nations (as, for example, a lower-wage workforce).

Considering this section as a prologue, I think that Figure 4.2, a political cartoon appearing in the *Boletín Mexicano de la Crisis* on September 23, 1995, sums up eloquently this NAFTA story of crisis and critique. In the figure, one eagle, the national symbol of the United States of America, wearing the hat of Uncle Sam,[32] is flying off with the other eagle, the national symbol of the United Mexican States; on the Mexican coin, the inscription reads, "We Mexicans are sunk." Despite the upbeat reading of the crisis by President Zedillo in defense of his administration's neoliberal policies, this cartoon represents the majority

Ill. 4.2 We Mexicans are sunk (Alán, *Boletín Mexicano de la Crisis*, September 23, 1995)

of explanations I heard: that the United States had benefited from NAFTA already, at Mexico's expense.

Stories of Plurinational Action

Ironically, NAFTA has given rise both to plurinational social movements (e.g., labor and environmental groups from Mexico, Canada, and the United States that propose alternatives to the trade agreement and its administration) and a kind of hypernationalism in which the state is seen as a buffer against the actions of transnational corporations,[33] even as it is criticized for promoting closer bonds with multinational entities like the International Monetary Fund and the World Bank. It is, of course, not enough simply to make moral judgments about multinational or plurinational actions as good or bad; it is necessary to look at exactly what *kind* of actions they are and who and what interests the agents of decisionmaking represent. Guillermo Delgado has studied binational social movements, particularly those of pueblos indígenas, in which a social force is raised as leverage against particular nation-states that may be violating the rights of some citizens. I consider these movements to be nongovernmental organizations, just as much as those registered with particular states as nonprofit organizations (e.g., the World Wildlife Fund). Lucy Luccisano (1995), along with other social scientists, has argued that NGOs are poised to become more important political bodies than national governments themselves, particularly as they take on more and more services of the State with privatization. One example of nongovernmental, plurinational organizing follows.

A few days after the 1995 celebration of Mexican Independence, there was a gathering in Mexico City to discuss more recent international events: globalization and its effect on workers.[34] Representatives of labor organizations in the "Little Tiger" nations and in Canada (another Pacific Rim nation) met with workers representing thirty different labor organizations in Mexico to discuss free trade and human rights. At a press conference at the end of the second day, spokespersons told this collective story about conditions for workers under free-trade policies: changes were needed in NAFTA and other free-trade policies to better accommodate workers' human rights. It was difficult even to articulate the effects of neoliberalism on human rights; a meeting on workers' rights in Indonesia the month before, for example, had been clandestine, because one could be persecuted even for talking about workers' human rights. Representatives announced that workers in Indonesia, Thailand, and Mexico had been—as a whole—better off a decade before than in the era of NAFTA. Globalization means an influx of capital for these nations, but it has not resulted in a recognition of the human rights of workers. The administering bodies overseeing NAFTA had the responsibility to oversee these rights as well, but did they really have the desire to do so? These policies must not be realized at the cost of the workers. The labor side agreements negotiated as part of NAFTA gave other nations an example to follow in crafting future accords and an ability to learn from mistakes. For those watching conditions for Mexican workers closely, the story appeared to be about falling salaries (between 80 percent and 300 percent from 1986 to 1995, depending on the sector); one representative said that average earnings for Mexican workers had been $70 (U.S.) weekly before the devaluation of the peso in 1994 and had fallen to $35 after the crisis. It was also a story about fewer protections for workers: those representing workers from the maquiladoras said that union participation and salaries had gone down, while subcontracting and accidents, including chemical ones, had gone up.

Points made during the conference included the fact that multilateral organizations and national governments could have very different reasons for pursuing neoliberal policies, so the process of globalizing free trade needed to be studied very closely (Graciela Bensusán). Also noted was the need for not only a North American alliance (of Mexican, Canadian, and U.S. workers) but also a global alliance of workers (Manuel Fuentes), and the need to look at the sectoral effects of NAFTA as a way of anticipating the effects on international workers of a renegotiated GATT (Bertha Luján). Luján, representing the RMALC, said that plurinational administrative entities, actually representing workers' interests, were important in making lawyers and judges in specific countries more accountable for their interpretations of changes made in national labor laws in accordance with neoliberal models. What was being argued for here was a very different kind of plurinational accountability than the control of the IMF and the World Bank (also plurinational entities, in constitution if not in the final word) over Mexico's national decisionmaking powers discussed in the previous section.

Information given out during the conference included a circular analyzing the Uruguay Round of the GATT and the powers of the World Trade Organization to administer, with the IMF and the World Bank, "the future of the economy of the whole globe" (Osorio y Quiroz 1995). The social clause introduced in the Uruguay Round was left under debate there, and the authors of the circular distributed by the RMALC explained that the Organización Internacional del Trabajo (International Labour Organization) saw the GATT social clause as a hopeful opportunity for addressing the human rights of workers. The RMALC, having monitored closely the effects of NAFTA on workers in Mexico, proposed that GATT could be amended in the next round of discussions to foster trade agreements more amenable to sustainable economic development; to reform the World Trade Organization itself to "guarantee its independence from the interests of transnational corporations, its internal democracy and transparency, and its effective commitment to a just and sustainable development" (Osorio y Quiroz 1995) [author's translation]; to address conditions of child labor and forced labor in all nations; to improve equality for male and female workers, the right of free association and the health and safety of all workers; to include social organizations in the panels that oversee international trade; to set up international funds to improve conditions for workers in developing nations; and to set up "Codes of Conduct for transnational corporations, universally applied, that would guarantee that they meet minimum requirements concerning environmental protection and respect for workers' rights" (Osorio y Quiroz 1995) [author's translation]. The RMALC publishes a bimonthly magazine called *Alternativas: Integración, Democracia y Desarrollo* (*Alternatives: Integration, Democracy, and Development*) in which specific alternatives to neoliberal policy statements, such as the National Development Plan 1995–2000 issued by President Zedillo and his cabinet, were elaborated.[35] This story—of a concrete set of alternatives to (or reformulations of) NAFTA[36] and GATT—was a plurinational one, since NGOs such as the RMALC and its counterparts around the world were meeting in conferences like those held in Mexico City in September 1995 and soon thereafter in Osaka, Japan, to discuss positive alternatives.

Bertha Luján, an activist in both the FAT and the RMALC, spoke with me in the UNAM cafeteria on September 27, 1995, about the plurinational effort. I have translated the whole interview here because I think her views on the scope of plurinational organizing are an essential NAFTA story to include.

In response to my question, "How and when did the Red Mexicana de Acción frente al Libre Comercio get started?" Bertha Luján answered:

It began in April of 1991 when they began to negotiate the North American Free Trade Agreement. It is a coalition of nongovernmental organizations and social organizations. In the RMALC, there are labor unions, environmental organizations, human rights groups, and organizations of campesinos that want to present an alternative trade agreement to the Mexican government. When NAFTA was signed, and the contents became known, the Red [RMALC] opposed this treaty and the organization is still fighting for a renegotiation.

I asked her, "Is the level of participation the same now or has it changed in some respect?" She said:

It has changed in some respect, yes. Obviously, participation was greatest during the negotiation of the treaty. The groups had a lot more interest, and they had an immediate objective, which was to have an influence on the negotiation of the treaty. That is to say, the goal was to try to introduce into NAFTA aspects dealing with a social agenda and treaty features that would actually benefit the people of Mexico, not just the transnational corporations.

I think that today, participation [in the RMALC] is less. Nevertheless, there is ongoing interest because of the economic crisis, and whatever relationship might exist between the crisis we are living through and the treaty they signed. So the work we are developing currently is that of monitoring the effects of NAFTA, and we continue elaborating an alternative.

A.K.: *Was that monitoring work trinational [between Mexico, Canada, and the U.S.A.] as well?*
B.L.: Yes, the participation continues to be trinational. However, in the United States and Canada, there has also been a decrease in activity. The networks of organizations are restructuring themselves. In the U.S.A., other groups have appeared working on the same themes. And today the challenge is to try to establish relations between all the groups that are concerned with free trade and the process of economic integration, which are two complementary issues.

The work of monitoring is work we are doing through various routes. One is the collaboration of the different organizations within the RMALC itself, each one in its own subject area. For example, the labor groups have concerned themselves with whether the transnational companies that have benefited from the trade opening have been complying with labor regulations. The environmental groups have each been monitoring conditions in their own community or region. The organizations along the border, for example, on both sides, are studying the impact of the neoliberal model's opening [of the economy to free trade] on the environment.

A.K.: *Was there equal participation in the RMALC by women and men, by those from different social classes, and by representatives of different regions of Mexico, or not?*
B.L.: Obviously, no. Men have participated more strongly because there is a culture [encouraging them to do so] and they have more real possibilities for participating. Nevertheless, if we compare the participation of women today with that of ten or fifteen years ago in Mexico, we will see an enormous jump in the quality and quantity of participation, because questions of gender are now on the agenda and because there are women's organizations participating in various areas of the political and social life of the country. Women have consolidated their organizing experiences in urban and rural areas. Because in plural organizations, in groups where there are both women and men, participation of women is greater and greater. We can't really compare participation in terms of regions. I think that there is less participation by women in rural areas, for example, naturally. And I think that in the southeastern part of Mexico, for example in the indigenous zones, women and young people still participate a lot less in matters of public policy. So participation is not equal.

A.K.: *Have sources of information about NAFTA changed between 1993 and 1995?*
B.L.: I don't think they have changed much. The Mexican state continues to have a monopoly on the primary media of communication. And the media will only change if the country is democratized. So there is not much difference from year to year.

A.K.: *What have been the most significant changes in the lives of workers, and all Mexican citizens, between 1993 and now?*
B.L.: Well, the crisis that took its hardest fall with the devaluation of December 1994 has worsened living conditions for the Mexican

people. Simply put, the drop in earnings this year alone has been more than 30 percent. A million jobs have been lost just in these past eight or nine months, and new sources of jobs have not been sufficient to absorb the 1,200,000 young people who are among the economically active population.

And so I believe, in relation to 1993, that the situation is even more grave, that there are more poor people, that there are more people in extreme poverty, and the worst thing is that there is even less possibility in the short run of improving the working conditions of the people. Obviously, everything having to do with health, education, public services, and social needs has been worsening. And today, state services to deal with social needs and problems are worse than the services available in 1993.

A.K.: *Would it be possible to say that the crisis of December 1994 was related to NAFTA or not?*
B.L.: I think there is a very direct relationship between NAFTA and the crisis. I believe that through its agreement on investment, NAFTA facilitated the entrance of speculative capital into Mexico. And it was this speculative foreign capital that contributed to the development of the financial crisis. In addition, much of the crisis was due to the deficit in the trade balance and the balance of payments, and this was related to the incredible increase in imports and the very, very poor increase in Mexican exports. NAFTA facilitated the arrival of merchandise in great volume. So the nation's overall imports grew. That same opening [of the market] signed into effect with NAFTA allowed the importation of goods that displaced national goods in the Mexican market. So part of the crisis was due to the displacement of national products, and this was associated with a loss of internal markets, of infrastructure, and of jobs. So there was a very direct relationship between NAFTA and the crisis.

A.K.: *Which sectors of workers were the most and the least affected by NAFTA?*
BERTHA LUJÁN finished her coffee, and answered: I think there are important sectors, like the rural workers, that have been affected directly by NAFTA—by the importation of agricultural products, including basic grains—because NAFTA does not permit access to new technologies and inexpensive technologies to modernize the rural sector. There are industrial sectors, auto parts, for example,

that are directly affected by the treaty; they are in complete crisis. Why? Because today the automotive industry imports a fair amount of auto parts.

A.K.: *From where?*
B.L.: From the U.S. Before, they were made in Mexico. And now all that is done here is automobile assembly. So the auto parts industry is an industry in crisis, and this crisis has been accelerated fundamentally due to the signing of NAFTA. There are crises in other industrial sectors, like textiles, tailoring, and shoes that have to do with the GATT and have to do with the indiscriminate opening [of the market] that Mexico has been engaged in since 1986. And what's missing are supports for national industry. But these crises, I think, were made even worse by NAFTA. So, the treaty—instead of helping the agricultural sector out of crisis or helping certain branches of the industrial sector—has helped to deepen this crisis. Some will say that NAFTA is not responsible for causing the crisis, and they may be right. It is a trade opening that goes much further than the treaty with the U.S. and Canada. But let us say that the Mexican government said that NAFTA was going to support national industry and that it was going to help the country recover levels of growth and development, and from the moment they signed the treaty, what we have seen is the complete opposite. We have seen a drop in exports. We have seen an overall increase in imports. There is a deficit in the trade balance and in the balance of payments. Yes, there has been an increase in investment, but it was speculative investment, not productive investment. We have seen an overall reduction in national productive capacity. We have today a crisis in national productivity, derived from various political and financial factors, and so on, and added to by the devaluation, intermediary costs, and interest rates. But I think that the trade opening via NAFTA had a very important role in bringing about this crisis.

A.K.: *How can one compare working conditions in the European Union with those in North America? Could there ever be an economic or cultural North American community?*
B.L.: In the European Union, they gave special attention to the asymmetries between countries. Less-developed countries like Spain, Portugal, or Greece have special status within the European Community. There are compensatory funds; there are longer peri-

ods of adjustment for salaries; there are technological supports.
Also in the integration agreement, there is a special treaty having to
do with labor that deals with workers as human beings. It is not
only an agreement about free trade or investment; it also has to do
with people, with the theme of migration, with the rights of
migrants, and so on.

In the case of the North American Free Trade Agreement, there
was none of this consideration of asymmetries, of differences.
There is not a special status for Mexico as a less developed country.
There is no possibility of access to new technologies. On the contrary, what there is in NAFTA is a chapter about intellectual property that maintains or decreases the differences. There is no consideration of migrant labor, that is to say, those persons left outside of
the treaty. In sum, I think that NAFTA is a treaty much more clearly
in the interests of corporations, and that it left completely aside
social aspects and, even more gravely, aspects having to do with
development. With this treaty, differences have widened, not only
between classes but also between countries.

Regarding the question about a North American community, I
think that there are many differences . . . , and I'll tell you something: in the case of Europe, there is a greater respect for the rights
of workers. Even though there are also government policies that
attack unions, that try to weaken the voice of unions as representatives of the collective interests of workers. . . . Even though there is
also this, there is a very big difference between the observance of
labor laws there in Europe and here in North America.

And even at the level of North America, there is a big difference between what happens in Canada, for example, and what happens in Mexico. In Mexico, the rights of the freedom to associate in
unions, to strike, and to have a contract are not observed [even
though the laws are on the books]. Definitely, there is not the right
to be free to join a union. In Canada and in the U.S.A., there is a
medium level of compliance with labor laws. I don't want to put
them up as examples to follow. I think that there are also a lot of
failures and that there are many problems—not only having to do
with the freedom to organize, but with labor laws, you see? And I
think this is a common struggle [in North America].

A.K.: *What would the process be if the North American Free Trade
Agreement were to be broken?*

B.L.: We are proposing a renegotiation of the treaty. We think that Mexico has to act in relation to the disappointments and the safeguards not so much in NAFTA as in the World Trade Organization. There must be established the possibility of making changes in trade agreements when they are affecting directly the balance of payments or the trade balance, when there are recurrent and each time more serious deficits. I think that these resources exist and that Mexico must pay attention to them. And this, in the short and medium term, is going to be a social and political demand that gets stronger and stronger. Today, for example, there are broad sectors of businesspeople who are proposing changes in NAFTA. And they are not alone. For example, small- and medium-sized industries, not only in the auto parts sector, have been hit very hard because there are no national policies supporting them. They are hanging us with financial policies and also with this free-trade treaty. Those in small- and medium-sized industries are saying, give us time [to pay in installments], give us supports, in order to make ourselves competitive and to be able to survive. So I think they are playing today with the productive capacity of the nation and, to a great extent, with what agricultural production means to Mexico. There are very important sectors mobilizing to protect their interests.

A.K.: *What do you see as the basis of hope for this country?*
B.L.: In the organization of the people, in the possibilities of constructing a democratic country. This is only going to be successful with the organized action of the separate social sectors. I think that the challenge is not only in the political parties. Today in Mexico there is a civil society that is very mobilized and that is acting to democratize this country, and it is going to be in the confluence of social groups, civil society, and political society that we will succeed in making changes in this country. I would say that there are even very strong changes coming about in the party of the state, that is to say the PRI. There are those inside that party who are interested in making profound changes in the political life of Mexico, and they will also make important contributions in this process of making the transition to democracy. That will be the hope for everyone. [author's translation]

I thanked her for her time, and she gave me a ride in the rain to the Metro station. I have not spoken with Bertha Luján since 1995, but I wonder if she saw the 1997 election of PRD candidate Cuauhtémoc Cárdenas as mayor of the Federal District, or Mexico City,[37] and the 2000 election of President Vicente Fox Quesada (candidate of the PAN, the conservative National Action Party) as steps in that process of democratization.

Bertha Luján's analysis reflected a critical difference in interpretation of the economic crisis between herself and President Zedillo. While he was careful to distance his own administration from responsibility for the crisis, Luján made it plain that she thought both the economic restructuring associated with NAFTA and the privatization of social services that was part of the more general neoliberal reform agenda (continuing from the Salinas into the Zedillo administration) were to blame for the crisis and the worsening living conditions for many Mexicans. One analytical advantage that Luján had, in working with a plurinational alliance of activists, was the ability to compare notes on how neoliberal structural adjustment policies had affected or were affecting workers in other countries. She could openly acknowledge what President Zedillo could or would not: "Differences have widened, not only between classes but also between countries." Through the ties between the RMALC and counterpart organizations in Canada, the United States, Europe, and Asia, Luján was able to examine closely the processes that had created those gaps (for instance, the difference between stated and practiced labor compensation rules in each country), and she participated in designing plurinational alternative policies to address them. As she said in the interview, social welfare and long-term internal economic development goals must inform the negotiation and implementation of transnational treaties such as the NAFTA in order to avoid the kind of worsening conditions so many Mexicans had experienced from the recent economic crisis. She and her counterparts in Mexico and other nations were prepared to continue advancing those alternative policies through both governmental and nongovernmental forums.

A NAFTA story of democratization that has been heard around the world is the process initiated by the EZLN in Chiapas for recognizing and amplifying the rights of citizens to land, identity, and indigenous sovereignty assigned by the Mexican constitution but denied in political practice—and especially eroded under recent neoliberal policies. This is a plurinational NAFTA story not only because international attention has been brought, through the Internet, print, and television media, to the EZLN's militant demands for political and social change, but also because included in what was glossed as EZLN concerns was also the long-building, broadly expressed set of concerns of members of nations that straddle the dominant political boundaries of North America: the pueblos indígenas. Within Mexico, and in coalition with indigenous nations across the Americas, a plurinational movement for observing human, land, language, and governance rights for indigenous communities gained popular attention and strength when the EZLN initiated a dialogue for change with the Mexican government, even though the interests and participation of every indigenous nation overlain by Mexico's political boundaries were not necessarily synonymous with the EZLN. As Miguel León-Portilla put it in 1995, when asked about the possibilities for success in the upcoming talks between the EZLN and the Mexican government regarding indigenous rights[38] and culture: "The most important issue right now is that the indigenous people themselves, who have among them many leaders . . . , do the talking. They are the ones who have the ultimate right, and the voice with which to speak"[39] (Flores Aguilar 1995). [author's translation]

One way to follow the NAFTA story on indigenous and rural rights, and on democratization in general, is to look at the proposed constitutional changes being discussed in 1995, as the EZLN met with representatives of the PRI government and a popular referendum was being administered—as a signal of the possibilities for democratization—by the Alianza Cívica. In 1992, President Salinas and the Mexican congress had rewritten Article 4 of the constitution to read:

> The Mexican nation has a pluricultural composition, sustained originally in its indigenous peoples. The law will protect and promote the development of their languages, cultures, uses, customs, resources, and specific forms of social organization, and will guarantee their members effective access to the jurisdiction of the state. In the trials and agrarian proceedings in which they take part, their practices and judicial customs will be taken into account in the terms established by the law. (Krieger 1995, 25-A) [author's translation]

According to Krieger, this article was never supported by implementing legislation that would have permitted even this extent of a nod to plurality in Mexican culture, even though the administration found time to create and pass all the implementing legislation related to the NAFTA and other neoliberal reforms. Creating the legal structure to recognize this paragraph added to Article 4 still remained to be carried out in 1995, by the next administration. A federal government proposal to further revise the article (and Article 115, concerning municipal government) and to enact implementing legislation, was published in *La Jornada* on September 22, 1995. The proposal recognized the popular demand for stronger legal recognition of the rights of indigenous communities, through the careful wording, "in January of 1994 interest [in translating the constitutional mandate into law] grew"; acknowledging the specific concerns of members of indigenous nations as Mexican citizens, further amendments to Article 4 were made. The proposed text (Poder Ejecutivo 1995b) included these changes, italicized in my translation:

> The Mexican nation has a pluricultural composition, sustained originally in its indigenous peoples. *[The nation] recognizes and will promote the development* of their languages, cultures, uses, customs, *natural* resources, and specific forms of organization both social and *political, their normative system of conflict resolution,* and will guarantee to their members effective access to the jurisdiction of the State. *In any federal or local trial in which they take part*, their legal practices and customs will be taken into account.

While it is clear that the public discourse regarding democratization and indigenous rights had moved the Zedillo administration to be even more attentive legislatively to the demands for indigenous sovereignty, Antonio Hernández, secretary of the Commission of Indigenous Affairs of the House of Representatives (and a representative of the PRD), denounced the administration's legislative project in advance, saying:

> President Ernesto Zedillo's proposal to convoke the legislature in order to, along with the administration, elaborate a Law of Indigenous Rights, is one more sign of paternalism, and there exists the risk that it represents a step backwards, because it will be others who are going to make decisions about our destiny and not the Indian communities themselves. (Correa 1995, 18) [author's translation]

Secretary Hernández, the EZLN, the National Plural Indigenous Assembly (ANIP), and others proposed to make much stronger legal provisions for indigenous sovereignty through the creation of Autonomous Indian Regions (Regiones Autónomas Indias). These would not only be in the state of Chiapas, since, the authors of the proposal pointed out, "of the 2,403 municipalities in the nation, a third of them, 803, have indigenous residents comprising more than 30 percent of their population" (Correa 1995, 23). They also made the direct link between NAFTA and challenges to indigenous sovereignty, saying: "For neoliberal plans, indigenous peoples are an obstacle" (1995, 24).

As the proposals went back and forth between Chiapas and Mexico City, a more inclusive discussion of Mexicans' rights was being enacted through the Consulta Nacional por la Paz y la Democracia (National Poll for Peace and Democracy). It was proposed by the EZLN's Subcomandante Marcos in June 1995 (César López 1995, 37). The purpose of the poll was to find out whether the goals the members of the EZLN had been fighting for had the support of a broad base of Mexican citizens, as was supposed but had not been demonstrated democratically. The Consulta Nacional was held a year after the Convención Nacional Democrática (National Democratic Convention), and was administered by the Alianza Cívica, an independent entity (César López 1995, 37) working for democratization in Mexico. The Civic Alliance was only one of a growing number of organizations promoting democracy in civil society, as demonstrated by the Encuentro Nacional de Organizaciones Ciudadanas (ENOC, National Meeting of Citizens' Organizations),[40] "with the participation of more than fifty civic organizations from all over the country" (Gómez-Hermosillo 1995, 4). [author's translation]

Citing NAFTA and the constitutional change in Article 27, Yolanda Massieu Trigo (1995) stated that the agricultural producers of Mexico, for whom the right to communal lands had been won in the 1910 Mexican Revolution, were desperate for positive change and that perhaps the transition of the EZLN from a revolutionary army to a political party would represent such a change for them; indeed, one of the questions asked in the Consulta Nacional was whether the EZLN should transform itself into a political party.[41] The popular vote on this question would guide the EZLN in deciding the organization's specific form in future contributions to Mexico's ongoing process of social and political change, and the vote itself would demonstrate the process of democratization.

Subcomandante Marcos pointed out in an interview with Carmen Lira (1995, 11), published on the day of the Consulta Nacional (August 27), that the EZLN itself represented a process of creating a culture of increasing democratic participation in decisionmaking in the Chiapas region. He said, "What the EZLN has to offer to Mexican society is someone who will listen to its demands and make a case for them, take them into account. And yes, we are constructing this culture, and yes, we are learning to do it, because that's how we grew; if we hadn't, we would have remained eight or twelve." (Lira 1995; 11) [author's translation]

Political cartoons and commentaries stated that Subcomandante Marcos controlled the Consulta Nacional, but Carlos Monsiváis argued against this view, saying that from his observations in Mexico City, those members of civil society who stood all day at the polling booths were not revolutionaries with abstract goals, but residents of the city—mostly women—who were relieved to finally contribute something concrete to the palpable process of social change (Monsiváis 1995b). That was certainly the experience of the Alianza Cívica member I interviewed the week after the Consulta Nacional.

There were three unofficial plebiscites, or polls, administered in August and September 1995: a national poll, an international poll, and a youth poll. They took place at different times. The ballots were signed by the voters, who had to present valid identification, and while the Mexican federal government did not recognize the results as a vote, the three-part Consulta was monitored and counted carefully by civic organization members, and it was used widely to discuss public opinion on the specific pathways to democratization—a word used equally by those in all political parties and many civic organizations, with a range of meanings regarding inclusiveness and goals for public action.

The National Referendum for Peace and Democracy administered by the Civic Alliance throughout the nation on Sunday, August 27, 1995, consisted of ballots with the following six questions, each answered with a check in one of three boxes: yes, no, or I don't know:

1. Do you agree that the principal demands of the Mexican people are: land, housing, work, food, health, education, culture, information, independence, democracy, liberty, justice, peace, security, combatting corruption, [and] defense of the environment?
2. Should the separate democratizing forces unite in a broad citizens' social and political front of opposition, and fight for these sixteen principal demands?
3. Should we Mexicans make profound political reforms that guarantee democracy? (Respect for the vote, trustworthy leadership, impartial and autonomous administration of elections, free citi-

zen participation—including nongovernmental organizations and those not in political parties, recognition of all the national political forces, regional and local, equity for all.)

4. Should the EZLN convert itself into a political force, independent and new, without uniting itself with other political organizations?
5. Should the EZLN unite itself with other organizations and together form a new political organization?
6. Should the presence and equal participation of women be guaranteed in all offices in civil organizations and in the government? (Reproduced in *Boletín Mexicano de la Crisis* 1995) [author's translation]

The Alianza Cívica set up 10,032 voting tables in thousands of towns (with no government support), and approximately 1,200,000 Mexican citizens went to those tables to vote (Semo 1995b). Among them were some of the Mexican government representatives responsible for negotiating with the EZLN (Zamarripa 1995, 8). Small signs of the Consulta Nacional were evident throughout Mexico City that day: a runner in the marathon wore a ski mask, and flyers reminded those wanting to vote what forms of identification they needed to take to the booths and where to find them—near churches, parks, markets, shopping centers, and Metro stations.

The majority of voters (53 percent) in the Consulta Nacional said they wanted the EZLN to become an independent political force, not joining with other parties. This was, of course, interpreted in various ways—including calls for the EZLN to lay down arms, which did not happen during the ongoing peace talks. After all three Consultas, Subcomandante Marcos published his analysis on behalf of the EZLN. His statement again made it clear to me that this, too, was a plurinational NAFTA story:

> For us there were not three plebiscites; for us, there was one big plebiscite with three parts. For that reason, now that we have the results of the young people's poll and the international poll, we can say that the Consulta is over and we are taking this opportunity to thank all of you. For us, there was not a first-class, second-class, and third-class poll. We value the view of the twelve-year-old person and the eighty-six-year-old person; we value the view of the Greeks, the Spaniards, the French, the Italians, the British, the

North Americans, the South Americans, the Asians, and the
Islanders. (Subcomandante Marcos 1995) [author's translation]

Marcos's letter reported that questions 1, 2, 3, and 6 were answered yes
by a majority of voters and that the answers to 4 and 5 (yes to an independent political force, no to joining with other political parties)
required thought within the EZLN. In another communication, Marcos
called for a national dialogue between the EZLN, civil society groups,
the Ruta 100 strikers, the students excluded from the National
University, El Barzón, and other groups without the national government's participation (Henríquez y Martínez 1995). The response to the
Consulta did seem emblematic of a strengthening of civil society in
Mexico, although there were regional differences, and—as a worker I
spoke with in Mexico City pointed out—discussions of democracy did
not necessarily turn into solutions to the crisis.

On September 1, 1995, "Carmen," a volunteer for the Alianza
Cívica, agreed to be interviewed about the Consulta Nacional and the
social context that had led to it. We were standing in the Zócalo, in the
booth of the Convención Nacional Democrática where she had been
volunteering. I asked her about the history of the Consulta Nacional.
Carmen said it had originally been the idea of the EZLN and that the
Alianza Cívica had administered it so it would be an independently
monitored vote. The Alianza had approved the ballot questions because
they appeared to give Mexican people a way to provide public opinion
on the real necessities in the country—economic, social, political, and
those not conforming with government policies. Carmen continued in
the following excerpts:

> Unfortunately, we are very backward here in our understanding of
> politics. We do not participate, we do not want to get involved
> because of fear; there has been a lot of government intimidation.
> But what happened last Sunday was lovely, because so many peo-
> ple voluntarily came to the balloting tables in order to express their
> views by voting. That is very important. Even though most of the
> media represented the Consulta as a failure, that was a lie. Because
> I was right here in this polling place [in the Zócalo], one of the best
> attended, and I saw that people from all social classes were here.
> . . . I saw students, and I saw children who came and wanted to par-
> ticipate . . . from six-year-olds on up.
>   There is going to be a youth referendum later. . . . But one

could see people's enthusiasm and desire to do something about what is happening in Mexico right now. I talked with some of the adults who came to vote. I would ask, "And you, why did you come to vote today?" And they would say, "Because I want a change." The sense one got from talking with people is that things are bad in this country. And we are the only ones who can begin to make a change, ourselves . . . each one of us. . . . So last Sunday was a good beginning. [author's translation]

I asked her if people were afraid their votes would become known. She answered that yes, some people asked if there would be consequences from the government for their votes in the Consulta, including one man who said "OK, I'm going to vote, but I don't want to put my name on the ballot or show my ID." Carmen said she explained to him that it was important that everyone show their identification and sign their ballots, so that the Alianza Cívica could demonstrate it had been a fair balloting process and people had come of their own will. He decided to vote. She said everyone had to do something, as they were able, because the crisis in Mexico was impossible for anyone to ignore—whether they were poor, from the middle class, or rich, everyone was being affected in some way or other. It's important, she explained, that people see that it is the crisis that is bad, and not the EZLN.

CARMEN: First, one must know, then one can express an opinion, and then later, if one wants, one can criticize. But you can't start off criticizing without knowing anything. . . .

A.K.: *How can people find a true account of what is happening in Mexico if, as you say, the newspapers are lying?*
CARMEN: Yes, and [there are lies] in the television, too. Look, what is happening is that people are very apathetic because each person is engrossed in his or her own economic problems. I have seen this myself. What I want to do is to make things better in some way—to help people find new media to read, for example, because that is very important. People don't like to read and aren't used to it, because it's hard to tell something good from something mixed up. A lot of sources end up confusing one more instead of helping one figure out what's going on. So people say no, it's better not to know anything about it. And that's bad, isn't it? What I say is, you don't have to be a politician and you don't have to know politics, but you

can begin in your own home. I try to look for sources of information and to talk with people who know about what is happening but who are neutral politically. I am neutral myself: I don't belong to any political party. I believe in the ideals expressed by the Zapatistas, but I see those things as my own individual responsibility. I have to do something for myself, for my country, because I love my country. [Here she stopped for a minute, looking across the square.] I'm crying. . . .

Look, this is what is bad. People are wearing T-shirts from the U.S.A. and feel like they are almost gringos. This is bad. Things from that country have been promoted so much here. For me, that's very sad. We need to feel proud, truly proud, of the culture that we have *here*.

A.K.: *Do you think this change in national pride and consumption is due in part to the North American Free Trade Agreement?*
CARMEN: That was a lie, that's all—a lie in the interests of some powerful people. The lie was we were told that we were going to become part of the first world. How could people possibly believe this when we can't even compare ourselves with the U.S.A.? The two nations are two different worlds. The lie is that through your pal the market you can become part of the first world: by putting on a pair of tennis shoes. It's a lie. We can't actually be at the same level as the U.S.A. because they are much more advanced technologically, and in many other areas. You can't change into that from one day to the next. And we are seeing the results: this country is poorer than ever. And the U.S. is growing at our expense. Many people have continued believing the lies because we are accustomed to believing the lies the government tells us. But we should not. We have the responsibility not to. We are accustomed to paternalism.

For example today [in the primer informe], Zedillo said that we had touched bottom in the crisis and that everything would get better, as if he were a magician who could wave a wand and make everything better for the country. People go on believing this because they have to believe in *something* . . . There is a lot of repression, and people are not themselves. They go on believing and believing and avoiding reality. They would rather dream than confront reality. It's very hard to [see what is actually happening], and one suffers, but one cannot live in a lie. You have to confront it.

Carmen went on to tell me how she herself was acting to confront the reality she saw in Mexico. She was concerned about the suspension of schooling for many children in Chiapas (for over a year, by that time). Schoolbooks written in Spanish had been sent by the government to Chiapas, when most of the children there do not read Spanish, she said. She was interested in supporting efforts to create libraries in Chiapas, some of which had been destroyed in the war, with books in the languages of the many indigenous nations represented there.

I asked her again about the Consulta Nacional she had helped administer the week before. She said the vote was fair and that newspapers had underrepresented popular participation in the Consulta. The over one million votes recorded by the Alianza Cívica really represented quite a few more people than that, since one adult often was voting on behalf of a whole household. Carmen said that the vote in the first Consulta had resulted in a call for a new political force for change in Mexico, not necessarily for the EZLN to integrate itself into the existing set of political parties. Change would happen step by step, and since the majority of the Mexican population was under twenty-five, the Consulta that asked young people their opinions would be important.

I then asked her about the Consulta Juvenil (the balloting of young people), and she explained that only persons over eighteen had been allowed to cast ballots in the Consulta Nacional; in the next referendum, those twelve to eighteen years old would be able to vote. She said that what was happening was more important than marches and protests: young people were being asked to really participate (in determining the future of Mexican politics).

A.K.: *Has participation in the Consulta Nacional varied by region in the nation?*

CARMEN: Look, it depended on the identity [of the region]. There are very politicized states, in which people are much more informed than others regarding their internal problems. There are many populations in which people are completely isolated. . . . So it's very unequal. There are regions in very great need. The Tarahumara, for example, are dying from hunger.[42] Because they are in isolated communities, they are cornered. [Powerful people] have taken away their lands from them to enrich themselves. What the Tarahumara are concerned with, and what they ask, is that they be allowed to sustain themselves with what they produce. . . . That is how it is all over the country; each community wants to be allowed to live according to their own customs and to be respected by everyone else. I, for example, living here in the city, don't have any right to tell them how they should live or to change their customs, which they have been following for many years. . . . Some states are very politicized, and others have very little participation [in a national political conversation]. So it is impossible to generalize what percentage is interested, what percentage participates, because there are so many inequalities between regions.

A.K.: *Do you think there is a Mexican cultural or national identity, or a plurality of identities?*
CARMEN: Well, I think yes, it is a plurality. But I could not venture an opinion about what percentage is interested or not [in the work of the EZLN, from different regions of Mexico]. I, for example, am worried about the Tarahumara and I want to do something. But I also have to worry about my own area, right here in the capital district. I cannot resolve the problems of those in Chiapas, nor of the Tarahumara, because I live here. In this city, I am worried about assaults, about the lack of public safety. So you see, I think that each person in his or her own place, own community, has to be concerned with his or her community. I am worried about the country, but I am also worried about what is happening right here. I have an eighteen-year-old son, and I am worried that something will happen to him in the street. He is a student. Those of us who live in Mexico City also have to solve our own problems.

Because Carmen needed to get home to her son and her work as an artesan, I asked my last question—the one I ended most interviews with that fall: "In what step, or from what source, does hope exist, do you think?" Her thoughtful response (on the same day as President Zedillo's *primer informe*) demonstrates the kind of analysis of the crisis and the future of Mexico occurring in civil society at that moment.

I agree with those who are convinced that a change is coming. I think that naturally, historically, there has to be a change. Because everything revolves, right? It's all a circle. Right now, the circle is closed. But it has to open. . . . If you think about it, the conditions in which we are living are associated with revolution. Only the names have been changed. But one has to analyze how far we have come since the Revolution [of 1910]. And we have not advanced much. . . . Right now we are in a very important moment of change, but it has to be to make things better, because nobody wants a war. There are very violent things going on in the world right now, aren't there? It is not only here; the whole world is in crisis. But this country needs a change. It needs to turn over a new leaf. Because there are intelligent, talented people in this country, but they are not given any opportunities—not politically, not in any sense. I think, from what we can see historically and on all levels, a change is coming now. Whether we want it or not, this change has to be. I hope it is for the better! None of us wants a war. But I'm not going to be passive either. Because although one works, there is no option but to just barely survive. Right now, there is still food, but when there is even more unemployment, even less food, more homelessness . . . when you are hungry, you have a stomach for action.

But it doesn't have to come to that. Right now would be a good time for a peaceful change. But a reasonable one, with conscience. Right now, everybody's talking about conscience, but I think this word is very difficult to understand precisely and in all its vastness. . . . Does it mean to act with reason? In what country? Wherever one is, as a Mexican, as a human being, one has the right to live well. And this country is too rich to have people who have nothing to eat, children who can't go to school. This country has an immense wealth, the potential of which we are only using 10 percent. . . .We are accomplished, but with a sense of inferiority that makes us believe we are worthless. This is the time to rise up and say, "I belong to this country and this country belongs to me." So, yes, I feel secure and hopeful that we are going to be able to do it. Probably very slowly, but yes, change has to come.

Carmen acted on her commitment to civic participation, even in relation to this interview. As I tried to do with all interviews, I transcribed our conversation that night and delivered it to her the next day at the CND booth in the Zócalo—for her approval, rejection, or amendment as one of the NAFTA stories for this book. She read the transcript, discussed it with other Alianza Cívica volunteers, taking into account their responses, then retyped our interview and returned it to me with slightly revised answers to the questions. The new answers reflected discussions of current conditions such as the demand for public education, in practice and not just in written policy, for all Mexican citizens.

Carmen revised her answer to the final question, for example, in this way:

> In this country, there should be no one who has no bread to put in his or her mouth, no one who does not have at least a basic education, given the immense wealth that we have as a nation and which any other nation on this planet would want. We should stop believing that we are a stupid people, and cast off the inferiority complexes.

The process she demonstrated for negotiating a representation (rather than it being single-authored and individually commodified—with symbolic capital, at least—in a capitalist context) is a model for future participatory transnational research.

Carmen's statements on the same day as President Zedillo's address provided a strong counterpoint to his analysis of conditions in, and the future of, Mexico, just as Bertha Luján's analysis did. Her examination of the morality or "conscience" of capitalist development, for example, and her conviction (like Luján's) that ultimately social welfare *must* be taken into account in national and transnational policy expressed very effectively the aspect of neoliberal capitalist policy that leaders in all three North American nations had been silent about. The violence Carmen mentioned, both actual and potential, against the Mexican state and beyond it, was in protest of a neoliberal economic agenda that touted equality but actually promoted inequality. Many people in all three nations were finding mostly nonviolent ways—as Carmen was doing through her work with the Alianza Cívica—to *act* on what Saskia Sassen (1998) would call their discontent with globalization. I mean to imply here not that local or plurinational organizing efforts in response to NAFTA and related conditions were in effortless agreement or were based on the same thinking (Ortiz 1999), but that one NAFTA story was about people like Carmen who found themselves, for the first time, becoming part of a collective political response to regional, national, or transnational policy.

If the nation of Mexico (like the other two nations of North America) can be seen as a plurality of constituencies or publics, then a majority constituency is young people. On September 13, the Alianza Cívica administered another plebiscite, this time the Consulta Nacional Juvenil. More than two hundred thousand young people voted, at tables largely staffed by them, with these results: 93.25 percent answered yes, they agreed with the principal demands articulated in question 1; 78.21

percent responded positively to the second question, on a united front working to achieve those demands; and 83.72 percent wanted reforms guaranteeing democracy (question 3). On question 4, whether the EZLN should become an independent political force, 48.73 percent voted yes, 33.14 percent no, and 18.13 percent said they didn't know; on question 5, whether the EZLN should integrate itself with existing political parties, 37.69 percent responded affirmatively, 46.72 percent negatively, and 15.59 percent were unsure; and on question 6, regarding the participation of women, 80.56 percent voted yes. In the Consulta Juvenil, two additional questions appeared on the ballot: 88.52 percent said yes to number 7, on the right to a free and public education at all levels, with respect for student rights, and to the eighth question, on the federal government's proposal to shift the age that one could be prosecuted as an adult to sixteen, 52.77 percent said yes.[43]

During the Consulta Nacional Juvenil, I visited the polling place on the Zócalo and talked with a group of five friends (three young women, two young men), all sixteen years old, after they had cast their ballots. They were very excited about the opportunity to vote and told me they saw it as a step toward taking young people more seriously. One said that the president, in his primer informe, did not seem to be addressing the young people who comprise the national majority at all and that young people should be consulted in formulating national and international policies. The young people I spoke with all attended the same school. They told me that newsmagazines like the *Forum* (published by the CND) and any information published by the EZLN was prohibited by the government from being distributed in zones around high schools and polytechnic schools. And yet, according to the person who was staffing the polling booth at that time, eighty-five young people had come to the Zócalo to vote thus far that day, even though there were no schools in that area.

Circulation Stories

In the last section, I focused on NAFTA stories told in Mexico City. Here, I will end the chapter on 1995 with stories of circulation—of citizens and resources transnationally. I revisited the farm of Leonardo and Diana in rural Morelos, with Miguel Morayta M., and heard about the circulation of farm labor between Mexico and Canada; I also revisited the farm of Tommy and Dot in rural Kentucky and heard about the circulation of farm commodities. And I heard about currency circulation from an undersecretary in President Zedillo's government who was among those responsible for overseeing financial matters through the crisis.

Miguel Morayta M. saw the 1994–1995 crisis as severely affecting subsistence farmers. He wrote:

> The economic catastrophe of 1994–1995 is taking a high toll on rural people in Morelos. The cost of fertilizer, before the rise of the dollar, has now doubled. Now fertilizer costs more than corn. There is no possibility of getting enough credit from the government, and the bank is charging 130 percent annual interest on loans.
> (Kingsolver and Morayta M. 1995, 15) [author's translation]

In the fall of 1995, Miguel Morayta M. and I talked with Diana about the changes that had occurred since we had last talked with the couple on their ejido plot. She was working there alone, since their labor resources were stretched even further this year. The two younger children had joined their older brother as migrant farmworkers in Canada. She said conditions there were good for them and that their cash contributions were making it possible for the family in Morelos to survive. The older son had earned 32,000 pesos in Canada the season before, and his airfare was paid by the farm owner. Of the 16,000 pesos he had sent thus far this season, they had used 12,000 to pay for the harvest. Diana and Leonardo had to hire workers, some of whom may have been migrant workers coming from more economically depressed states like Guerrero. The pump installed the year before had enabled them to keep the tomato crop alive, although the tomatoes they sold brought only 30 new pesos per box, half the price of the year before. Diana pointed out two kinds of corn growing in the field; the white corn paid the rent on the second burro required to pull the plow, and blue corn (which she called black corn) was for household consumption. Crops being grown to pay the high interest rates and other costs could not be counted on— both because they were bringing lower prices in the market and because the drought was reducing the yield so severely.

Diana did not blame NAFTA directly for the crisis, but in Kentucky, where farmers were also experiencing crisis conditions, Dot and Tommy did. The Argentinian tobacco they had been concerned about had not come in (through NAFTA openings in the market) to displace theirs, but the bottom had fallen out of the beef market, which they relied on to pay labor costs at specific times in the annual production cycle of the tobacco crop.[44] Dot and Tommy blamed the fall in prices on Mexico and on NAFTA. They also told me they thought the United States was losing its agrarian identity because of increasing interdependence between the nations of North America.

Another person I interviewed in 1995 who, like Diana, did not blame NAFTA for economic problems, including the Mexican financial crisis, was a member of the Zedillo administration. He attributed the crisis to events in Chiapas and to the assassination of leaders within the PRI, and said it would have been much worse had Mexico not been a signatory to NAFTA and able to rely on financial assistance from the United States and the IMF. When I asked about the administration's position vis à vis globalization, the undersecretary, "Cristóbal," answered:

> We think that the new international tendency is to have greater integration between all countries, and that's the direction in which things have been going, isn't it? So we have been trying to increase our trade relations not just with the U.S. and Canada, but the idea is also to make agreements of that kind with other Latin American nations. There has already been one signed with Colombia and Venezuela. We have another one with Chile. We have another one with Bolivia. And we think this will continue to be the tendency. Nevertheless, I think that economic interchange, and even more strongly, cultural interchange, will continue to be most strongly with other North American countries because they are closer and because they offer different kinds of economic support. [author's translation]

I asked him if he thought NAFTA had affected national identity or culture, and he replied:

> Yes, I think there have been important changes. For example, in the financial sector, one of the most important aspects of NAFTA has been that it opened financial services to external competition. Because for more than sixty years, even when banks were private or had not yet been nationalized, foreign banks were not allowed to operate in Mexico. So NAFTA is the first policy that allows this. And since it passed, foreign banks have opened a number of branches in Mexico.

Now, in terms of national culture or identity, which was the topic of your question, I think that it has not been permeated as much and that the influence of other countries already existed before NAFTA. Because basically that happens through TV programs, through the radio, where there is foreign programming. And that already existed. So NAFTA has encouraged those kinds of changes, but they were already happening before NAFTA.

Cristóbal would not have agreed then, in his NAFTA story, with the one told earlier in the cartoon of the U.S. eagle flying off with the Mexican eagle (and thus national sovereignty). But what was happening with the circulation of other visual symbols of nationalism in 1995?

There was a dance going on between California Governor Pete Wilson, the Mexican press, and the Statue of Liberty. When Governor Wilson announced his campaign for the U.S. presidency, journalists in Mexico were critical of his use of the Statue of Liberty in campaign ads, because that symbol was supposed to represent openness to immigrants, and as explained in Chapter 3, his position had been contrary to that in 1994. The constitutionality of California Proposition 187 was still under debate, but a law had been proposed in the U.S. Congress that would take the selective anti-immigrant policies in that proposition to the national level (Cornejo 1995). In the United States, not only that symbolic wall but a physical wall along the U.S.-Mexican border was being proposed (*El Financiero* 1995c). The PRI denounced the plan (Ureña 1995), even as a "wall" of border officials every twenty meters along the Mexican-Guatemalan border was being proposed to address the problem of undocumented immigration across North America's actual southern border (Victorio 1995). Pat Buchanan, another candidate running for the U.S. presidency, announced after a meeting with Christian conservatives, that he would definitely construct a wall along the U.S.-Mexican border and that he would cancel NAFTA if elected (*Excelsior* 1995). The circulation of images of national identity went on, even as the circulation of Mexican citizens through North America and other regions of the world was being discussed in relation to a policy of dual citizenship for Mexicans outside Mexico who had had to renounce their Mexican citizenship when taking citizenship in other countries—primarily the United States (Pérez Canchola 1995).

As Carmen, the artesan who volunteered with the Alianza Cívica, said, profound changes—especially in the relationship between civil society and the state—were in process in 1995, in Mexico and elsewhere in North America. In the concluding chapter, these changes will be considered more extensively.

Notes

1. One way to think about the economic crisis in Mexico is in terms of the devaluation of the peso. Another is to regard it, in the context of Mexico's position as a signatory to the NAFTA, in terms of the overvaluation of the U.S. dollar, as Jorge Castañeda (1995, 32) put it:

> The NAFTA debate in the United States obscured a crucial trade-off: in order for Mexico to become a dynamic market for American exports— thus providing "good jobs at good wages" for U.S. workers—it had to maintain an overvalued currency that would eventually drive *Mexican* firms out of business, and *Mexican* workers out of *their* jobs. All of this was calculated, stated, and denounced by countless Mexican and Latin American economists and pundits; it simply was not paid attention to north of the border, except by a few Bush, Salinas, or Clinton administration critics whose views were dismissed as partisan, resentful, or simply out to lunch.

2. I have quoted people who either were making comments intended to be public information or who knew I was working on this project, as is consistent with ethnographic ethics.

3. See note 26 in Chapter 3 on Day of the Dead celebrations and Halloween elements.

4. Whether these products were manufactured in the United States or in Mexico is unclear, as a reader has asked me to note. More U.S. name brands were being both produced and consumed in Mexico all the time, at least from what I saw and was told.

5. This and all quotes in this chapter, unless otherwise indicated, I have translated from Spanish.

6. Daniel noted figures from the United Nations stating that half the population of Mexico was under twenty (similar to Turkey, Ethiopia, and Bangladesh). Emilio Alanis Patiño (1995, 55) predicted dire consequences for "Mexican, and international, finances" if there did not immediately develop "a political and administrative will to recognize the obligation that the currently active generation has to the unavoidable rights of the population growing toward age sixty-five" [author's translation]. Alanis Patiño went on to say that starting in 1995, the money supposedly in retirement funds needed to be accounted for and that funds that would actually correspond to the need of future retirees must be developed and managed honestly.

7. After the sudden devaluation of the Mexican peso, Anthony DePalma, writing on the crisis for the *New York Times* (1995), said this about the Mexican middle class:

But many of the most disillusioned are among the more than 40 million
in the rapidly expanding middle class—defined here as everyone who
earns enough to keep from being hungry, but not enough to be considered
among the richest 10 percent. The steep rise in interest rates that has
accompanied the devaluation has hurt them. Monthly payments on
adjustable-rate mortgages suddenly eat up an entire salary; credit cards
are charging interest rates as high as 80 percent; payments on car loans
have ballooned.

In a nation with a perceived middle-class identity, such as the United States, the
notion that middle-class Mexicans were suffering with the crisis somehow
seemed to pierce a perceptual first-third world wall in that thought style, and
stories of the middle-class debtors' movement were picked up in the international press, often with very different contextualization than stories about the
(also NAFTA-related) demands of coalitions of indigenous nations.

8. For a discussion of the barzón movement, see Greider (1997).

9. Carlos A. Heredia and Mary E. Purcell (1995, 2), writing about the
political repression and increasing inequalities resulting from structural adjustment policies in Mexico that were encouraged by the World Bank and the
International Monetary Fund, said this:

A series of events in 1994, including the Declaration of War by the EZLN
in January, the assassination of Luis Donaldo Colosio, PRI presidential
candidate, in March, and the assassination of José Francisco Ruiz
Massieu, general secretary of the PRI, in September, illustrate the inabili-
ty of the Mexican political system to resolve the extreme economic polar-
ization and internal political disputes. It is becoming more and more clear
that the imposition of policies that concentrate wealth among a few people at the same time as supporting austerity for everyone else, is no
longer feasible in Mexico without causing even more and greater social
upheavals. [author's translation]

10. One journalist compared the financing plan the United States offered
to Mexico to junk-bond sales. In an article called "Has the U.S. Got a Horse for
You: Mexico," Allen R. Myerson (1995) said that NAFTA had caused investors
to believe that investments in Mexico were as safe as those in U.S. and
Canadian markets and that when the peso was devalued, many investors lost
earnings (including a Chemical Banking loss of $70 million). Myerson said:

That the United States is now looking like Mexico's junk-bond financier,
under arrangements being hashed out last week, reflects the nation's huge
stake south of the border. Banks, corporations and mutual funds, and their
ma-and-pa investors, sent tens of billions to Mexico, and the United States
has to bail them out. Mexican debt, which flirted with investment-grade
ratings last year, now looks about as solid as the bonds pumped out by
many a tottering savings and loan.

Last week, members of Congress derided the Clinton Administration's

$40 billion rescue plan, on top of an $18 billion international package, as a welfare program for bumbling Mexican leaders and gullible American investors. President Clinton responded that the country has no choice. To hold back, he said, would ravage the American economy, devastate Latin American markets and send hundreds of thousands more illegal immigrants swarming northward.

This was clearly a moment of xenophobic retrenchment for some in the United States and another battleground for President Clinton and the Republican-dominated Congress. After Congress refused to support a $40 billion loan-guarantee package, according to the *New York Times* (1995), the Clinton administration "promised $20 billion from its Exchange Stabilization Fund" and encouraged the IMF to put together a $17.8 billion loan package that officials in Britain, Belgium, the Netherlands, Germany, and Switzerland refused to support, saying that the rescue package was too hastily assembled and made large IMF loans look too available to other nations verging on crisis. Globalization and balkanization are two sides of the same coin, it seems.

11. President Ernesto Zedillo said in his first annual address to the nation that the economic crisis had not begun in 1994 [during his administration] but in 1992, with the signing of the Agreement [by President Salinas de Gortari]. "The opening of trade, with the signing of the NAFTA, was indiscriminate in its effects on the Mexican business sector," as Camacho (1995) summed up President Zedillo's explanation of the economic crisis at the end of 1994.

12. The internet address for SIPRO is www.laneta.apc.org/sipro.

13. Freire and Horton were mentioned in Chapter 1, no. 8. Paulo Freire wrote *Pedagogy of the Oppressed* (1984), *Education for Critical Consciousness* (1973), and other texts on critical pedagogy and led literacy circles among workers in Brazil. He authored the concept of *conscientização* (conscientization), or critical education for democratic action, and along with Myles Horton is associated with the tradition of participatory research, in which research questions come from communities rather than from researchers. Horton was a founder of the Highlander Center in Tennessee, which was a site for key conversations during the civil rights movement and which has become known for connecting workers with information to better understand and improve their situations (Adams with Horton 1975). For example, after the Union Carbide accident in Bhopal, India, workers in Institute, West Virginia, wondered whether they were working with the same chemicals that had caused the tragedy. They approached Highlander, and through its resources they learned how to use chemical reference books and what they needed to do to protect themselves physically and legally from harm in the workplace (Horton, personal communication to author 1985). In working with other workers as a union activist, Monroy decided that an important task for helping workers to know and act on their situation would be to provide accessible information on economic issues, which he was doing through SIPRO.

14. In this case, I was tagging along on an interview they had arranged because Luccisano was researching NGOs and public services in Mexico.

15. Democracy, in the sense being called for by those distributing *Forum,*

is a concept equated with equality and accountability. As Freire (1973, 58) expressed it:

> One subverts democracy (even though one does this in the name of democracy) by making it irrational; by making it rigid in order "to defend it against totalitarian rigidity"; by making it hateful, when it can only develop in a context of love and respect for persons; by closing it, when it only lives in openness; by nourishing it with fear when it must be courageous; by making it an instrument of the powerful in the oppression of the weak; by militarizing it against the people; by alienating a nation in the name of democracy.
>
> One defends democracy by leading it to the state Mannheim calls "militant democracy"—a democracy which does not fear the people, which suppresses privilege, which can plan without becoming rigid, which defends itself without hate, which is nourished by a critical spirit rather than irrationality.

More and more calls like that of the CND were being made in Mexican civil society in 1995 for ending the subversion of democracy by the national government.

16. In another analysis of Mexico's neoliberal policy, Asa Cristina Laurell (1995) said that the EZLN rebellion had been a dramatic wake-up call signaling the tremendous social crisis in Mexico. She argued:

> The context in which one must evaluate the Mexican social question is that of a medium-developed country that is characterized by great inequalities, between classes and social groups, between regions, and between rural and urban areas. While Mexico is certainly not a First World nation, neither is it a poor country that lacks resources and wealth. Therefore, the intense social problems derive from a highly regressive distribution of income and wealth, and not from underdevelopment in the abstract.

Additional sources on the economic crisis that followed the wake-up call, with specific sectoral figures and a range of explanations, include: Gómez, Alemán, y Román (1995); Urrutia (1995); Fernandez Santillan (1995); Guajardo Touché (1995); García y Rubalcalva (1995); Cruz Serrano (1995); Mentado Contreras (1995); Berumen y Asociados S.C. (1995); Morales y Concheiro (1995); Alcocer V. (1995); Pérez Vences (1995a); Mora Tavares (1995); Guerrero Chiprés (1995); *El Financiero* (1995a); SEPPI (1995); Silverstein and Cockburn (1995); Rosenthal (1995); Nasar (1995); and Beltrán del Río (1995).

17. The ski mask worn by Subcomandante Marcos (as just one of the members of the EZLN) as he spoke with journalists from Chiapas served to transform his voice into that of Everyman: an interchangeable social actor for change in Mexico and elsewhere. Alfredo Velarde (1995) wrote that in unmasking Marcos and vilifying him, President Zedillo had actually unmasked himself as belonging to a national government that had repeatedly forgotten that sover-

eignty constitutionally rested with the *people* of Mexico. The armed conflict between the EZLN and the national government was an overlay on a much more complex renegotiation in the 1990s—in Mexico and elsewhere in North America—of the relationship between sovereign rights of national publics and the decisionmaking powers of their elected and appointed representatives.

18. I saw this personally while traveling to another rural Morelos community and our car was stopped by demonstrators. Stuffed figures representing the investors in a golfing resort (for which the national government had taken land from ejidatarios and sold to the investors) were hanging from a tree, and demonstrators approached the car with a coffee can and asked for money to allow us to pass. I asked about the demonstration, and they said that the resort would bring increased economic disparity and ecological destruction and would take subsistence lands from many Tepoztecos without replacing that form of subsistence with alternative jobs. The money collected on the roads was being used to bring international attention to the Tepoztlán situation; the publicity eventually brought pressure on the backers and halted the construction plans. For further discussion of the Tepoztlán golf resort plans, the controversy regarding the investors, and the social mobilization against the plan in the region, see these sources: Martinez Olais (1995); Vera (1995); Gutiérrez Oropeza (1995); Zebadúa (1995); Jiménez Trejo (1995); Bogin (1995); Guerrero Garro (1995); Trejo (1995); Sánchez (1995); Villegas, Rico, y Sánchez (1995); Enciso (1995); Garduño Espinosa y Enciso (1995); Ambriz y Ortega Pizarro (1995); Cruz y Rodríguez (1995).

19. The 11,000 strikers referred to generally as Ruta 100, who maintained a presence throughout the capital by leafleting on buses and demonstrating, were actually in an organization called SUTAUR–Sindicato Unico de Trabajadores de Autotransportes Urbanos de Pasajeros Ruta 100 (Becerril 1995).

20. The fact that the word pueblo can be translated as village, town, people, or nation indicates a relationship between place and identity (especially in the construction of indigenous sovereignty) that was recognized in Article 27 of the 1917 Mexican Constitution and challenged in the neoliberal privatization of communally held ejido lands. El Movimiento de los 400 Pueblos had been fighting for ejido lands since 1988, had been promised land by President Salinas, and had been refused an audience with President Zedillo (Pérez 1995).

21. This was a national referendum, which also went to Mexican citizens outside the nation; it was administered independently by the Alianza Cívica and inspired by proposals of the EZLN. I discuss the Consulta Nacional, which was administered in several days of specific balloting, below, in note 27.

22. *The News* includes figures on the Mexican *Bolsa,* or stock market, and from the New York Stock Exchange; when I asked people in Mexico City their perception of its readership, they generally see it as serving businesspeople and tourists from the United States, Canada, and other English-speaking nations.

23. Zedillo probably found it necessary to stress this point because voices in the press and other public venues had been linking the economic crisis and the loans of 1995 to a decrease in national sovereignty ultimately connected to NAFTA and other neoliberal policies.

24. Even though the president announced in this address that the econom-

ic crisis had reached its worst point and was improving, economic conditions actually continued to worsen, which further challenged his credibility according to those I interviewed about the crisis.

25. These changes were no doubt accelerated by public scrutiny of what were seen as miscarriages of justice in the Salinas administration; in fact, former President Salinas was himself persona non grata, in exile at the time of this speech.

26. At this point in the speech, one might think, on first reading, that Zedillo reached the closest discursive parity with the EZLN and other organizations within Mexico who were calling for democratization; however, the rhetoric more closely resembles state's-rights discourse in the United States than a call for greater recognition and representation in the Mexican government of, for example, a federation of autonomous indigenous nations.

27. In his summary, Alemán Alemán (1995) observed that it had been the shortest state of the nation address in Mexican history. Rene Delgado (1995) commented that it was neither informative nor a message to the nation, leaving clouds on the horizon and bodies (those of Luis Donaldo Colosio and José Francisco Ruiz Massieu, among others) unburied; he said the president had not advised the nation of what might be coming after the structural adjustment program was in place. (A political cartoon on the same page explored the topic of "neorhetoric.") In that same issue of *Reforma,* a new newspaper aiming for more independent discussions of current events, twenty prominent writers for the paper summed up their views of what was best, worst, and missing from the speech. Several saw as promising the president's self-criticism, a recognition of the seriousness of the crisis, and commitments to electoral and judicial reform. What was missing, according to the *Reforma* writers, included mention of the army (since there had been armed conflict in Mexico); more specifics on how some of the proposals—such as decentralization—might be carried out; ecological and labor issues; and a long-term vision for the country that included improving conditions for all Mexicans. Cárdenas (1995) pointed out that President Zedillo, in outlining a new federalism, had neglected to mention exactly *who* would need to agree on the new changes, which he saw as an important question.

Bueno Soria (1995) observed that Zedillo had spoken of Mexico as though it were a completely isolated entity, with no mention of international relations. Pérez Vences (1995b) reported that at a press conference held by President Zedillo's cabinet after the primer informe, Herminio Blanco categorically rejected the possibility of renegotiating the North American Free Trade Agreement. Herminio Blanco said that exports to the United States had increased by about 30 percent, and exports to Colombia, Venezuela, and Bolivia (through other trade agreements) had increased even more. A report in *El Financiero* (1995b) said that public finances had indeed improved during 1995, but at the cost of consumers who, in general, were becoming more impoverished and facing higher taxes and increased costs for fuel, electricity, and other goods and services. Monsiváis (1995) noted in *El Financiero* that President Zedillo had creatively found someone to blame for the economic crisis: the Mexican people themselves, for not saving and spending more money.

Maza (1995) examined closely the economic figures used in the address and raised questions about social welfare, which were minimized by Zedillo. He asked, for example, whether it made a difference, when it came to going hungry, if people able to work were officially counted as unemployed or simply had no income (together, those figures amounted to eight million Mexicans).

A number of analyses related the address to the issues of recognition and democratization that were being discussed widely in Mexican public discourse. An article in *Mira* (1995) raised questions about the commitment to indigenous education and cited Fausto Guadarrama López—a writer in the Mazahua community—who asked if extremes had to be reached before national attention would be turned to indigenous communities; only in 1992 were indigenous languages officially recognized in Mexico. The September 11th issue of *Mira* also published photographs from the primer informe ceremony showing protestors in the legislative chamber holding signs that called for punishment for the PRI members responsible for the political assassinations, for President Salinas to be brought to justice, and for solutions in Chiapas. García Colín (1995) indicated that the silent protests during the address (by students not admitted to UNAM, demonstrators calling for an end to hunger and unemployment, and others holding up banners) may have made them more effective. *Uno más uno* published the entire address on September 2, 1995, along with a photo of President Zedillo delivering it and two men in front of the dais holding a large sign saying that the dialogue with debtors was unjust and insufficient. *Proceso* came out four days before the speech with an issue called *Primer Informe: nueve meses de pesadilla* (nine months of nightmare), with its own analysis of the state of the nation nine months into 1995. Romero (1995) reported in *La Jornada* that after the address the opposition parties in congress—the PAN, the PRD, and the PT (labor party)—called for rapid democratization as the only way out of the crisis facing Mexico. Cano (1995) reported that President Zedillo had opened up a possibility, through announcing electoral reforms, for the EZLN's transition to a political party (one of the questions on the Consulta Nacional) with representatives in congress, but Cano wondered if the PRI government would actually allow that. Chávez (1995) summed up the speech by saying that it sounded a lot like President Salinas's primer informe, with promises of happiness, democracy, economic growth, controlled inflation, security, justice, and peace just around the corner.

28. Another translatation of *viva* would be "long live," but I have included here the text of Zedillo's grito exactly as it was transcribed by Monroy Aguirre (1995) because the analysis of the exact wording in Spanish, rather than how it would be translated into English, is important.

29. In an article in a political cartoon weekly, *El Papá del Ahuizote*, Magú (1995) reported that Zedillo raised a cheer for independence, liberty, and the priest Hidalgo, then went to bed. He said the heroes who had struggled for Mexican Independence along with Hidalgo had disappeared from the grito as led by the president in 1995. The other four traditionally mentioned in the commencement of the grito are Ignacio Allende, Aldama, Morelos, and Vicente Guerrero.

30. The cartoonists involved in the publication of *el chahuistle* are El

Fisgón, El Riús, El Patricio, and Helguera; it is published by Editorial Posada S.A. de C.V.

31. Former president Miguel de la Madrid Hurtado stated, one week after the Noche Mexicana, that improving education levels in Mexico was essential to preserving the nation's sovereignty (Lino Ramos 1995).

32. Uncle Sam, another U.S. national symbol, was also employed by political cartoonists in commentaries on the crisis and the grito. In several depictions of events in the Noche Mexicana, Uncle Sam imprisoned Mexican characters in his hat; in another, he allowed Mexicans to go on with the grito on September 15, but it was implied that with the "bailout plan," *Tío Sam* had bought Mexican national sovereignty.

33. R. S. Ratner (1997, 275) has suggested that globalization has spurred activist possibilities for "rediscovering a positive role for [the state]: of holding transnational corporations accountable for the consequences of their policies across all levels of citizen involvement."

34. The conference was called the "Consulta Nacional Sobre Comercio Internacional y Derechos de los Trabajadores" (National Consultation on International Trade and Workers' Rights), and it featured panel discussions on "Globalization and Labor Rights," "Social Clauses: National and International Mechanisms for the Protection of Workers' Rights," and "National and International Strategies to Protect Workers' Rights" during the two days. Representatives from major networks of (or including) labor organizations in Mexico participated: ICHRDD, RMALC, COCENTRA, ANAD, FAT, Red de Trabajadores de la Maquila, CMDPDH, and ASPA, as well as workers in several countries employed by the same corporation, for example, SONY.

35. Peñalosa Méndez (1995) pointed out that the biggest inconsistency in the National Development Plan was its call for sustainable development that would reinforce national sovereignty and promote justice and democracy, even as the neoliberal policies laid out in the document promote increasing disparities (concentration of wealth) in Mexico and abandonment of administration to the "forces of the market" and international economic interests. Peñalosa Méndez (1995, 7) called for policies that would comply with the Mexican constitution's stipulation that Mexico's administration follow a course of action that would actually promote the interests of all citizens (which he felt neoliberal policies did not).

36. While breaking the North American Free Trade Agreement was discussed at the Mexico City conference among representatives of labor, environmental, health, and human rights organizations, it is important to note that the plurinational effort was to make the trade agreements *better* in terms of actual social welfare rather than simply to disrupt them for the sake of disruption. As the national governments related through NAFTA considered fast-track legislation to incorporate Chile, these representatives of plurinational organizations were considering the detrimental effects on workers of the Agreement already in place, as well as what possible victories it had facilitated for workers. A binational committee had just been established, according to NAFTA rules, to consider, for example, a complaint by leatherworkers and to make a financial award (Rodríguez Trejo 1995).

37. The PRI had controlled that office for many decades, and Cárdenas had long been a spokesperson for those critical of PRI policies. In Mexico City, for example, one of his campaign promises was to decrease police repression—which had been particularly brutal in recent years in the treatment of the growing homeless population and street vendors. Whether he has been able to control the police force is another question. As Bertha Luján said, change will happen only through the joint, sustained actions of multiple groups, not simply with an election.

38. The Spanish word *derecho* translates into English as either "right" or "law"; both were on the table at the proposed talks between the EZLN and the Mexican government.

39. I assume he was stressing the participation of indigenous people themselves as a critical note on the readiness to subsume all EZLN voices under the romanticized rubric of Subcomandante Marcos (who was aware of this problem himself, in his communications), who was interpreted through an ethnic lens to be *ladino* (or mestizo). I realize that even using this quote by León-Portilla to make the point is further paternalization, but I was not working in Chiapas and did not talk with indigenous leaders of the EZLN.

40. ENOC produced a Citizens' Rights Charter, in which participants stated: "The democracy that we citizens demand is based in the complete exercise of the rights that belong to us. The solution to the crisis of our country cannot be found without the active participation of citizens. Mexican civil society has given clear demonstrations of its maturity" (Encuentro Nacional de Organizaciones Ciudadanas 1995). [author's translation] The charter outlined citizens' rights in the areas of democracy and citizen participation; human rights and the dispensation of justice; political economy and workers' rights; social development, subsistence, and health; education; culture; communication; rural development; and the environment; as well as for indigenous peoples; women; the disabled and the elderly; youth and children; gays and lesbians; prostitutes; and persons with AIDS.

41. If the EZLN became a political party, commented Jean Meyer of the Centro de Investigación y Docencia Económicas, there would be choices to be made by the political left in Mexico: either the EZLN would incorporate its interests with those of the PRD, or in becoming its own party, it would split the PRD, taking the younger and more radical PRD members with it (Inclán 1995).

42. At that time, this indigenous group in northern Mexico was suffering from a prolonged drought and a dearth of food supplies from any source.

43. These figures are from an uncredited article in *La Jornada* (1995). Other analyses of the Consulta Nacional Juvenil were published by Icela Rodríguez y Saldierna (1995), Gil Olmos (1995), and Saldierna (1995). Those writing after the event reported that the organizers viewed the Consulta Juvenil as a success in terms of the participation of young people—particularly in Mexico City.

44. Since virtually all burley tobacco is sold to tobacco corporations in early January through the cooperative warehouses, all costs related to its production during the year—especially the labor-intensive "setting" period in early summer and the "cutting and hanging" period at the end of the summer—have

to be paid with either the promise of the January check or by some other means. Increasingly, Dot and Tommy and other small farming families in rural Kentucky were hiring Mexican migrant workers when they could not cover the labor themselves or through their community networks of labor exchange. One way tobacco farmers raise cash for such labor costs during the season is by selling a calf from the small beef cattle herds that can be pastured on the region's steep hillsides.

5

Conclusion:
Stories of Accountability

During a rally in Washington, D.C., on April 16, 2000—the purpose of which was to question the social accountability of the International Monetary Fund, the World Bank, and the World Trade Organization—Richard Trumka, secretary-treasurer of the AFL-CIO, said, "It's time for the people's business to be conducted in public, and nothing less is acceptable" (C-SPAN broadcast). This call for transparency in the process of negotiating transnational trade and loan agreements, and for more attention to human welfare than to the welfare of capital, echoed a dominant chord in the NAFTA stories I heard between 1993 and 1996 in Mexico and the United States.

In this chapter, I follow several meanings of the word *accountability* in relation to transnational agreements like NAFTA and GATT. Who is accountable to whom? Is the role of the nation changing in relation to capital, transnational entities like the World Trade Organization, and nongovernmental organizations? Who constitutes the public for agreements like NAFTA? What are new venues for marginalization and integration in post–Cold War global capitalism?

Those endorsing neoliberal free-trade policies are no doubt pursuing that strategy for various reasons. A central one I discern is to position nations well in relation to "the market," at least appearing to cooperate with structural adjustment plans imposed with loans given through the International Monetary Fund and the World Bank since World War II. One goal of such loans has been to "structurally adjust" in another sense the economies and—by association, it is hoped—the political inclinations of third-world countries. In the fourth week of October 1994, a cartoon appeared in *Los Caricaturistas (Periodismo Gráfico de*

199

Actualidad) (see Figure 5.1), in which "Nostragamus" (the cartoonist/
commentator) depicted President Carlos Salinas de Gortari dreaming of
the World Trade Organization (OMC–Organización Mundial de
Comercio) and saying to himself, "On second thought, unemployment
insurance is not such a bad idea." In other words, Nostragamus saw
Salinas making that decision according to what OMC members would
think of him and the policy, rather than what the Mexican people would
think. I believe the NAFTA/GATT story being told here is a broad-
reaching one: many national leaders have come to see themselves as
more accountable to transnational entities—in this case, the World
Trade Organization, which Salinas still hoped to head—than to their
own publics.

In the U.S. public education industry, in which I am a worker, we
have heard the word *accountability* quite a lot in recent years, through
the kind of accountability legislation that swept through the United
Kingdom earlier, during Thatcher's administration.[1] Here, fiscal
accountability has meant more than, say, moral accountability to the
students in facilitating their education. The project of fiscal accountability, whether of nations to the World Bank as part of structural adjustment programs or of state workers to legislatures in U.S. universities,
has been an encompassing one in a neoliberal agenda.

What seemed to be in question as a theme running through NAFTA
stories, as well as in other accounts of neoliberal restructuring (e.g., the
privatization of industries, the financing of social programs by the participants themselves, and giving the market more free rein), was what
constituted the bottom line in measuring accountability. For some, this
has meant balancing national budgets; for others such as holders of
Internet company stocks, it has been the promise of future profits; and
for still others, the bottom line has not been financial at all. The major
division I see running through NAFTA stories is not the first-
world/third-world schema inherited from the Cold War era but another
cultural and conceptual division that has been playing itself out right
along (as we say in Kentucky): the division between those whose bottom line is capitalist profit, no matter what, and those whose bottom
line is the well-being of humans and environments.

Accounting language carries the rhetorical power of objectivity and
other empirical leftovers, but as an interpretive ethnographer I see it as
just another cultural logic organizing a social world that, among other
things, assigns value and tasks to people, even as the same people perpetuate it. Throughout the NAFTA stories in this book, I hear play—in

Ill. 5.1 President Salinas dreaming of the World Trade Organization: "On second thought, unemployment insurance is not such a bad idea." (Nostragamus, *Los Caricaturista [Periodismo Gráfico de Actualidad]*, 4th week of October 1994)

the sense that anthropologists think of the word.[2] It's not always fun. Through discussions of free trade and other neoliberal transnational policy, there has been play with the nation's role in regulating capital or being regulated by it, with the role of NGOs from the EZLN to the Pioneer Fund to the Sierra Club, and with the notion of citizenship— whether indicating the agency of individuals in shaping policies that affect their livelihoods or connoting a reconfiguration of citizenship in relation to transnational bodies (e.g., the European Union, the North American free-trade area, or confederations of indigenous peoples). There also seems to be cultural play (in its serious sense) with the meaning of *real* U.S. citizenship, in which some would seek to impose additional, if invisible, requirements: whiteness, for example, or market citizenship (the ability to be a free trader).

Running through the responses to neoliberal policy I heard in many NAFTA stories, I discern a feeling that the emperor (however defined) has no clothes—or at least no reason to brag about fiscal accountability. For example, if we think about how the "globalizing economy"[3] depends on inexpensive fuel to transport goods between export process-ing zones and if we adjust for what is argued are the true costs of rely-ing on fossil fuels, then the bottom line might dramatically shift. The same would apply if we adjusted the bottom line to reflect the social costs of racialization and racism, gender inequality, the development of underdevelopment,[4] and long-term environmental degradation for short-term profits.

The most recent round of free-trade policies (not a new story in themselves) has led to an even greater concentration of wealth and, as pointed out in Chapter 3, to a resurgence of white supremacist and other meritocratic reasoning to justify the inequitable distribution of resources; it is not surprising there has been such a surge of popular movements calling for accountability of capital, transnational entities, and national governments to social rather than financial bottom lines. It will not be without a fight, but it is possible that the logic through which many have argued that a capital surplus is the polestar for guid-ing decisionmaking within and between nations is being revealed in the public sphere as just that—not "the truth" but simply another logic, which benefits some but not most of those affected by it. This is not to say that neoliberal logic does not include considerations of people's well-being.[5] What is exposed through the myriad stories told about NAFTA and the World Trade Organization and various levels of sover-eignty[6] is that there are different ways to account for and different decisions to be made about what is best for social collectivities. According to some NAFTA stories, it is increasing competitiveness, productivity, and efficiency but according to others, like Don Hugo's, it is being able to feed one's family through multiple generations.

One of the things I have found interesting, in following NAFTA stories through the first several years of its implementation, is that social movements contesting government officials' rights to negotiate such agreements in secret or at all have not just negated NAFTA and provisions of the GATT, but they have written and circulated (often on the Internet, a venue for transnational free trade of everything from commercials to political organizing to viruses) carefully conceptualized and negotiated alternatives to these policies—with social accountability as the bottom line. Public attention in the United States to the protests in Seattle and Washington, D.C., in the fall of 1999 and the spring of 2000 did not necessarily acknowledge many years of transnational meetings paralleling the negotiations of NAFTA, GATT, and other agreements/treaties. Such meetings have brought together environmental, human rights, labor, and other advocates to negotiate agreements that have solidified a transnational network of those concerned with globalizing long-term, socially accountable collectivities (without separating out economic activities as the sole means of valorization). No matter how powerful the McCarthy-like rhetoric against a social bottom line may be,[7] the numbers of people in the world who agree that we need long-term planning about livelihoods and provisions for more, not less, equitable resource distribution far surpass those who insist that a fair playing field exists in free-trading capitalist economic development.

If so many North Americans expressed concerns about NAFTA, then why did it pass? Because there is a rift between popular consensus and those who insist they represent the interests of the majority. As many have noted, the prevalence of organized alternatives to neoliberal policies—the RMALC's alternative NAFTA proposal, for example—shows that whatever social contracts national governments believed they had, in order to negotiate advantages for capital, are in question and will continue to be. Isn't the United States better off now with at least some neoliberal policies, than it has been in the past? Part of the way neoliberal logic, like any other, works is to strategically emphasize some aspects of experience and suppress others. It is very difficult, I think, for some U.S. residents to articulate at present that they are *not* thriving. Low unemployment figures (which do not continue to count those who have gone off the unemployment insurance rolls), neoliberal rhetoric of individual responsibility and thus personal rather than social failure, and other factors contribute to silencing those who are not benefiting from the miracle of the unregulated market.

There are new ways to be marginalized in the configuration of post–Cold War, transnational free-trade relations and new ways to be integrated. In 1991, I was studying the parallel development of the European Community—now the European Union—and a possible North American community and read in the *Eurobarometer,* or *European Omnibus Survey,* sent out from Brussels twice a year that citizens in Greece and Ireland, for example, tended to see themselves as marginal to the new transnational entity. Similarly, in the NAFTA stories I solicited, I was told it was silly (stated more politely, usually) even to ask about the possibility of a political North American community emerging concurrently with the economic ties forged through NAFTA. I was told this in numerous ways, in response to my asking if the person thought there could ever be a North American community similar to the European Union, some of which follow.

First, though, I will explain why I asked the question.[8] Octavio Paz wrote in 1990 that he saw membership in an American community (one in North America, one in South America) as an inevitable choice for Mexico:

> The question of a possible American Community does not depend only on nations and governments. It is the expression of a deep and widespread trend in contemporary history. We have a choice between two distinct and contradictory things: one is association; the other, historical solitude. (Paz 1990, 36)

I wondered if others saw full association, or integration, between the three nations of North America (at least) as inevitable. On one hand, President Salinas had promised to penetrate a definitional barrier and make Mexico part of the first world, joining that insider's club with the United States and Canada. On the other, the Spanish linguistic convention referred to Canadians and U.S. residents, not Mexicans, as *norteamericanos.* Did neoliberals expect cultural and linguistic realignment over the fifteen years of the Agreement's implementation? Could the imagined first-world/third-world line, which required an extraordinary act of compartmentalized imagination in the first place, really be dissolved in North America, or had the point of the Agreement all along been to realign the capital and status of a single class? After all, the very wealthy in Mexico benefited most from it—President Salinas's own family, for example. He left Mexico to live in Ireland and Canada after putting NAFTA in place, and hearsay states that his family members profited enormously from the privatization of such industries as the telephone company.

Sharing Salinas's and Paz's vision of transnational integration in perhaps a more utopian way, a Mexican architect interviewed by Steve Spellman and Calvin Aurand (members of our 1993 fieldschool team) offered his view of a North American and world community:

> Really, NAFTA is something beneficial for all three countries, isn't it? There will arrive a moment in which—and I'm talking about thirty or forty years from now—there will be a single currency in America and maybe the world. Then we won't need passports any more. We will be in a situation of complete communication. And then we in Mexico will not be forgotten like China was one hundred years ago, or in the last century when no one could enter China. We have to forget all this, and we have to be united, all countries; really, that's the only solution. That's the only way we could avoid hunger, war, and other problems. That's reality. So no one is worried about NAFTA. [author's translation]

Most of the NAFTA storytellers who were asked about the possibility of a North American community, however, did not envision it happening—not soon anyway. The first person of whom I asked this question was a businessman in Cuernavaca, Mexico, in 1993. He said that a North American community would not be created with NAFTA, if it were passed, but that it would take much, much longer than a few years to create such an entity, because it had taken the Europeans fifty years—and they were still working it out.

Also in 1993, I put this question to an undersecretary of the Labor Department in Mexico who had helped draft parts of what became the NAFTA document. He said that a very strong difference existed between what was proposed in the Agreement and what existed in the European Union. First of all, NAFTA is a commercial agreement, not a social one, and the European Community has laws concerning the protection of workers and of investments, neither of which was written into the central NAFTA document.

Cristóbal, another government undersecretary in a different department, gave a similar response in 1995 to my question about the possibility of a North American community facilitated by NAFTA:

> I think that the process of European integration is different from what is happening in North America. The European process is much more advanced because there is more cultural homogeneity, and it is a much smaller territory with much better communications, which facilitates integration. In the European Union, economic integration is much better. Under the European Economic Community's agreement, at some point in the future there is going to exist a single currency, a single passport, and government bodies that oversee the directives that are obligatory for every country. So in that sense, the NAFTA is exclusive. It does not deal with political aspects; it is only regulating an interchange of goods and investments. This is a much lesser kind of integration than in the European Union, and for the time being, I don't think that kind of integration is possible in North America; that would take a lot more time. [author's translation]

Bertha Luján, the labor activist, agreed with these government workers that there was no parallel between the European Union and a North American community (which she, too, saw as impossible). As one who helped draft a socially accountable alternative to NAFTA, however, she had a different view than the undersecretaries of the distance between the process of transnational integration in the EU and the strictly economic integration in North America. In 1995, Luján compared the European Union with the idea of a North American community, as reported earlier (see Chapter 3). She particularly noted the financial compensation and technological support for economically disadvantaged countries within the EU—not provided in NAFTA—and the attention to the rights of workers, including migrant workers.

Others emphasized cultural differences in their negative responses to the possibility of a North American community. A newspaperwoman with dual Mexican and U.S. citizenship told me in 1995:

> I don't think culturally [that a North American community] is possible, because I think the cultures are too diverse. In Canada you have the Québecois who are voting on whether or not they are staying within the nation; Canadians and Americans, somehow I don't

know why they don't get along. And Mexico is so far from those two that I don't think it is possible. It's just too much diversity.

In 1994, a Mexican sociologist who has been following that cultural diversity through plurinational, indigenous sovereignty movements in North America said this about the possibility of a community:

I don't think there will ever be one, really, because there is not the desire to get to that point. There is a theory about integration that says that when economic integration is initiated, there is the necessity to initiate other kinds of integration—political, social, and so on. I think that, to date, what has happened in North America is a limited move toward economic integration but that there will never be a formal recognition of a North American community because [those in power] do not want to plant the idea of a political project [between the three countries]. They do not want to believe in an institution like a North American community, only insofar as it facilitates trade. For example, in North America, the idea of the free circulation of workers will never be accepted. Nor will they ever legalize voting between the three countries. Nor a common currency. . . . This is to say that the goals are much more limited. They are concentrated on what is convenient for a few to do business—it is a very different project [from the European Union]. [author's translation]

After asking this question many times, I realized it was very much framed within a particular class experience. All of the above answers were from middle- to upper-class speakers, as was the question itself. Sometimes in these semistructured interviews, it would be reframed to fit the storyteller's agenda better.[9] An example was the way Dot, the middle-class Kentucky farmer, interpreted my question (about the possibility of a North American community in comparison with the European Community) as asking her to compare the notion of community itself in Europe and the United States. She said that communities are better integrated in Europe than in the United States, where one could work and starve and nobody would care. She was angry that people were not buying local farm products, and she blamed NAFTA and GATT, in part, for a general breakdown she saw in community in the United States.

Just as Don Hugo made me realize that neoliberal policies in

Mexico at the end of the twentieth century were very much related to liberal policies and popular responses to them at its beginning, Dot and others have shown that the story of NAFTA is as much about the integrity of local communities as it is about the World Trade Organization or the possibility of a North American community. The plurinational activists who have been struggling for indigenous sovereignty, for a worldwide living wage, and for other socially accountable policies to be recognized by states and transnational bodies have been saying this all along.[10] It is time for dialogue, if not harmony, between the cultural logics of fiscal and social accountability.

It is also time, as many of these storytellers have implied, to recognize the cultural implications of neoliberal economic policy on a world scale: xenophobia; the masking of inequality as individual or national "failure"; and the official promotion of simplified representations of national identities countered by new possibilities for constructing plurinational identity and for political action. NAFTA has served as a metaphor (as has the WTO) for the valorization of the financial surplus for *some* over the welfare of *all* national or world citizens, and as such, it has been met with anger and articulate alternatives. Others have seen in NAFTA the possibilities of the free market to democratize prosperity, although I think few remain who are "waiting for the miracle" (see Figure 2.1).

Responses to this symbolic NAFTA, the space of hopes and fears, have ranged from the anti-immigrant (and, I argue, white supremacist) citizen campaigns, Lights on the Border and FAIR, in the United States to the boycott organized across the California-Mexico border the week before Proposition 187 passed. Critical NAFTA stories were told far beyond the margins of newspapers and textbooks; they were told in political cartoons, youth "zines," and songs across North America. Critiques of NAFTA, both the document and the social meanings it took on in public discourse in the document's absence, did not simply say no to a neoliberal structural adjustment agenda. Just as those crafting the Agreement thought about what policies would best serve the people of North America, members of organizations critical of it and the long-term structural adjustment obligations it represented took their own call for accountability seriously. Participants in networked nongovernmental organizations opposing NAFTA proposed what they saw as viable alternatives to it, for example, calling on their nations to enforce earlier agreements such as the 1990 UN agreement on the protection of the rights of migrant workers and their families. They also proposed a

North American trade commission, parallel to the regulatory body established by the NAFTA's three signatory nation-states, which would consist of NGOs including the RMALC, the Fair Trade Campaign, the Canadian Action Network, and the Quebéc Coalition Against NAFTA. The purpose of the trade commission would be to harmonize labor and environmental standards and to be as vigilant of human rights and social welfare as the current NAFTA oversight commission is of intellectual property rights.

The North American Free Trade Agreement will not be fully implemented until 2009, and by that time it may have been amended or replaced to reflect popular calls for attention to the rights of workers and not just the rights of capital. There have already been major changes in the political landscape of North America unforeseen by NAFTA negotiators. After seven decades in power, the PRI lost the Mexican presidency in 2000 with the election of PAN candidate Vicente Fox Quesada. President Fox is known as a businessman, not as a political reformer, but he has appointed a principal critic of the NAFTA, Jorge Castañeda, his minister of foreign affairs and has called for an open border between the United States and Mexico.[11] In the United States, major public demonstrations have taken place against the World Trade Organization, the World Bank, and the International Monetary Fund,[12] which I venture to say were not necessarily household words at the time the Agreement was signed in 1992. In the case of these protests, as in the earlier NAFTA debates, the World Bank, the WTO, and the IMF served as lightning rods for public anxiety about what can seem to be a faceless and uncontrollable process of economic globalization. Through this book, I suggest that one way to address that anxiety is to construct multilocal understandings of what is glossed as "globalization," by doing collaborative, activist social documentation.

Notes

1. Novelists David Lodge and John Mortimer have written about the effects of this legislation on various public industries, and Doreen Massey (1984), a geographer, wrote about the spatial implications of restructuring in the UK.

2. See Schultz and Lavenda (2001, 127–132) for a review of the anthropological literature on play. In this case, I am thinking of play as transformative and as having serious societal consequences.

3. Globalizing economy is in quotes because I agree with those social scientists who speak of multiple processes glossed as globalization, and of the

problems with contributing to the naturalization of the category "the economy," as a separate domain of human experience. Those of us who think about culture and change are trained to compartmentalize our thinking so well that many have adopted postmodern analyses and question the big stories about identity (re-theorizing race, gender, and ethnicity, for example) while continuing to uncritically perpetuate what, through economic discourse, is still the big story of a totalizing global capitalism, even when that story contradicts our own experience. I join many others in saying this, especially Arturo Escobar in his genealogy of development discourse and his point that "anthropologists have been complicit with the rationalization of modern economics, to the extent that they have contributed to naturalizing the constructs of economy, politics, religion" and other domains of society deemed universal (Escobar 1995, 61).

4. The *development of underdevelopment* is a term that André Gunder Frank (1966) used in his articulation of dependency theory. He argued that third-world nations were not simply undeveloped economically but that they had been actively underdeveloped by "the most developed" nations. By seeing those processes of development and underdevelopment as linked, largely through colonial and neocolonial relationships of (a) the extraction of natural resources and surplus labor and (b) the suppression of infrastructure for "development," this thesis allows us to think about the consequences of capitalist globalization for everyone.

5. Milton Friedman (1962), for example, whom many see as an architect of neoliberal capitalist logic, wrote in *Capitalism and Freedom* that a market freed from government regulation would lead to a *reduction* in discrimination. He really did believe in the democratizing power of free-market capitalism.

President Ernesto Zedillo Ponce de León made a strong contemporary statement of this dimension of neoliberal capitalist logic. In his final state of the nation address, Zedillo praised both the democratization of the electoral process that had removed his own party, the PRI, from the Mexican presidency that summer and the democratizating potential of the free market. On the first point, he said:

> Mexico has completed its journey toward democracy. After a long process that has included crucial struggles by our people in the 19th and 20th centuries, today's Mexicans now have all the ingredients of a modern democracy: individual guarantees, civil liberties, a multi-party system, free and fair elections, pluralism, and now, as a result of the determination of our citizens, the alternation of parties in power. (Zedillo Ponce de León 2000, 9)

And about the democratizing potential of the free market, Zedillo had this to say:

> I see the market economy as a very powerful means for any nation to achieve progress. I believe that the freedom to participate in economic exchange is an essential freedom, one of great intrinsic value to every cit-

izen. That freedom thus has a high social value, regardless of its material import. (2000, 3)

6. By "various levels of sovereignty," I mean indigenous nations and nongovernmental organizations and also different levels of municipal and state government. I interviewed a member of Governor Wilson's cabinet in 1996, for example, who stated that "in a sense, California is the seventh largest economy in the world and you take that kind of economy and it is going to be a player and there is no way to avoid that." He spoke of California's lobbying, as a state government, regarding NAFTA and the World Trade Organization.

7. Jorge Castañeda, for example, who published an alternative to NAFTA that emphasized social accountability (and who was named President Fox's minister of foreign affairs in 2000), was "called a communist by Jesse Helms, a powerful senator of the Republican Party" in the United States (Cevallos 2000).

8. I was by no means the only anthropologist asking this sort of question. Ethnographers have been looking at attempts to construct transnational entities by studying the discourse makers directly to learn how arguments about changing sovereignty and identity are made and whether they "take" in social and political life. In the early 1990s, Cris Shore and Annabel Black, for example, were studying the European Commission—the "would-be architects of the new Europe" (Shore and Black 1992, 11). They chronicled the functionaries' systematic marketing of a European identity through the manipulation of symbols:

> Since the 1980s the EC has created the European passport, the twelve-star European flag, a standardized European driving license, and a (supranational?) anthem in the guise of Beethoven's "Ode to Joy." At international airports it has replaced customs signs, erected the EC logo next to notices welcoming passengers in the various languages of the Community, and streamlined incomers into categories of "EC nationals" and "Others." Community printing presses have published hundreds of thousands of posters, leaflets, and mass-circulation booklets informing people of their rights as Europeans. In Brussels there are "EC shops" where one can buy all the Europaraphernalia items imaginable. We now have European cities of culture, a series of new European sporting trophies, and a European postage stamp. There have even been attempts to invent a new ritual calendar, partly through the creation of "European Weeks" and the European Years of Cinema and Television, but more significantly, through the invention of Euro-holidays. (Shore and Black 1992, 11)

Shore and Black note that the considerable efforts by the European Commission "promoting the idea that Europeans are heirs to a common cultural heritage may simply add to the tide of xenophobia and racism currently sweeping through Europe" (1992, 11). I wonder, for example, how evenly the pamphlets on European citizens' rights were being distributed among recent migrants to the European Union.

9. This is one of my favorite aspects of the ethnographic process. I prefer semistructured interviewing to completely structured conversations (such as following a questionnaire) because of the ways the interviewer can be surprised by the person being interviewed and educated about how to ask questions in the future. In this project, I chose semistructured over unstructured interviews about NAFTA so that I could compare responses to a particular question whenever it came up in the conversation, as in this section.

10. Vandana Shiva, for one, said in the 1999 International Forum on Globalization, "Some of us never even *think* about the profit motive." That forum, held December 2, 1999, in Seattle, was broadcast on C-SPAN (from which I took these notes); it was organized in conjunction with the protests of the preliminary meetings of the World Trade Organization. Speakers included Ralph Nader (representing Public Citizen); Jagdish Bhagwati (Department of Economics, Columbia University); David Aaron (U.S. undersecretary of commerce for international trade); John Cavanagh (Institute for Public Studies); and R. Scott Miller (Procter and Gamble). Among the issues debated was whether the WTO was in a position to protect smaller nations from the economic power of the United States, as Jagdish Bhagwati argued, or whether it facilitated the imposition of corporate interests on unwilling citizens of communities in smaller nations, as Vandana Shiva argued—an example being the intellectual property provisions that prevent individual farmers from saving their seed.

Vandana Shiva, an environmental and human rights advocate from India, said: "The new trading system has removed the lid on limits to the profit motive." She pointed out that "for every dollar of free trade profit, there are $10 in environmental costs." Shiva called for considering products and policies on the basis of social values and for paying close attention to how words like "productivity" and "growth" are used. She said, "The WTO agreement is the ultimate climax in the wrong direction of what life is about and of how you measure growth."

Ralph Nader has consistently argued for the need to negotiate transnational trade agreements publicly, not behind closed doors, and to consider human interests over economic interests in negotiating trade. He, too, has participated in drafting alternative trade agreements. Nader has long pointed out that the public must be consulted in policy decisions at all levels. He said in this forum: "There's never been a national referendum in *any* country on the WTO."

R. Scott Miller and David Aaron agreed with Vandana Shiva that close attention to how particular words are used in trade documents is necessary, and Aaron advised those protesting WTO policies to read those policies closely and be prepared to debate specific points.

In this forum, I saw echoed many points made in Mexico by those who called for increased accountability of the national government to the citizens who would be affected by neoliberal policies.

11. "All this is part of [President Fox's] larger vision: that in twenty years' time, maybe less, maybe more, the border will no longer be a barrier, fortified by armed guards, but a mere line on a map dividing two partners in a common

market, and with much more in common than what divides the United States and Mexico today" (Weiner 2000, A12).

12. In early December 1999, a preliminary meeting of the World Trade Organization in Seattle was blocked by protests, with at least six hundred people arrested (Egan 1999; Kahn and Sanger 1999). In mid-April 2000, demonstrators from the United States and many other nations protested the joint meeting of the World Bank and the International Monetary Fund in Washington, D.C., calling for environmental and social accountability in global economic policy. The umbrella organization for that protest was the Mobilization for Global Justice, and NGOs ranging from Witness for Peace to the Rainforest Action Network to the Mexico Solidarity Network participated. Some, as in a *USA Today* editorial (2000), felt that blaming the problems of globalization on the IMF and the World Bank was inappropriate, because those institutions are in a position to attach conditions to loans that would improve human rights, labor, and environmental conditions in particular countries.

Appendix: Proposition 187

This is the text of Proposition 187, taken from the California Ballot Pamphlet, which was mailed to all registered voters in California. It was on the ballot for the November 8, 1994, general election.

This initiative measure is submitted to the people in accordance with the provision of Article II, Section 8 of the Constitution.

This initiative measure adds sections to various codes; therefore, new provisions proposed to be added are printed in *italic type* to indicate that they are new.

PROPOSED LAW

SECTION 1. Findings and Declaration.

The People of California find and declare as follows:

That they have suffered and are suffering economic hardship caused by the presence of illegal aliens in this state.

That they have suffered and are suffering personal injury and damage caused by the criminal conduct of illegal aliens in this state.

That they have a right to the protection of their government from any person or persons entering this country unlawfully.

Therefore, the People of California declare their intention to provide for cooperation between their agencies of state and local government with the federal government, and to establish a system of required notification by and between such agencies to prevent illegal aliens in the United States from receiving benefits or public services in the State of California.

SECTION 2. Manufacture, Distribution or Sale of False Citizenship or Resident Alien Documents: Crime and Punishment.

Section 113 is added to the Penal Code, to read:

113. Any person who manufactures, distributes or sells false documents to conceal the true citizenship or resident alien status of another person is guilty of a felony, and shall be punished by imprisonment in the state prison for five years or by a fine of seventy-five thousand dollars ($75,000).

SECTION 3. Use of False Citizenship or Resident Alien Documents: Crime and Punishment.

Section 114 is added to the Penal Code, to read:

114. Any person who uses false documents to conceal his or her true citizenship or resident alien status is guilty of a felony, and shall be punished by imprisonment in the state prison for five years or by a fine of twenty-five thousand dollars ($25,000).

SECTION 4. Law Enforcement Cooperation with INS.

Section 834b is added to the Penal Code, to read:

834b. (a) Every law enforcement agency in California shall fully cooperate with the United States Immigration and Naturalization Service regarding any person who is arrested if he or she is suspected of being present in the United States in violation of federal immigration laws.

(b) With respect to any such person who is arrested, and suspected of being present in the United States in violation of federal immigration laws, every law enforcement agency shall do the following:

(1) Attempt to verify the legal status of such person as a citizen of the United States, an alien lawfully admitted as a permanent resident, an alien lawfully admitted for a temporary period of time or as an alien who is present in the United States in violation of immigration laws. The verification process may include, but shall not be limited to, questioning the person regarding his or her date and place of birth, and entry into the United States, and demanding documentation to indicate his or her legal status.

(2) Notify the person of his or her apparent status as an alien who is present in the United States in violation of federal immigration laws and inform him or her that, apart from any criminal justice proceedings, he or she must either obtain legal status or leave the United States.

(3) Notify the Attorney General of California and the United States Immigration and Naturalization Service of the apparent illegal status and provide any additional information that may be requested by any other public entity.

(c) Any legislative, administrative, or other action by a city, county, or other legally authorized local governmental entity with jurisdictional boundaries, or by a law enforcement agency, to prevent or limit the cooperation required by subdivision (a) is expressly prohibited.

SECTION 5. Exclusion of Illegal Aliens from Public Social Services.

Section 10001.5 is added to the Welfare and Institutions Code, to read:

10001.5 (a) In order to carry out the intention of the People of California that only citizens of the United States and aliens lawfully admitted to the United States may receive the benefits of public social services and to ensure that all persons employed in the providing of those services shall diligently protect public funds from misuse, the provisions of this section are adopted.

(b) A person shall not receive any public social services to which he or she may be otherwise entitled until the legal status of that person has been verified as one of the following:

(1) A citizen of the United States.

(2) An alien lawfully admitted as a permanent resident.

(3) An alien lawfully admitted for a temporary period of time.

(c) If any public entity in this state to whom a person has applied for public social services determines or reasonably suspects, based upon the information provided to it, that the person is an alien in the United States in violation of federal law, the following procedures shall be followed by the public entity:

(1) The entity shall not provide the person with benefits or services.

(2) The entity shall, in writing, notify the person of his or her apparent illegal immigration status, and that the person must either obtain legal status or leave the United States.

(3) The entity shall also notify the State Director of Social Services, the Attorney General of California, and the United States Immigration and Naturalization Service of the apparent illegal status, and shall provide any additional information that may be requested by any other public entity.

SECTION 6. Exclusion of Illegal Aliens from Publicly Funded Health Care.

Chapter 1.3 (commencing with Section 130) is added to Part 1 of Division 1 of the Health and Safety Code, to read:

Chapter 1.3. Publicly-Funded Health Care Services

130. (a) In order to carry out the intention of the People of California that, excepting emergency medical care as required by federal law, only citizens of the United States and aliens lawfully admitted to the United States may receive the benefits of publicly-funded health care, and to ensure that all persons employed in the providing of those services shall diligently protect public funds from misuse, the provisions of this section are adopted.

(b) A person shall not receive any health care services from a publicly-funded health care facility, to which he or she is otherwise entitled until the legal status of that person has been verified as one of the following:

(1) A citizen of the United States.

(2) An alien lawfully admitted as a permanent resident.

(3) An alien lawfully admitted for a temporary period of time.

(c) If any publicly-funded health care facility in this state from whom a person seeks health care services, other than emergency medical care as required by federal law, determines or reasonably suspects, based upon the information provided to it, that the person is an alien in the United States in violation of federal law, the following procedures shall be followed by the facility:

(1) The facility shall not provide the person with services.

(2) The facility shall, in writing, notify the person of his or her apparent illegal immigration status, and that the person must either obtain legal status or leave the United States.

(3) The facility shall also notify the State Director of Health Services, the Attorney General of California, and the United States Immigration and Naturalization Service of the apparent illegal status, and shall provide any additional information that may be requested by any other public entity.

(d) For purposes of this section "publicly-funded health care facility" shall be defined as specified in Sections 1200 and 1250 of this code as of January 1, 1993.

SECTION 7. Exclusion of Illegal Aliens from Public Elementary and Secondary Schools.

Section 48215 is added to the Education Code, to read:

48215. (a) No public elementary or secondary school shall admit, or permit the attendance of, any child who is not a citizen of the United States, an alien lawfully admitted as a permanent resident, or a person who is otherwise authorized under federal law to be present in the United States.

(b) Commencing January 1, 1995, each school district shall verify the legal status of each child enrolling in the school district for the first time in order to ensure the enrollment or attendance only of citizens, aliens lawfully admitted as permanent residents, or persons who are otherwise authorized to be present in the United States.

(c) By January 1, 1996, each school district shall have verified the legal status of each child already enrolled and in attendance in the school district in order to ensure the enrollment or attendance only of citizens, aliens lawfully admitted as permanent residents, or persons who are otherwise authorized under federal law to be present in the United States.

(d) By January 1, 1996, each school district shall also have verified the legal status of each parent or guardian of each child referred to in subdivisions (b) and (c), to determine whether such parent or guardian is one of the following:

(1) A citizen of the United States.

(2) An alien lawfully admitted as a permanent resident.

(3) An alien admitted lawfully for a temporary period of time.

(e) Each school district shall provide information to the State Superintendent of Public Instruction, the Attorney General of California, and the United States Immigration and Naturalization Service regarding any enrollee or pupil, or parent or guardian, attending a public elementary or secondary school in the school district determined or reasonably suspected to be in violation of federal immigration laws within forty-five days after becoming aware of an apparent violation. The notice shall also be provided to the parent or legal guardian of the enrollee or pupil, and shall state that an existing pupil may not continue to attend the school after ninety calendar days from the date of the notice, unless legal status is established.

(f) For each child who cannot establish legal status in the United States, each school district shall continue to provide education for a period of ninety days from the date of the notice. Such ninety day period shall be utilized to accomplish an orderly transition to a school in the child's country of origin. Each school district shall fully cooperate in this transition effort to ensure that the educational needs of the child are best served for that period of time.

SECTION 8. Exclusion of Illegal Aliens from Public Postsecondary Educational Institutions.

Section 66010.8 is added to the Education Code, to read:

66010.8. (a) No public institution of postsecondary education shall admit, enroll, or permit the attendance of any person who is not a citizen of the United States, an alien lawfully admitted as a permanent resident in the United States, or a person who is otherwise authorized under federal law to be present in the United States.

(b) Commencing with the first term or semester that begins after January 1, 1995, and at the commencement of each term or semester thereafter, each public postsecondary educational institution shall verify the status of each person enrolled or in attendance at that institution in order to ensure the enrollment or attendance only of United States citizens, aliens lawfully admitted as permanent residents in the United States, and persons who are otherwise authorized under federal law to be present in the United States.

(c) No later than 45 days after the admissions officer of a public postsecondary educational institution becomes aware of the application, enrollment, or attendance of a person determined to be, or who is under reasonable suspicion of being, in the United States in violation of federal immigration laws, that officer shall provide that information to the State Superintendent of Public Instruction, the Attorney General of California, and the United States Immigration and Naturalization Service. The information shall also be provided to the applicant, enrollee, or person admitted.

SECTION 9. Attorney General Cooperation with the INS.

Section 53069.65 is added to the Government Code, to read:

53069.65. Whenever the state or a city, or a county, or any other legally authorized local governmental entity with jurisdictional boundaries reports the presence of a person who is suspected of being present in the United States in violation of federal immigration laws to the Attorney General of California, that report shall be transmitted to the United States Immigration and Naturalization Service. The Attorney General shall be responsible for maintaining on-going and accurate records of such reports, and shall provide any additional information that may be requested by any other government entity.

SECTION 10. Amendment and Severability.

The statutory provisions contained in this measure may not be amended by the Legislature except to further its purposes by statue passed in each house by rollcall vote entered in the journal, two-thirds of the membership concurring, or by a statute that becomes effective only when approved by the voters.

In the event that any portion of this act or the application thereof to any person or circumstance is held invalid, that invalidity shall not affect any other provision or application of the act, which can be given effect without the invalid provision or application, and to that end the provisions of this act are severable.

References

ABC News Investigative Unit. 1994. *ABC World News Tonight* story on *The Bell Curve* and the Pioneer Fund. 22 November. Transcript available from ABC News Investigative Unit, 47 West 66th Street, New York, NY, or at website <http://www.intnet.net/pub/HUMAN-RIGHTS/Pioneer.Fund.info>.

Ackerman, Bruce, and David Golove. 1995. *Is NAFTA Constitutional?* Cambridge, MA: Harvard University Press.

Acosta-Belén, Edna. 1995. Hemispheric remappings: Revisiting the concept of Nuestra América. In *Identities on the Move: Transnational Processes in North America and the Caribbean Basin.* Liliana R. Goldin, pp. 81–106. Albany, NY: Institute for Mesoamerican Studies, State University of New York–Albany.

Adams, Frank, with Myles Horton. 1975. *Unearthing Seeds of Fire: The Idea of Highlander.* Winston-Salem, NC: John F. Blair, Publisher.

Adler Hellman, Judith. 1994. *Mexican Lives.* New York: The New Press.

Alanis Patiño, Emilio. 1995. Ejercicio demográfico: Reto estadístico. *Este País* 53(3): 48–55.

Alarcón González, Diana. 1994. *Changes in the Distribution of Income in Mexico and Trade Liberalization.* Tijuana, Mexico: El Colegio de la Frontera Norte.

Alcocer V., Jorge. 1995. El "modelo" y sus fantasmas. *Proceso* 987(2 October): 45.

Alemán Alemán, Ricardo. 1995. El avance democrático ha residido básicamente en la ciudadanía: Zedillo. *La Jornada* 2 September, p. 3.

Alliance for Responsible Trade/Citizen Trade Campaign. 1992. Letter to President-elect Clinton. 15 December.

Almaguer, Tomás. 1994. *Racial Fault Lines: The Historical Origins of White Supremacy in California.* Berkeley: University of California Press.

Alvarez, R. Michael, and Tara L. Butterfield. 2000. The resurgence of nativism in California? The case of Proposition 187 and illegal immigration. *Social Science Quarterly* 81(1): 167–179.

221

Ambriz, Agustín, and Fernando Ortega Pizarro. 1995. La transnacional tele-
fónica GTE, parte medular del megaproyecto Tepoztlán-Cuernavaca; el
campo de golf es sólo la fachada. *Proceso* 984(11 September): 33–34.
Amigón, Edgar. 1995. Jubilados en plantón; piden pensión mínima de 2
salarios. *El Financiero* 8 September, p. 21.
Amit, Vered, ed. 2000. *Constructing the Field: Ethnographic Fieldwork in the
Contemporary World.* London: Routledge.
Anderson, A. L. 1999. Who's zooming who(m)? Resituating filmic representa-
tions and the decolonization of critical viewing. Lecture given at the
University of South Carolina, 16 July.
Andonaegui, Ricardo H. 1993a. No seremos agencia migratoria de EU: Andrés
Rozental. *El Día* 19 July, pp. 1, 8.
———. 1993b. El TLC no afecta la propiedad de México sobre el petróleo:
Lozoya. *El Día* 19 July, pp. 1, 3.
Annis, Sheldon. 1989. *God and Production in a Guatemalan Town.* Austin:
University of Texas Press.
Bain, George. 1988. The free flow of news information. *Maclean's* 101 (24
October): 55.
Ballinas, Víctor. 1995. En 1995, 7.7 movilizaciones por día en la ciudad. *La
Jornada* 3 October, p. 40.
Barajas, Rafael (El Fisgón). 2000. The transformative power of art: Mexico's
combat cartoonists. *NACLA Report on the Americas* 33 (6)May/June:
6–14.
———. 1993. *¡Me lleva el TLC! El tratado retratado.* Mexico City: Editorial
Grijalbo.
Barrera, Eduardo. 1996. The U.S.-Mexico border as post-NAFTA Mexico. In
Mass Media and Free Trade: NAFTA and the Cultural Industries. Ed.
Emile G. McAnany and Kenton T. Wilkinson, pp. 187–217. Austin:
University of Texas Press.
Bátiz V., Bernardo. 1993. El tratado de ayer y el de hoy. *La Jornada* 14 June.
Beaucage, Pierre. 1998. The third wave of modernization: Liberalism,
Salinismo, and indigenous peasants in Mexico. In *The Third Wave of
Modernization in Latin America: Cultural Perspectives on Neoliberalism.*
Ed. Lynne Phillips, pp. 3–27. Wilmington, DE: Scholarly Resources, Inc.
Becerril, Andrea. 1995. Barco: no ha habido diálogo ni negociación con autori-
dades. *La Jornada* 4 September, p. 42.
Behar, Ruth. 1993. *Translated Woman: Crossing the Border with Esperanza's
Story.* Boston: Beacon Press.
Behar, Ruth, and Deborah A. Gordon, eds. 1995. *Women Writing Culture.*
Berkeley: University of California Press.
Beltrán del Río, Pascal. 1995. La deuda externa mexicana creció un tercio en
este año y ya es impagable. *Proceso* 983(4 September):16–19.
Benitez, Rodolfo. 1993. Provocaría una "guerra de bloques comerciales," el
fracaso del GATT. *El Universal* 15 July, pp. 1, 4.
Berumen y Asociados S.C. 1995. Impacto de la crisis económica en los jefes de
hogar: Encuesta. *Este País* 53(3) August: 12–20.
Bickers, Chris. 1993. Price wars strike global tobacco market. *Progressive
Farmer* (September): 60.

Black, George. 1988. *The Good Neighbor: How the United States Wrote the History of Central America and the Caribbean.* New York: Pantheon Books.

Blee, Kathleen M. 1991. *Women of the Klan: Racism and Gender in the 1920s.* Berkeley: University of California Press.

Bliss, Michael. 1987. The lessons of history. *Maclean's,* 100 (19 October): 23.

Boffil Gómez, Luis A. 1995. Trece detenidos y cinco lesionados al dispersar con gas lacrimógeno una manifestación panista en Oxkutzcab. *La Jornada* 1 September, p. 9.

Bogin, Magda. 1995. Skirmishes from Mexico's "Golf War." *New York Times,* Op-Ed. sec., 8 October, E-13.

Bognanno, Mario F., and Kathryn J. Ready, eds. 1993. *The North American Free Trade Agreement: Labor, Industry, and Government Perspectives.* Westport, CT: Quorum Books.

Boletín Mexicano de la Crisis. 1995. [Publicación de las preguntas de la] Consulta Nacional por la Paz y la Democracia. 2(26 August): 43.

Bonfil Batalla, Guillermo. 1966. Conservative thought in applied anthropology: A critique. *Human Organization* 25:89–92.

Bonilla, Frank, Edwin Meléndez, Rebecca Morales, and María de los Angeles Torres, eds. 1998. *Borderless Borders: U.S. Latinos, Latin Americans, and the Paradox of Interdependence.* Philadelphia: Temple University Press.

Bonnett, Alastair. 1999. Constructions of whiteness in European and American anti-racism. In *Race, Identity, and Citizenship: A Reader.* Ed. Rodolfo D. Torres, Louis F. Mirón, and Jonathan Xavier Inda, pp. 200–218. Malden, MA: Blackwell Publishers, Inc.

Bostwick, Robert, Don Newquist, and Alan Reynolds. 1992. Job growth in North America under a NAFTA. In *The North American Free Trade Agreement: Spurring Prosperity and Stability in the Americas.* Ed. Michael G. Wilson and Wesley R. Smith, pp. 23–40. Washington, D.C.: The Heritage Foundation.

Bourdieu, Pierre. 1977. *Outline of a Theory of Practice.* Cambridge: Cambridge University Press.

Brandes, Stanley. 1988. *Power and Persuasion: Fiestas and Social Control in Rural Mexico.* Philadelphia: University of Pennsylvania Press.

Brodkin, Karen. 2000. Global capitalism: What's race got to do with it? 1998 keynote address of the American Ethnological Society meeting. *American Ethnologist* 27(2): 237–256.

———. 1998. *How Jews Became White Folks and What That Says About Race in America.* New Brunswick, NJ: Rutgers University Press.

Bueno Soria, Juan M. 1995. Política exterior, eliminada del informe presidencial. *El Financiero* 4 September, p. 74.

Calva, José Luis. 1995. Plan Nacional de Desarrollo 1995–2000; los fines, los medios, y las alternativas. *Revista Latinoamericana de Economía; Problemas del Desarrollo* 26(12): 29–55.

———. 1991. *Probables Efectos de un Tratado de Libre Comercio en el Campo Mexicano.* Mexico City: Distribuciones Fontamara, S.A.

Calzada Falcón, Fernando, and Abelardo Aníbal Gutiérrez Lara, with José

Manuel Herrera Núñez. 1992. *Un Tratado en Marcha.* Mexico City: El Nacional, S.A. de C.V.

Camacho, Carlos. 1995. La caída se inició en 1992, tras la firma del TLC. *La Jornada* 3 September.

Cameron, Duncan. 1993. Introduction. In *Canada Under Free Trade.* Ed. Duncan Cameron and Mel Watkins. Toronto: James Lorimer and Company, Publishers.

Cameron, Duncan, and Mel Watkins, eds. 1993. *Canada Under Free Trade.* Toronto: James Lorimer and Company, Publishers.

Cameron, Maxwell A., and Brian W. Tomlin. 2000. *The Making of NAFTA: How the Deal Was Done.* Ithaca, NY: Cornell University Press.

Cano, Arturo. 1995. Tiempo de estrenos. Enfoque sección de *la Reforma,* 10 September, p.13–14.

Cárdenas, Jaime. 1995. Nuevo o viejo federalismo. *Epoca* 11 September, p. 18–19.

Carmichael, Elizabeth, and Chloë Sayer. 1992. *The Skeleton at the Feast: The Day of the Dead in Mexico.* Austin: University of Texas Press, in cooperation with British Museum Press.

Carrásco Araizaga, Jorge. 1993. Yupitecas y tecnoburócratas. *El Financiero* 2 July.

Carrásco Araizaga, Jorge, and David Torres. 1992. Free-trade double-hype. *San Francisco Bay Guardian.* 21 November.

Carreño Figueras, José. 1993. Refuta Clinton el fallo del juez Richey contra el TLC. *El Universal* 21 July, pp. 1, 20.

Carrizales, David, Carlos A. Gutiérrez, Livia Díaz, Emanuel Salazar, and Alberto Espinosa. 1995. El Barzón publicará un periódico nacional, informó. *La Jornada* 28 September, p. 56.

Castañeda, Jorge G. 1995. *The Mexican Shock: Its Meaning for the U.S.* New York: The New Press.

———. 1993. *La Casa por la Ventana: México y América Latina Después de la Guerra Fría.* Mexico City: Cal y Arena.

Césaire, Aimé. 1972. *Discourse on Colonialism.* New York: Monthly Review Press.

César López, Julio. 1995. La consulta nacional en un paraje zapatista: unanimidad. *Proceso* 982(28 August): 37–38.

Cevallos, Diego. 2000. Politics—Mexico/U.S. relations to change little under Bush/Fox. Mexico City: Inter Press. Service, 15 December. Online. LEXIS-NEXIS® Academic Universe. 1/11/01.

Chávez, Elías. 1995. Avizora Zedillo un nuevo país, con democracia, crecemiento, ahorro, empleo, justicia, paz, seguridad . . . y todo lo necesario para la felicidad. *Proceso* 4 September, p. 6–15.

Chávez, Victor, Sergio Leñero, and Víctor González. 1995. 2 de octubre: vandalismo, quema de autobuses y 200 detenidos. *El Financiero* 3 October, p. 26.

Chavolla Nava, Gustavo. 1993. Se ratificará el TLC por la globalización comercial: Sinclair. *El Universal* 21 July, p. 3.

Citizen's Forum on Canada's Future. 1991. *Report to the People and Government of Canada.* Ottawa: Canadian Government Publishing Center.

Coffey, Peter. 1987. Co-operation between the European Economic Community (EEC) and Latin America—with special reference to Mexico: A European view. In *The EEC and Mexico*. Ed. Peter Coffey and Miguel S. Wionczek, pp. 29–36. Dordrecht: Martinus Nijhoff Publishers.

El Colegio de la Frontera Norte y la Universidad Autónoma de Ciudad Juárez. 1992. *Economia Fronteriza y Libre Comercio*, Vol. I. Jorge A. Bustamante, prologue, and Joseph Hodara, introduction. Mexico: El Colegio de la Frontera Norte y la Universidad Autónoma de Ciudad Juárez.

Collins, Patricia Hill. 2000. *Black Feminist Thought: Knowledge, Consciousness, and the Politics of Empowerment*. 2nd ed. New York: Routledge.

Collins, Richard. 1990. *Culture, Communication, and National Identity: The Case of Canadian Television*. Toronto: University of Toronto Press.

Congress of the Thirteen United States of America. 1776. *The Declaration of Independence*. Philadelphia.

Contracting Parties to the General Agreement on Tariffs and Trade. 1949. *The Attack on Trade Barriers: A Progress Report on the Operation of the General Agreement on Tariffs and Trade, from January 1948 to August 1949*. Geneva: Interim Commission for the International Trade Organization.

Cornejo, Jorge Alberto. 1995. Con la ley de inmigración de EU habría una frontera militarizada. *La Jornada* 21 September, p. 42.

Correa, Guillermo. 1995. Organizaciones independientes proponen reformas y adiciones a la Constitución para reconocer Regiones Autónomas Indias. *Proceso* 984(11 September): 18–24.

Croucher, Sheila L. 1997. *Imagining Miami: Ethnic Politics in a Postmodern World*. Charlottesville: University Press of Virginia.

Cruz, Noé, and Raúl Rodríguez. 1995. El proyecto de un Club de Golf polariza a Tepoztlán. *Epoca* 11 September, p. 23–24.

Cruz Serrano, Noé. 1995. Infraestructura en mal estado, obstáculo para el desarrollo económico. *Epoca* (4 September): 26–31.

Daly, John. 1990. A triple threat? Canada is pushing ahead with three-way free trade with the United States and Mexico. *Maclean's* 103 (8 October 8): 48–49.

Dávila-Villers, David R., ed. 1998. *NAFTA on Second Thoughts: A Plural Evaluation*. New York: University Press of America.

de Beauvoir, Simone. 1999. Woman as other. In *Social Theory: The Multicultural and Classic Readings*. Ed. Charles Lemert, pp. 337–339. Boulder, CO: Westview Press.

de la Peña, Guillermo. 1981. *A Legacy of Promises: Agriculture, Politics, and Ritual in the Morelos Highlands of Mexico*. Austin: University of Texas Press.

Delgado, Rene. 1995. Ni informe, ni mensaje. *Reforma,* 2 September, p. 8A.

Delgado, Richard. 1999. Citizenship. In *Race, Identity, and Citizenship: A Reader*. Ed. Rodolfo D. Torres, Louis F. Mirón, and Jonathan Xavier Inda, pp. 247–252. Malden, MA: Blackwell Publishers, Inc.

de Marrais, Kathleen Bennett, ed. 1998. *Inside Stories: Qualitative Research Reflections*. Mahwah, NJ: Lawrence Erlbaum Associates, Publishers.

De Mateo, Fernando. 1987. Mexico and the European Economic Community: Trade and investment. In *The EEC and Mexico*. Ed. Peter Coffey and Miguel S. Wionczek, pp. 3–28. Dordrecht: Martinus Nijhoff Publishers.

DePalma, Anthony. 1995. In Mexico, hunger and woe in crisis; dashed middle-class hope and disaster for the poor. *New York Times* 15 January, pp. Y-1, Y-7.

de Tocqueville, Alexis. 1838. *Democracy in America.* 2nd ed. New York: G. Adlard.

El Día. 1994. Expresa México a EU su preocupación por el clima antimexicano de la 187. Enviado por Notimex. 29 October, p. 3.

Domínguez, Virginia R. 1986. *White by Definition: Social Classification in Creole Louisiana.* New Brunswick: Rutgers University Press.

Douglas, Mary. 1986. *How Institutions Think.* Syracuse, NY: Syracuse University Press.

Dreiling, Michael. 1997. Remapping North American environmentalism: Contending visions and divergent practices in the fight over NAFTA. *Capitalism, Nature, Socialism* 8(4): 65–98.

Dreiling, Michael, and Ian Robinson. 1998. Union responses to NAFTA in the U.S. and Canada: Explaining intra- and international variation. *Mobilization: An International Journal* 3(2): 163–184.

Dyson, Michael Eric. 1999. The labor of whiteness, the whiteness of labor, and the perils of whitewashing. In *Race, Identity, and Citizenship. A Reader.* Ed. Rodolfo D. Torres, Louis F. Mirón, and Jonathan Xavier Inda, pp. 219–224. Malden, MA: Blackwell Publishers, Inc.

Eco, Umberto. 1986. Language, power, force. In *Travels in Hyperreality.* Trans. William Weaver, pp. 239–255. New York: Harcourt, Brace, Jovanovich.

The Economist. 1993. NAFTA: The showdown. 13–19 November, pp. 23–26.

El Economista. 1993. Equivocados quienes piensan que se cederá soberanía ante el TLC: Lozoya. *El Economista* 19 July, p. 34.

Egan, Timothy. 1999. Free trade takes on free speech. *New York Times* Sec. 4, pp. 1, 5.

Enciso, Angélica. 1995. Suspenden el club de golf en Tepoztlán: Incompleta, la autorización de uso del suelo: Azuela y Quadri. *La Jornada* 9 September, pp. 1, 16.

Encuentro Nacional de Organizaciones Ciudadanas. 1995. *Carta de los Derechos Ciudadanos.* Mexico City: Encuentro Nacional de Organizaciones Ciudadanas.

Erfani, Julie A. 1995. *The Paradox of the Mexican State: Rereading Sovereignty from Independence to NAFTA.* Boulder, CO: Lynne Rienner Publishers.

Escobar, Arturo. 1995. *Encountering Development: The Making and Unmaking of the Third World.* Princeton, NJ: Princeton University Press.

Excelsior. 1995. Construiré un muro entre EU y México, si gano: Buchanan. 11 September, p. 5-A.

Executive Office of the President, United States of America. 1993. "North American Free Trade Agreement Between the Government of the United

States of America, the Government of Canada, and the Government of the United Mexican States." Vols. I-V.

Fanon, Frantz. 1991. *Black Skin, White Masks.* Preface by Jean-Paul Sartre. Trans. Charles Markman. New York: Grove Press.

Farmer, Paul. 1992. *AIDS and Accusation: Haiti and the Geography of Blame.* Berkeley: University of California Press.

Fernández de Castro, Rafael, Mónica Verea Campos, and Sidney Weintraub, eds. 1993. *Sectoral Labor Effects of North American Free Trade/TLC: Los Impactos Laborales en Sectores Clave de las Economías.* Austin, TX, and Mexico City: U.S.-Mexican Policy Studies Program, The University of Texas at Austin; El Centro de Investigaciones Sobre Estados Unidos de América, Universidad Nacional Autónoma de México.

Fernández Santillan, José. 1995. La crisis económica y política en México. *Este País* 54(2): 35–42.

Ferreyra, Carlos. 1993. Será presentado en otoño ante el Congreso: Brown. *El Universal* 21 July, pp. 1, 20.

El Financiero. 1995a. México pagará y lo hará a tiempo, asegura Camdessus. *El Financiero,* 2 October, p. 4.

———. 1995b. Reporte semanal: el primer informe de Zedillo. 4 September, p. 6A.

———. 1995c. Inicia EU la construcción del muro antiinmigrantes. *El Financiero* 14 September, p. 43.

Finnigan, David. 1995. Hate crimes up since Proposition 187, group says. *National Catholic Reporter* 29 December, 32(10):6(1).

Fischel, Jack. 1995. Strange "bell" fellows. *Commonweal* 122(10 February), 16–17.

Fischer, Michael M. J. 1999. Worlding cyberspace: Toward a critical ethnography in time, space, and theory. In *Critical Anthropology Now: Unexpected Contexts, Shifting Constituencies, Changing Agendas.* Ed. George E. Marcus, pp. 245–304. Santa Fe, NM: School of American Research Press.

Fleischmann, Jessica. 1992. The U.S.-Mexican Border in the U.S. Press, 1980–1992: Image, Identification, and Identity. M.A. thesis, University of Chicago.

Flores, Richard. 1995. Alamo images and the birth of "otherness." Paper presented at the annual meeting of the American Anthropological Association, Washington, D.C., November.

Flores Aguilar, Verónica. 1995. Está despertando la conciencia del mexicano: Miguel León-Portilla. *El Día* 4 October, p. 23.

Foley, Douglas E., with Clarice Mota, Donald E. Post, and Ignacio Lozano. 1988. *From Peones to Politicos: Class and Ethnicity in a South Texas Town, 1900–1987.* Austin: University of Texas Press.

Foucault, Michel. 1980. *Power/Knowledge: Selected Interviews and Other Writings, 1972–1977.* Ed. Colin Gordon; trans. Colin Gordon, Leo Marshall, John Mepham, and Kate Soper. New York: Pantheon Books.

Frank, André Gunder. 1966. The development of underdevelopment. *Monthly Review* 18(4):17–31.

Frank, Dana. 1999. *Buy American: The Untold Story of Economic Nationalism.*
New York: Beacon Press.

Fraser, Steven, ed. 1995. *The Bell Curve Wars: Race, Intelligence, and the
Future of America.* New York: Basic Books.

Freire, Paulo. 1984. *Pedagogy of the Oppressed.* Trans. Myra Bergman Ramos.
1968. Reprint, New York: Continuum.

———. 1973. *Education for Critical Consciousness.* New York: Continuum.

Friedman, Milton. 1962. *Capitalism and Freedom.* Chicago: The University of
Chicago Press.

Friedman, Thomas L. 1993. Clinton maintains U.S. standing rides on trade
accord. *New York Times* 7 November, pp. A-1, 12.

García, Brigida, and Rosa Maria Rubalcava. 1995. Empleo y mercado de trabajo: Desigualdad de ingresos y pobreza. *Este País* 54(17): 1–11.

García Canclini, Néstor. 1993. *Transforming Modernity: Popular Culture in
Mexico.* Austin: University of Texas Press.

García Canclini, Néstor, coordinador. 1996. *Culturas en Globalización:
América Latina–Europa–Estados Unidos: Libre Comercio e Integración.*
Caracas, Venezuela: Editorial Nueva Sociedad (CNCA/CLACSO).

García Colín, Margarita. 1995. Primer informe de gobierno: la promesa de la
esperanza. *Epoca* 4 September, p. 10–12.

Garduño Espinosa, Roberto, and Angélica Enciso. 1995. Zapata cabalga de
nuevo, aseguran en Morelos: Día de fiesta y de protesta vivió ayer
Tepoztlán. *La Jornada* 11 September, p. 45.

Gibson-Graham, J. K. 1996. *The End of Capitalism (as we knew it): A Feminist
Critique of Political Economy.* Cambridge, MA: Blackwell Publishers.

Gillespie, Ed, and Bob Schellhas, eds. 1994. *Contract with America: The Bold
Plan by Rep. Newt Gingrich, Rep. Dick Armey and the House Republicans
to Change the Nation.* New York: Times Books.

Gil Olmos, José. 1995. El EZLN fuerza política, 47% en la consulta juvenil. *La
Jornada* 17 September, p. 7.

Giménez, Gilberto. 1993. Apuntes para una teoría de la identidad nacional.
Sociológica 8(21):13–29.

Gluckman, Max, ed. 1962. *Essays on the Ritual of Social Relations.*
Manchester: Manchester University Press.

Goldberg, David Theo, ed. 1990. *Anatomy of Racism.* Minneapolis: University
of Minnesota Press.

Goldin, Liliana R. 1995. Transnational identities: The search for analytic tools.
In *Identities on the Move: Transnational Processes in North America and
the Caribbean Basin.* Ed. Liliana R. Goldin, pp. 1–11. Albany, NY:
Institute for Mesoamerican Studies, State University of New York.

Gómez, Laura, Ricardo Alemán, and José Antonio Román. 1995. Advierte Frei
sobre los riesgos de mantener los actuales índices de pobreza en América
Latina. *La Jornada* 8 September, p. 18.

Gómez-Hermosillo, Rogelio. 1995. Una oportunidad para la sociedad civil:
Encuentro nacional de organizaciones ciudadanas. *Rostros y Voces de la
Sociedad Civil* (July–August): 4–6.

Gómez-Quiñones, Juan. 1994. Inmigración y cambio cultural. La participación
cívica, la sindicalización y la educación. En *Mitos en las relaciones*

México—Estados Unidos. Ed. Esther Schumacher, pp. 329–398. Mexico City, Secretaría de Relaciones Exteriores, Fondo de Cultura Económica.

Gordon, Charles. 1986. Trading in the Canadian identity. *Maclean's* 99 (7 July): 27.

Gould, Stephen Jay. 1996. *The Mismeasure of Man.* Rev. ed. New York: W. W. Norton and Company.

Gouvernement du Québec. 1993. *Québec and the North American Free Trade Agreement.* Quebec: Ministère des Affaires Internationales.

Gramsci, Antonio. 1971. *Selections from the Prison Notebooks.* Ed. and trans. Quintin Hoare and Geoffrey Nowell Smith. New York: International Publishers.

Greider, William. 1997. *One World, Ready or Not: The Manic Logic of Global Capitalism.* New York: Simon and Schuster.

Grindal, Bruce, and Frank Salamone, eds. 1995. *Bridges to Humanity: Narratives on Anthropology and Friendship.* Prospect Heights, IL: Waveland Press, Inc.

Guajardo Touché, Ricardo. 1995. La lección de las crisis. *Ejecutivos de Finanzas* 8(August): 29–33.

Guerrero, Francisco. 1995. Morelenses advierten que se harán justicia por su propia mano. *La Jornada* 8 September, p. 21.

Guerrero Chiprés, Salvador. 1995. La extrema pobreza, exacerbada por la crisis. *La Jornada* 28 September, p. 25.

Guerrero Garro, Francisco. 1995. Liberan a los 6 funcionarios del gobierno retenidos en Tepoztlán. *La Jornada* 6 September.

Gupta, Akhil. 1992. The song of the nonaligned world: Transnational identities and the reinscription of space in late capitalism. *Cultural Anthropology* 7(1): 63–79.

Gutiérrez Oropeza, Manuel. 1995. En el golf se juega empleo vs. ecología. *Mira* 18 September, p. 9.

Gutmann, Matthew C. 1998. For whom the Taco Bells toll: Popular responses to NAFTA south of the border. *Critique of Anthropology* 18(3): 297–315.

Handelman, Don. 1990. *Models and Mirrors: Towards an Anthropology of Public Events.* Cambridge: Cambridge University Press.

Harrison, Faye V. 1997a. Anthropology as an agent of transformation: Introductory comments and queries. In *Decolonizing Anthropology: Moving Further Toward an Anthropology for Liberation.* Ed. Faye V. Harrison, pp. 1–15. Arlington, VA: Association of Black Anthropologists and the American Anthropological Association.

————. 1997b. The gendered politics and violence of structural adjustment. In *Situated Lives: Gender and Culture in Everyday Life.* Ed. Louise Lamphere, Helena Ragoné, and Patricia Zavella, pp. 451–468. New York: Routledge.

————. 1995. The persistent power of "race" in the cultural and political economy of racism. *Annual Review of Anthropology* 24:47–74.

Hartigan, John, Jr. 1999. Establishing the fact of whiteness. In *Race, Identity, and Citizenship: A Reader.* Ed. Rodolfo D. Torres, Louis F. Mirón, and Jonathan Xavier Inda, pp. 183–199. Malden, MA: Blackwell Publishers, Inc.

Henríquez, Elio, and Néstor Martínez. 1995. Marcos: diálogo sin el gobierno. *La Jornada* 1 October, pp. 1, 6.

Herbert, Bob. 1996. Affront to black people. *New York Times* New York late ed., 12 February, A-15.

Heredia, Carlos. 1993. El TLC y el petate del muerto. *Cemos Memoria* (July): 24–28.

Heredia, Carlos A., and Mary E. Purcell. 1995. La polarización de la sociedad mexicana: Una visión desde la base de las políticas de ajuste económico del Banco Mundial. *Este País* 54(3): 2–26.

Hernández, Evangelina, and David Aponte. 1993. TLC, instrumento para el desarrollo fronterizo, afirman Colosio y Brown. *La Jornada* 15 July, p. 17.

Herrnstein, Richard J., and Charles Murray. 1994. *The Bell Curve: Intelligence and Class Structure in American Life.* New York: Free Press.

Hindley, Jane. 1996. Towards a pluricultural nation: The limits of *indigenismo* and Article 4. In *Dismantling the Mexican State?* Ed. Rob Aitken, Nikki Craske, Gareth A. Jones, and David E. Stansfield, pp. 225–243. London: Macmillan Press Ltd.

Holzinger, Albert G., and John L. Manzella. 1992. NAFTA by the numbers. *Nation's Business* (December): 25.

hooks, bell. 1992. *Black Looks: Race and Representation.* Boston: South End Press.

Hossfeld, Karen J. 1990. "Their logic against them": Contradictions in sex, race, and class in Silicon Valley. In *Women Workers and Global Restructuring.* Ed. Kathryn Ward, pp. 149–178. Ithaca, NY: ILR Press.

Howard, Leslie. 1997. Thinking globally, acting locally: The strategies of sub-national and transnational actors in Mexico and Canada in response to NAFTA. Paper presented at the Latin American Studies Association meeting, Guadalajara, Mexico, April.

Huchim, Eduardo. 1992. *TLC: Hacia un País Distinto.* Mexico City: Nueva Imagen.

Hurtado, Aída. 1999. The trickster's play: Whiteness in the subordination and liberation process. In *Race, Identity, and Citizenship: A Reader.* Ed. Rodolfo D. Torres, Louis F. Mirón, and Jonathan Xavier Inda, pp. 225–243. Malden, MA: Blackwell Publishers, Inc.

Hymes, Dell, ed. 1969. *Reinventing Anthropology.* New York: Random House.

Icela Rodríguez, Rosa, and Georgina Saldierna. 1995. Rebasó expectativas la repuesta juvenil a la consulta del EZLN. *La Jornada* 14 September, p. 14.

Inclán, Isabel. 1995. Integrarse al PRD o ser partido, encrucijada para el EZLN: Meyer. *El Financiero* 8 September, p. 38.

Jiménez Trejo, Pilar. 1995. Un problema ecológico que se volvió político. *Boletín Mexicano de la Crisis* 1(7): 16–20.

Johnson, John J. 1980. *Latin America in Caricature.* Austin: University of Texas Press.

Johnson, Kevin R. 1997. The new nativism: Something old, something new, something borrowed, something blue. In *Immigrants Out! The New Nativism and the Anti-immigrant Impulse in the United States.* Ed. Juan F. Perea, pp. 165–189. New York: New York University Press.

La Jornada. 1995. Más de 200 mil participaron en la consulta juvenil. 23 September, p. 13.

————. 1993. Sincronía en la relación comercial de México y España: Javier Gómez. 20 July, p. 24.

Kahn, Joseph, and David E. Sanger. 1999. Seattle talks on trade end with stinging blow to U.S.: Rebellions and a deadlock block an effort by Clinton for more liberalization. *New York Times* 5 December, sec. A1, p. 14.

Kearney, Michael. 1995. Neither modern nor traditional: Personal identities in global perspective. In *Identities on the Move: Transnational Processes in North America and the Caribbean Basin*. Ed. Liliana R. Goldin, pp. 69–79. Albany, NY: Institute for Meso-american Studies, State University of New York, Albany.

Kerr, William A. 1986. Creating a free trade illusion: Some economic facades in the Canada-U.S. Reciprocity Treaty of 1854. *British Journal of Canadian Studies* 1(2): 323–324.

Kingsolver, Ann E. 2000. Strategic alterity in neoliberal rhetoric, labor, and land use: Mexican and U.S.A. examples. In *Proceedings of the Perspectives on Race, Gender, and Social Class Conference*. Ed. Charles Menzies. Vancouver: University of British Columbia.

————. 1993. Passing the word on NAFTA: Policy and "the public" in Mexican, U.S., and Canadian contexts. Paper presented at the annual meeting of the American Anthropological Association, Washington, D.C., November.

————. 1992. Contested livelihoods: "Placing" one another in "Cedar," Kentucky. *Anthropological Quarterly* 65(3): 128–136.

————. 1991. Tobacco, Toyota, and subaltern development discourses: Constructing livelihoods and community in rural Kentucky. Ph.D. diss., University of Massachusetts–Amherst.

Kingsolver, Ann E., and Miguel Morayta M. 1995. Contextual borders: Two interpretations of identity and modernity in Morelos, Mexico. Paper presented [in English and Spanish] at the meetings of the American Ethnological Society, Austin, TX, April.

Klahn, Norma. 1994. Writing the border: The languages and limits of representation. *Travesia: Journal of Latin American Cultural Studies* 3(1&2).

Klor de Alva, J. Jorge. 1999. Cipherspace: Latino identity past and present. In *Race, Identity, and Citizenship: A Reader*. Ed. Rodolfo D. Torres, Louis F. Mirón, and Jonathan Xavier Inda, pp. 169–180. Malden, MA: Blackwell Publishers, Inc.

Krieger, Emilio. 1995. Régimen constitucional para los indígenas de México. *Excelsior* 15 August, pp. 25, 6-A.

Lamphere, Louise, Helena Ragoné, and Patricia Zavella, eds. 1997. *Situated Lives: Gender and Culture in Everyday Life*. New York: Routledge.

Lane, Charles. 1994. The tainted sources of "The Bell Curve." *New York Review of Books* 41(1 December): 14–19.

Lappé, Frances Moore, and Joseph Collins. 1977. Why can't people feed themselves? In *Food First: Beyond the Myth of Scarcity*, pp. 99–111. New York: Ballantine Books.

Laurell, Asa Cristina. 1995. La política social del neoliberalismo mexicano. *Ciudades* 26(April–May): 3–8.

LeCompte, Margaret D., Jean J. Schensul, Margaret R. Weeks, and Merrill Singer. 1999. *Researcher Roles and Research Partnerships.* Walnut Creek, CA: Altamira Press.

Limón, José E. 1994. *Dancing with the Devil: Society and Cultural Poetics in Mexican-American South Texas.* Madison: University of Wisconsin Press.

Lino Ramos, Manuel. 1995. Elevar la calidad del sistema educativo, esencial para mantener nuestra soberanía: De la Madrid. *Excelsior* 12 September, p. 17A.

Lins Ribeiro, Gustavo. 1995. Ethnic segmentation of the labor market and the "work site animal": Fragmentation and reconstruction of identities within the world system. In *Articulating Hidden Histories: Exploring the Influence of Eric R. Wolf.* Ed. Jane Schneider and Rayna Rapp, pp. 336–350. Berkeley: University of California Press.

Lira, Carmen. 1995. No pedimos a la gente que crea en nosotros, sino que haga algo nuevo, que nos use. Entrevista con el Subcomandante Marcos del EZLN. *La Jornada* 27 September, p. 10–11.

Locke, John. 1689. *Second Treatise of Government.* Ed. Richard Cox. Reprint, Arlington Heights, IL: Harlan Davidson, Inc., 1981.

Loeb, Hamilton, and Michael Owen, eds. 1992. *North American Free Trade Agreement: Summary and Analysis.* Prepared by the firm Paul, Hastings, Janofsky and Walker. Times Mirror Books.

Lomas, Emilio. 1993. Comparte México el desafío de América Latina: Carlos Salinas. *La Jornada,* sec. El País, 14 July, pp. 10–11.

Lomnitz, Claudio. 2000. Passion and banality in Mexican history: The presidential persona. In *The Collective and the Public in Latin America: Cultural Identities and Political Order.* Ed. Luis Roniger and Tamar Herzog, pp. 238–256. Brighton: Sussex Academic Press.

Lomnitz-Adler, Claudio. 1992a. Concepts for the study of regional culture. In *Mexico's Regions: Comparative History and Development.* Ed. Eric Van Young, pp. 59–89. San Diego, CA: Center for U.S.-Mexican Studies, University of California–San Diego.

———. 1992b. *Exits from the Labyrinth: Culture and Ideology in the Mexican National Space.* Berkeley: University of California Press.

Luccisano, Lucy. 1995. A comparison between the organization of philanthropy in the context of neoliberalism: Mexico and Canada case studies. Paper presented in the Centro de Investigaciones Sobre América del Norte, UNAM, Mexico City, August 30.

Lutkehaus, Nancy C. 1995. *Zaria's Fire: Engendered Moments in Manam Ethnography.* Durham, NC: Carolina Academic Press.

Maclean's. 1988. Bow to culture: Four key exceptions under the act. 101 (21 November): FT21.

Magú. 1995. De un grito desaparecieron cuatro héroes pátrios. *El Papá del Ahuizote* 12 October, p. 4.

Marcus, George E. 1999. Critical anthropology now: An introduction. In *Critical Anthropology Now: Unexpected Contexts, Shifting Constituencies,*

Changing Agendas. Ed. George E. Marcus, pp. 3–28. Santa Fe, NM: School of American Research Press.

Martin, Emily. 1994. *Flexible Bodies: Tracking Immunity in American Culture—From the Days of Polio to the Age of AIDS.* Boston: Beacon Press.

Martinez Olais, Heliodoro. 1995. Retienen 9 mil tepoztecos a cuatro funcionarios del Gobierno de Morelos. *El Día* 4 September, p. 12.

Marx, Karl. 1978. The German ideology. In *The Marx-Engels Reader.* 2nd ed. Ed. Robert C. Tucker, pp. 146–200. New York: W. W. Norton and Company.

Marx, Karl, and Frederick Engels. 1848. *Manifesto of the Communist Party.* Reprint, Peking: Foreign Languages Press, 1975.

Massey, Doreen. 1984. *Spatial Divisions of Labor: Social Structures and the Geography of Production.* New York: Methuen.

Massieu Trigo, Yolanda. 1995. Viabilidad de la transición de la vía armada a la vía pacífica. *Forum* 34(January): 25–27.

Mayer, Frederick W. 1998. *Interpreting NAFTA: The Science and Art of Political Analysis.* New York: Columbia University Press.

Maza, Enrique. 1995. Primer Informe de Zedillo: cifras del pasado, sin conexión con el presente. *Proceso* 984(11 September): 39–42.

Mehler, Barry. 1988. Rightists on the rights panel. *Nation* 246(May): 640–642.

Memmi, Albert. 1991. *Colonizer and the Colonized.* Expanded ed. Introduction by Jean-Paul Sartre. Boston: Beacon Press.

Menchaca, Martha. 1995. *The Mexican Outsiders: A Community History of Marginalization and Discrimination in California.* Austin: University of Texas Press.

Mentado Contreras, Pedro. 1995. El desempleo bancario, otra "piedra en el zapato." *Epoca* (4 September): 47.

Millán Núñez, Jaime, and Norma Z. Pérez Vences. 1995. Exito, si más del 50% se adhiere al ADE: Madariaga. *Epoca* (4 September): 44–46.

Miller, Adam. 1994. Academia's dirty secret: Professors of hate. *Rolling Stone,* Fall college ed., 20 October, 106–108, 110–114.

Mills, Charles W. 1997. *The Racial Contract.* Ithaca, NY: Cornell University Press.

Mira. 1995 Educación básica para grupos indígenas. 11 September, p. 24–25.

Moisés Beltrán, Jesús. 1995. Los derechos laborales y la protección ambiental en las negociaciones del Tratado de Libre Comercio de América del Norte. *Frontera Norte* 7(14): 81–94.

Monroy Aguirre, Hilario. 1995. Ceremonia sencilla y republicana en el Zócalo. *Uno más uno* 17 September, p. 7.

Monroy Gómez, Mario B. 1995a. *Los Saldos de la Crisis.* Mexico City: Servicios Informativos Procesados, A.C.

———. 1995b. Un buen negocio. La otra cara de la crisis. *Rostros y Voces de la Sociedad Civil* (July–August): 16–20.

———. 1993. *¿Socios? ¿Asociados? ¿En sociedad? Asimetrias entre Canada, EEUU, México.* Mexico City: Servicios Informativos Procesados, A.C.

Monsiváis, Carlos. 1995a. Aproximaciones y reintegros: la repartición de poderes. *El Financiero* 2 September, p. 3.

―――. 1995b. Aproximaciones y reintegros: la consulta y los consultados. *El Financiero* 10 September, p. 26.

Montero, Ernesto. 1995. Tepoztecos se resisten a convertirse en servidumbre de multinacionales. *El Día* 5 September, p.12.

Mora Tavares, Eduardo. 1995. Tomará tiempo la recuperación de México: Estudio de la OCDE sobre la crisis económica. *Epoca* 2 October, pp. 54–56.

Morales, Sonia. 1995. Ambas partes, rectoria y excluidos, aflojan, ceden, conceden y se avizora la solución. *Proceso* 987(2 October): 10–19.

Morales, Josefina, and Elvira Concheiro. 1995. Una crisis en otra. *Revista Latinoamericana de Economía y Problemas del Desarrollo* 26(102): 255–273.

Morquecho, Gaspar, Raúl García, Manuel Enríquez, *La Jornada de Oriente,* Gerardo Rico, David Carrizales, Rubén Villalpando, Carlos Camacho, Antonio González Vázquez, Federico Velio Ortega, and Alejandra Gudiño. 1995. Conmemoraron en varios estados la matanza de Tlatelolco. *La Jornada* 3 October, p. 23.

Myerson, Allen R. 1995. Has the U.S. got a horse for you: Mexico. *New York Times* 22 January, p. E-3.

Nader, Ralph. 1993. Introduction: Free trade and the decline of democracy. In *The Case Against Free Trade: GATT, NAFTA, and the Globalization of Corporate Power,* pp. 1–12. San Francisco, CA: Earth Island Press.

Nader, Ralph, William Greider, Margaret Atwood, Vandana Shiva, Mark Ritchie, Wendell Berry, Jerry Brown, Herman Daly, Lori Wallach, Thea Lee, Martin Khor, David Phillips, Jorge Castañeda, Carlos Heredia, David Morris, and Jerry Mander. 1993. *The Case Against Free Trade: GATT, NAFTA, and the Globalization of Corporate Power.* San Francisco, CA: Earth Island Press.

Nájera-Ramírez, Olga. 1997. *La Fiesta de los Tastoanes: Critical Encounters in Mexican Festival Performance.* Albuquerque: University of New Mexico Press.

Narayan, Kirin. 1995. Shared stories. In *Bridges to Humanity.* Ed. Bruce Grindal and Frank Salamone, pp. 87–98. Prospect Heights, IL: Waveland Press, Inc.

Nasar, Sylvia. 1995. A prophet of financial doom who was right. *New York Times* 22 January, p. F-8.

Nash, June. 1992. Interpreting social movements: Bolivian resistance to economic conditions imposed by the International Monetary Fund. *American Ethnologist* 19(2): 275–293.

New York Times. 1995. Some European countries withheld Mexican aid. Reported in the *Santa Cruz Sentinel* 3 February, p. B-10.

Notimex (news service). 1993. El TLC y los paralelos deben estar antes del 15 de diciembre: Kantor. *La Jornada* 14 July, p. 37.

O'Beirne, Kate, and Senator John McCain. 1992. Improving America's global competitiveness under a NAFTA. In *The North American Free Trade Agreement: Spurring Prosperity and Stability in the Americas.* Ed. Michael

G. Wilson and Wesley R. Smith, pp. 73–77. Washington, D.C.: The Heritage Foundation.

Office of the U.S. Trade Representative. 1992a. *Overview: The North American Free Trade Agreement.* Pamphlet distributed by the Office of the U.S. Trade Representative, 600 17th Street, NW, Washington, D.C. 20506. August.

————. 1992b. *Myths and Realities: The North American Free Trade Agreement.* Pamphlet distributed by the Office of the U.S. Trade Representative, 600 17th Street, NW, Washington, D.C. 20506. July.

Omi, Michael, and Howard Winant. 1994. *Racial Formation in the United States from the 1960s to the 1990s.* Second ed. New York: Routledge.

Orme, William A., Jr. 1996. *Understanding NAFTA: Mexico, Free Trade, and the New North America.* Austin: University of Texas Press.

Ortiz, Victor M. 1999. Only time can tell if geography is still destiny: Time, space, and NAFTA in a U.S.-Mexican border city. *Human Organization* 58(2): 173–181.

Ortner, Sherry. 1973. *Sherpas Through Their Rituals.* Cambridge: Cambridge University Press.

Osorio, Victor, and Alejandro Quiroz. 1995. Comercio internacional y derechos de los trabajadores: Elementos para la definición de una postura sobre la clausula social. Red Mexicana Frente al Libre Comercio, circulated materials.

Paredes, Américo. 1993. *Folklore and Culture on the Texas-Mexican Border.* Ed. and intro. Richard Bauman. Austin: Center for Mexican American Studies.

Pastor, Robert A. 1993. *Integration with Mexico: Options for U.S. Policy.* New York: The Twentieth Century Fund Press.

————. 1992. ¿Del big brother al buen vecino? *Nexos* (December): 21–28.

Paz, Octavio. 1990 The case for an "American Community": Geography brings together what history has divided. *World Press Review* (April): 34–36.

————. 1950. *El Laberinto de la Soledad.* Mexico City: Cuadernos Americanos.

Peñalosa Méndez, Andrés. 1995. PND 1995–2000: Sector externo y proyecto de crecimiento económico. *Alternativas: Integración, Democracia y Desarrollo* 6(July/August): 1, 7–10.

Perea, Juan F., ed. 1997. *Immigrants Out! The New Nativism and the Anti-immigrant Impulse in the United States.* New York: New York University Press.

Pérez, María Luisa. 1995. Exigen solución al rezago agrario. *Reforma,* 4 September, p. 4A.

Pérez Canchola, José Luis. 1995. La doble ciudadanía y el voto en ausencia. *Forum* 36(May): 23–25.

Pérez U., Matilde. 1993. Búsqueda de consenso en 56 etnias sobre el artículo cuatro. *La Jornada* 18 July, p. 7.

Pérez Vences, Norma Z. 1995a. No se ve la salida inmediata a la crisis: Leopoldo Solís. *Epoca* 2 October, p. 44–46.

————. 1995b. Al inicio de 1996, la mayor parte del presupuesto. *Epoca* 11 September, p. 44–45.

Perot, Ross, with Pat Choate. 1993. *Save Your Job, Save Our Country: Why NAFTA Must Be Stopped – Now!* New York: Hyperion.

Petrich, Blanche, and Enrique Gutiérrez. 1993. Rechazan países iberoamericanos la presencia de EU como observador en la Tercera Cumbre. *La Jornada* 14 July, pp. 1, 42.

Poder Ejecutivo Federal, Estados Unidos Mexicanos. 1995a. Plan Nacional de Desarrollo, 1995–2000. Mexico City: Secretaría de Hacienda y Crédito Público.

———. 1995b. Desarrollo de los pueblos indígenas: Anteproyecto de reformas a los artículos 4o. y 115 constitucionales. Perfil de *La Jornada* 22 September.

Ratner, R. S. 1997. Many Davids, one Goliath. In *Organizing Dissent: Dissenting Social Movements in Theory and Practice.* Second ed. Ed. William Carroll, pp. 271–286. Chicago: Garamond Press.

Red Mexicana de Acción frente al Libre Comercio. 1993. *Agenda Social: Propuestas en Materia Laboral, Medio Ambiente y Derechos Humanos.* Mexico City: RMALC.

Reyes Heroles, Federico. 1996. Sovereignty: Concepts, facts, and feelings. In *NAFTA and Sovereignty: Trade-offs for Canada, Mexico, and the United States.* Ed. Joyce Hoebing, Sidney Weintraub, and M. Delal Baer, pp. 69–85. Washington, D.C.: The Center for Strategic and International Studies.

———. 1995. *Sondear a México.* Mexico City: Oceano.

Richardson, Laurel. 1990. Narrative and sociology. *Journal of Contemporary Ethnography* 19(1): 116–135.

Rodríguez, Luis Alberto. 1993. Indeclinable, la preservación de la soberanía en el TLC: Carlos Sales. *La Jornada* 20 July, p. 24.

Rodríguez O., Jaime E., and Kathryn Vincent, eds. 1997. *Common Border, Uncommon Paths: Race, Culture, and National Identity in U.S.-Mexican Relations.* Wilmington, DE: Scholarly Resources Books.

Rodríguez Trejo, Agustín. 1995. Primera victória dentro del TLC. *Excelsior* 19 September, p. 1-F.

Rojas, Guillermo. 1998. Nafta and California Proposition 187: Hegemony or cultural and political hypocrisy? In *NAFTA on Second Thoughts: A Plural Evaluation.* Ed. David R. Dávila-Villers, pp. 87–98. Lanham, MD: University Press of America.

Romero, Ismael. 1995. Transición democrática, camino contra la crisis: PAN, PRD y PT. *La Jornada* 2 September, p. 5.

Rosaldo, Renato. 1999. Cultural citizenship, inequality, and multiculturalism. In *Race, Identity, and Citizenship: A Reader.* Ed. Rodolfo D. Torres, Louis F. Mirón, and Jonathan Xavier Inda, pp. 253–261. Malden, MA: Blackwell Publishers, Inc.

Rosas, María Cristina. 1995. El "efecto NAFTA." *Uno más uno,* 3 October.

Rosenthal, A. M. 1995. U.S. knew Mexican bailout a bad gamble. Editorial. *Santa Cruz County Sentinel* 6 July, p. A-9.

Rosenthal, Steven J. 1995. *The Pioneer Fund: Financier of fascist research.* 39(September/October): 44–61.

Saldierna, Georgina. 1995. Instalarán mil 500 casillas en el DF para la Consulta Juvenil. *La Jornada* 13 September, p. 9.

Salinas de Gortari, Carlos. 1994. State of the Nation Address. *The News* (special supplement), 2 November, pp. 1–16.

Sánchez, Alfonso. 1995. Funcionarios, detrás del Club de Golf El Tepozteco: CCS. *El Financiero* 7 September, p. 25.

Sánchez L., Georgina. 1995. ¿Existe un futuro para la soberanía? *Este País* 54(September): 43–44.

Sassen, Saskia. 1998. *Globalization and Its Discontents: Essays on the New Mobility of People and Money.* New York: The New Press.

Schultz, Emily A., and Robert H. Lavenda. 2001. *Cultural Anthropology: A Perspective on the Human Condition.* Fifth ed. Mountain View, CA: Mayfield Publishing Company.

SECOFI (Secretaría de Comercio y Fomento Industrial). 1992. *¿Qué es el TLC?* Booklet based on speeches made by President Carlos Salinas de Gortari at the conclusion of the NAFTA negotiations.

Sedgwick, John. 1994. The mentality bunker. *Gentlemen's Quarterly* 64(November): 228–235, 250–251.

Semo, Enrique. 1995a. Neoliberalismo o crecimiento con equidad. *Cemos Memoria* 82(October): 5–11.

———. 1995b. Chiapas también es México. *Proceso* 986(25 September):48–49.

———. 1993. El TLC depende de lo que occura en la ronda Uruguay del GATT; México, de lo que pase en Estados Unidos. *Proceso* 864 (24 May): 6–9.

SEPPI. 1995. Explotó la bomba financiera. *Forum* 4(34): 2–8.

Shaiken, Harley. 1995. The NAFTA, a social charter, and economic growth. In *NAFTA as a Model of Development: The Benefits and Costs of Merging High- and Low-wage Areas.* Ed. Richard S. Belous and Jonathan Lemco, pp. 27–36. Albany: State University of New York Press.

Shiva, Vandana. 1993. Biodiversity and intellectual property rights. In *The Case Against Free Trade: GATT, NAFTA, and the Globalization of Corporate Power.* Ed. Ralph Nader et al. San Francisco, CA: Earth Island Press.

Shore, Cris, and Annabel Black. 1992. The European communities and the construction of Europe. *Anthropology Today* 8(3): 10–11.

Short, Thomas. 1991. Big brother in Delaware. *National Review* 43(18 March): 32.

Silverstein, Ken, and Alexander Cockburn. 1995. The killers and the killing: Who broke Mexico? *The Nation* 6 March, pp. 306–311.

Smedley, Audrey. 1993. *Race in North America: Origin and Evolution of a Worldview.* Boulder, CO: Westview.

Smith, Michael Peter, and Luis Eduardo Guarnizo, eds. 1998. *Transnationalism from Below.* New Brunswick, NJ: Transaction Publishers.

Sosa, Iván. 1995. "Yo juego con los héroes": Magú. *Boletín Mexicano de la Crisis* 16 September, p. 7.

Spivak, Gayatri. 1990. Gayatri Spivak on the politics of the subaltern. Interview by Howard Winant. *Socialist Review* 20(3): 81–97.

Stefancic, Jean. 1997. Funding the nativist agenda. In *Immigrants Out! The New Nativism and the Anti-immigrant Impulse in the United States*. Ed. Juan F. Perea, pp. 119–135. New York: New York University Press.

Subcomandante Marcos [EZLN]. 1995. Mesa nacional de diálogo independiente: Marcos. Una carta abierta. Perfil de *La Jornada* 1 October.

Taussig, Michael. 1993. *Mimesis and Alterity: A Particular History of the Senses*. New York: Routledge.

Tedesco, Theresa, and Marc Clark, with Hilary Mackenzie. 1989. Opening with a bang: An eventful first week in the free trade era. *Maclean's* 102 (16 January):15.

Terrazas, Ana Cecilia. 1995. La campaña publicitaria del gobierno y los banqueros acerca del ADE, una gran trampa. *Proceso* 983(4 September):39.

Third World Network. 1993. Modern science in crisis: A third world response. In *The "Racial" Economy of Science: Toward a Democratic Future*. Ed. Sandra Harding, pp. 484–518. Bloomington: Indiana University Press.

Thomas-Houston, Marilyn M. 1997. "Stony the Road": A Look at Political Participation in an African-American Community. Ph.D. diss., New York University.

Trejo, Ángel. 1995. Tepoztlán: una respuesta del *México Profundo. El Día* 5 September, p. 11.

Trueba Urbina, Alberto. 1974. *The Mexican Constitution of 1917 Is Reflected in the Peace Treaty of Versailles of 1919*. In English and Spanish. New York and Paris: N.p.

Turner, Victor W. 1957. *Schism and Continuity in an African Society*. Manchester: Manchester University Press.

Ureña, José. 1995. Critica el PRI el plan de erigir otra malla fronteriza. *La Jornada* 13 September, p. 3.

Urrutia, Alonso. 1995. Sin acceso a planes habitacionales, el 50% de la población urbana empleada. *La Jornada* 10 September, p. 39.

USA Today. 2000. Protestors target institutions most able to help the poor. Editorial, 14 April, p. A-14.

Valenzuela Arce, José Manuel. 1994. Identidad cultural en la frontera. Acción social e identidad de la población de origen mexicano en Estados Unidos. In *Mitos en las relaciones México—Estados Unidos*. Comp. Esther Schumacher, pp. 399–431. Mexico City: Secretaría de Relaciones Exteriores, Fondo de Cultura Económica.

Van Maanen, John. 1990. Great moments in ethnography: An editor's introduction. *Journal of Contemporary Ethnography* 19(1): 3–7.

Velarde, Alfredo. 1995. ¡Todos somos Marcos! *Pedimos la Palabra: Cultura, Crítica y Periodismo* 1(1): 16–18.

Vera, Rodrigo. 1995. El Club de Tepoztlán dividió a la diocesis de Cuernavaca: el obispo a favor; quince sacerdotes, en contra. *Proceso* 985(18 September): 39.

Victorio, Rafael. 1995. Necesario, un agente por cada 20 metros: Canacintra. *Excelsior* 3 September, p. 36-A.

Vila, Pablo. 2000. *Crossing Borders, Reinforcing Borders: Social Categories, Metaphors, and Narrative Identities on the U.S.-Mexico Frontier*. Austin: University of Texas Press.

Villegas, C., S. Rico, and A. Sánchez. 1995. En juego, intereses de Salinas en el club El Tepozteco: PRD. *El Financiero,* 8 September, p. 20.

Wallach, Lori. 1993. Hidden dangers of GATT and NAFTA. In *The Case Against Free Trade: GATT, NAFTA, and the Globalization of Corporate Power.* Ed. Ralph Nader, et al., pp. 23–64. San Francisco: Earth Island Press.

Weber, Max. 1980. *The Protestant Ethic and the Spirit of Capitalism.* Intro. Anthony Giddens. New York: Prentice Hall.

Weiner, Tim. 2000. Mexico chief pushes new border policy: Free and easy does it. *New York Times* 14 December, p. A-12.

Weintraub, Sidney. 1988. *Mexican Trade Policy and the North American Community.* Significant Issues Series X(4). Washington, D.C.: The Center for Strategic and International Studies.

Wetherell, Margaret, and Jonathan Potter. 1992. *Mapping the Language of Racism: Discourse and the Legitimation of Exploitation.* New York: Columbia University Press.

Whitaker, Mark P. 1996. Ethnography as learning: A Wittgensteinian approach to writing ethnographic accounts. *Anthropological Quarterly* 69(1): 1–13.

Whitaker, Reg. 1992. *A Sovereign Idea: Essays on Canada as a Democratic Community.* Montreal: McGill-Queens University Press.

Whiting, Van R., Jr., ed. 1996. *Regionalization in the World Economy: NAFTA, the Americas and Asia Pacific.* Delhi: Macmillan India Limited.

Williams, Brackette F. 1996. *Women Out of Place: The Gender of Agency and the Race of Nationality.* New York: Routledge.

———. 1991. *Stains on My Name, War in My Veins: Guyana and the Politics of Cultural Struggle.* Durham, NC: Duke University Press.

Wilson, Michael G., and Wesley R. Smith, eds. 1992. *The North American Free Trade Agreement: Spurring Prosperity and Stability in the Americas.* Proceedings of a Heritage Foundation Conference. Washington, D.C.: The Heritage Foundation.

Wilson, Pete. 1992. Remarks by Governor Pete Wilson to the Pacific Economic Cooperation Council. San Francisco, 23 September.

Witker, Jorge, coordinador. 1992. *Aspectos Jurídicos del Tratado Trilateral de Libre Comercio.* Mexico City: Universidad Nacional Autónoma de México.

Wolf, Eric R. 1982. *Europe and the People Without History.* Berkeley: University of California Press.

Zamarripa, Roberto. 1995. Entrevista con Marco Antonio Bernal: El problema es la vía, no las preguntas. Enfoque sección de *Reforma* 3 September, pp. 8–9.

Zavella, Patricia. 1997. The tables are turned: Immigration, poverty, and social conflict in California communities. In *Immigrants Out! The New Nativism and the Anti-immigrant Impulse in the United States.* Ed. Juan F. Perea, pp. 136–161. New York: New York University Press.

Zebadúa, Emilio. 1995. Tepoztlán vota. *La Jornada* 24 September, p. 1.

———. 1993. El momento latinoamericano. *La Jornada* 14 July, p. 48.

Zedillo Ponce de León, Ernesto. 2000. State of the Nation Address. *The News* (special supplement), 2 September, pp. 2–11.

————. 1995. State of the Nation Address. *The News* (special supplement), 2 September, pp. 2–8.

Zinn, Maxine Baca, and Bonnie Thornton Dill. 1999. Theorizing difference from multiracial feminism. In *Race, Identity, and Citizenship: A Reader.* Ed. Rodolfo D. Torres, Louis F. Mirón, and Jonathan Xavier Inda, pp. 103–111. Malden, MA: Blackwell Publishers, Inc.

Index

241

About the Book

Ann Kingsolver presents stories people have told about NAFTA—young people and old, urban and rural, with differing political perspectives, occupations, and other markers of identity—that demonstrate their expectations and imaginations of the sweeping trade agreement.

NAFTA, Kingsolver contends, both before and after its passage, became a catchall in public discourse for tensions related to neoliberal policies and to economic and cultural processes of globalization. The storytellers in her book, from Mexico, Kentucky, and California, imagined the meaning and possible effects of regional integration on topics ranging from agriculture, to the stereotyping of workers, to national sovereignty and identity. NAFTA became invested with possibilities far beyond the scope of its literal provisions.

Kingsolver analyzes the metaphorical meanings attributed to NAFTA, whether "a giant truck in your rear-view mirror" (in Ralph Nader's words) or a panacea for what they tell us about the changing relationship between national governments and their publics. She finds that, rather than strengthening national authority, the passage of NAFTA led to intense public questioning and deep political divisions in both Mexico and the United States.

Ann E. Kingsolver is assistant professor of anthropology at the University of South Carolina. She is the editor of *More than Class: Studying Power in U.S. Workplaces.*

252